Administering Education: International Challenge

Edited by

MEREDYDD HUGHES

Senior Lecturer in Education
University College, Cardiff, Wales

THE ATHLONE PRESS *of the University of London*
1975

Published by
THE ATHLONE PRESS
UNIVERSITY OF LONDON
at 4 Gower Street, London W C I

Distributed by
Tiptree Book Services Ltd
Tiptree, Essex

U S A and Canada
Humanities Press Inc
New Jersey

ISBN 0 485 12026 7

Printed in Great Britain by
W & J MACKAY LIMITED, CHATHAM

Contents

Part 2: Issues in Context

Part 3: Theory into Practice

Introduction

This book is an outcome of the third International Intervisitation Programme on Educational Administration (IIP 1974), an international conference held at three centres in the United Kingdom in July 1974. Though it cannot hope to capture within its covers the spirit of goodwill and mutual understanding which was an outstanding feature of the Programme, the volume provides a record of the joint efforts of scholars and practising administrators from many nations to respond creatively to the challenge and opportunities which arise, as never before, in administering education in the world of today.

The first International Intervisitation Programme was held in the United States and Canada in 1966, under the sponsorship of the University Council for Educational Administration (UCEA)[1] and with financial support from the Kellogg Foundation. It resulted from an initiative by Dr Jack Culbertson, Executive Director of UCEA, which was further developed in conjunction with Professor William Walker, Dean of the Faculty of Education at the University of New England, Australia. The Programme was attended by university teachers and practising educational administrators from the United States and from various Commonwealth countries (Australia, Canada, New Zealand and the United Kingdom). Trends and issues in education in the countries represented were explored, and consideration was given to means of encouraging the development in those countries of teaching and research in educational administration. The main papers were subsequently published in the volume, *Educational Administration: International*

[1] UCEA is an organization of fifty-nine universities in the United States and Canada. Its major objective is to advance research and development in educational administration through inter-university cooperation and communication. Among its publications are two journals, *Educational Administration Quarterly* and *Educational Administration Abstracts* (the latter in cooperation with the Ontario Institute for Studies in Education). The UCEA central office is located on the campus of the Ohio State University at 29 West Woodruff Avenue, Columbus, Ohio, U.S.A. UCEA representation at IIP 1974 was headed by Professor J. D. Scribner of the University of California, Los Angeles.

Perspectives (Baron, Cooper and Walker, 1969). Some communication difficulties experienced during the first IIP because of national differences in terminology gave rise to a further publication, *A Glossary of Educational Terms: Usage in Five English Speaking Countries* (Walker, Mumford and Steel, 1973).

A second International Intervisitation Programme was held in Australia in 1970 under the sponsorship of the University of New England, acting in association with UCEA. On this occasion the number of Commonwealth countries represented rose to fifteen, and the themes of common interest examined included planning and systems analysis, teacher negotiation and participation in policy making. The main papers have been brought together in the book, *Educational Administration in Australia and Abroad: Analyses and Challenges* (Thomas, Farquhar and Taylor, 1974), under three headings: crucial issues facing educational administrators, the administrator and the teacher, and the preparation of educational leaders.

An important outcome of the second IIP was the decision taken by participants from Commonwealth countries to set up their own organization, the Commonwealth Council for Educational Administration (CCEA).[2] Another outcome was a decision by some of the United Kingdom participants to explore the possibility of setting up an affiliated national association in the United Kingdom, which would, in addition to its domestic concerns, hope to act as host to a third International Intervisitation Programme to take place in Britain in 1974. As a result of these initiatives, the British Educational Administration Society (BEAS) was established in October 1971, with Dr Eric Briault as its first Chairman.[3]

The newly formed BEAS quickly established an IIP Steering Com-

[2] The primary objective of CCEA is to foster close links between those concerned with the improvement of educational administration in Commonwealth countries. It is assisted by grants from the Commonwealth Foundation and the University of New England, Armidale, New South Wales, Australia, where the headquarters of the Council are situated. The President is Professor William Walker, who is also Founding Editor of the *Journal of Educational Administration*.

[3] The constitution of BEAS states as its first aim 'to advance the practice of educational administration and to this end to promote high standards in the teaching of, and research into, educational administration in the United Kingdom'. Its journal, *Educational Administration Bulletin*, is edited by Dr Meredydd Hughes, with David Parkes (Further Education Staff College, Coombe Lodge, Blagdon, Bristol) as Associate Editor and Business Manager.

mittee, with Professor George Baron as Chairman, Gordon Wheeler as Vice-Chairman and Treasurer, and Mrs E. A. Wheeler as Secretary. Guided by George Baron, and relying also on the expertise and experience of its corresponding members, Jack Culbertson and William Walker, representing the co-sponsors U C E A and C C E A respectively, the Steering Committee sought to build on and extend the work of those who planned and carried out the first two Programmes.[4] In the event, I I P 1974 was attended by over a hundred educationists and administrators from twenty-one countries: Australia, Bangladesh, British Honduras, Canada, Cyprus, Ghana, Hong Kong, India, Kenya, Malawi, Malta, New Zealand, Nigeria, Papua New Guinea, Sierra Leone, Singapore, Sri Lanka, Uganda, the United Kingdom, the United States of America, and Zambia.

The essential purpose of the International Intervisitation Programmes, as it has emerged over the years, is to promote the development in an international setting of systematic study and research in educational administration, based on firm theoretical foundations in the social sciences and designed to improve teaching and practice at both system and institutional level. It is noted in the 1974 conference brochure that much of the content of each Programme is necessarily shaped by the thought and practice of the host country, but that the issues which emerge are discussed and interpreted within a designedly international frame of reference.

The theme of I I P 1974 is well expressed in the general title, 'Educational Administration: New Directions in Practice and Theory'. The standpoint adopted in framing the Programme was that educational administration involves more than regulatory and executive functions: it is to be viewed in the present age as being above all dynamic and innovatory. In order to increase opportunities of appreciating together some of the complex and far-reaching changes taking place within educational administration in Britain today, the conference was organized in three phases, each of one week's duration, in Bristol,[5]

---

[4] Other sponsoring bodies of I I P 1974 were: the Further Education Staff College, Jordanhill College of Education, the Ontario Institute for Studies in Education, Rank Xerox Ltd., the State University of New York at Buffalo, the University of Bristol School of Education, the University of London Institute of Education, and the United Kingdom Government through the Department of Education and Science and the Overseas Development Administration.

[5] The Bristol Local Committee, chaired by Professor Eric Hoyle, arranged visits to eight English and Welsh local education authorities (Avon, Devon, Gloucester-

Glasgow[6] and London,[7] visits being arranged from each centre to a wide variety of educational institutions and organizations. There were also opportunities for the pooling and appraisal of these experiences in small groups, and for testing the paradigms and perspectives of conference papers against the fresh empirical data brought back from visits by acute and experienced observers. The fact that each discussion group reflected in miniature the rich diversity of the whole IIP membership, both occupationally and geographically, enhanced the value of the occasions.

In preparing the present volume for publication the Editor found that the text at his disposal from the prepared addresses (many of them with very valuable, but lengthy, bibliographies), the responses to papers,[8] panel discussion reports and summaries by rapporteurs of group discussions,[9] was far in excess of the space available. All the major conference papers do in fact appear, except for one which is to be published elsewhere,[10] and the Editor is grateful to contributors for readily accepting with good grace that substantial cuts had to be made in nearly

[6] The Glasgow Local Committee, chaired by Dr Tom Bone, arranged visits to Open Plan Primary Schools in Glasgow; to two colleges of technology (Glasgow and Paisley); to Glasgow University and Moray House College of Education; to the Educational Institute of Scotland, the Robertson Centre, the Scottish Certificate of Education Examination Board, the Scottish Council for Research in Education, the Scottish Education Department, the Scottish Office Training Unit and the Thompson Foundation TV College.

[7] The London and South East Committee, chaired by Peter Judge, arranged visits to the Inner London Education Authority, its Television, Equipment and Media Resources Centres, the Rachel McMillan Teachers' Centre and the Non-Teaching Staff Training Centre; the Anglian Regional Management Centre, the National Foundation for Educational Research, the Open University and the House of Commons.

[8] Portions of summaries prepared by some of the respondents are given in Appendix 1.

[9] Short extracts from group discussion reports are given in Appendix 2.

[10] The paper, 'Problems of Educational Provision in Papua New Guinea: An Area of Scattered Population', by E. Barrington Thomas, Dean of the Faculty of Education of the University of Papua New Guinea, is currently being published by the Oxford University Press in a volume of papers on Papua New Guinea, (Thomas, 1975).

shire, Somerset; Mid, South and West Glamorgan, Gwent); to two primary schools (Birdwell and Perry Court); to two secondary schools (Castle and Nailsea); to two technical colleges (City of Bath and Filton); to Bristol Polytechnic, Redland College of Education and Bristol University.

all the papers.[11] For convenience of presentation they are grouped under three headings, 'Perspectives', 'Issues in Context' and 'Theory into Practice', though it is readily conceded that the categorization is a little 'rough' at the edges, and that the occasional paper might qualify for more than one group.

Part I consists of five papers in which consideration is primarily given to ways in which thinking about educational administration and its change processes may be structured. Lord Morris of Grasmere, Honorary President of BEAS, after officially opening IIP 1974 with a message from Her Majesty the Queen, invited us, in an address which forms the first chapter of the present volume, to define successful administration today in terms of its 'acceptability'. This is a concept which, sometimes translated into the language of 'participation' and 'accountability', remained with us throughout the conference. Chapter 2 consists of a wide ranging introductory paper by Professor George Baron, the Steering Committee Chairman, in which he sets out and discusses the approaches to thinking and research in educational administration which have developed in recent years and their significance for programmes of study and training.

In Chapter 3 Professor Eric Hoyle considers educational leadership and decision-making from the standpoint of organizational theory, and points to the relevance of a contingency model and a situational perspective in extending Organizational Development strategies. Dr Ross Thomas provides a comprehensive review of the literature of organizational change in Chapter 4, proposes a model of administrative action to effect change within a system, and also discusses Organizational Development approaches in this context.

Part I concludes with a chapter by Professor Barr Greenfield, in which he questions the basic assumptions of a 'natural systems' view of social reality and explores the implications for research and practice of an alternative 'phenomenological' perspective. The fact that for nearly a generation the study of educational administration has been

[11] For completeness it may be added that two unscripted papers, by Sir William Pile, Permanent Secretary at the Department of Education and Science, and by Peter Browning, Bedfordshire Chief Education Officer, were not available. Dr Luvern Cunningham, Executive Director of the Detroit Education Task Force, was unable to attend the IIP; he did, however, send a graphic tape-recorded account of citizen participation in Detroit to take the place of the paper on 'Community Involvement in the Education Service' which he would otherwise have placed before the conference.

placed by most scholars in a 'systems' frame of reference ensures that Greenfield's paper, whether judged to be 'perceptive' or 'naive', 'stimulating' or 'provocative', should certainly be of interest—as it proved to be at the IIP itself. It may be noted that Hoyle in Chapter 3 also recognizes the phenomenological view as 'an important perspective which is beginning to throw light on organizations and the behaviour of participants'; in further suggesting that one cannot, at the present time, simultaneously adopt a 'phenomenological' and a 'systems' perspective, he is again in accord with Greenfield. Those who are prepared to accept the validity of the antithesis may still wonder whether it might not be heuristically rewarding for the same student *on separate occasions* to examine an administrative situation both from a 'phenomenological' and a 'systems' viewpoint—just as physicists at Cambridge made rapid advances in the nineteen-thirties by being prepared, as Sir Arthur Eddington vividly put it, to assume a wave theory light on Mondays, Wednesdays and Fridays while adopting the seemingly irreconcilable 'photon' model of quantum dynamics on Tuesdays, Thursdays and Saturdays. Others are likely to argue that, in his presentation, Greenfield does less than justice to the refinement of concepts and elaboration of sub-systems which are possible within a 'systems' framework; thus Hills (1974), in reacting to Greenfield's paper, turns to the writings of Talcott Parsons to find support for his assertion that 'the fundamental tenets of the phenomenological view are integral parts of functional analysis'. As controversy continues, it is permissible to hope that the clash of ideas will lead to clarification and re-definition. It would be regrettable if the academics of educational administration formed themselves into rival doctrinal factions of one-eyed true believers, whether of an 'old' or of a 'new' ideology. Though our foci of interest may differ at a particular time, our understanding of complex issues will be enriched if we retain the ability and the will to appreciate that there are likely to be substantial merits, as well as demerits, in alternative perspectives.[12]

In Part 2 the focus changes to problems and issues as they arise in practice in specific contexts. This does not mean that it is to be assumed that papers in this group have no theoretical basis, though in some cases the perspective adopted is implicit, rather than explicitly stated. The primary emphasis, however, is on the actual situation as it appears to a

[12] Broadly similar views were expressed at the IIP by Alan Crane (see Appendix 1) and by Professor Walker at the final session.

well-informed observer, and on the difficult decisions which have to be made by the practitioners of educational administration, often in a limited time and with inadequate information.

Professor B. O. Ukeje in Chapter 6 draws on well recognized concepts of classical organizational theory to explicate the roles of central, regional and local authorities in educational decision-making. At the IIP his exposition was illustrated by detailed reference to the Nigerian situation at Federal and State levels, which, for reasons of space, regrettably appears in an abridged form in this volume.

Rien van Gendt and Dr Jinapala Alles in Chapters 7 and 8 are both concerned, though at different levels and in different national contexts, with the ability of educational organization to respond to change, to new practices and new ideas about the curriculum. Van Gendt's area of interest is the problem-solving capacity of the individual school. The approach which he advocates is somewhat similar to the Organizational Development ideology discussed in Chapters 3 and 4; he also reports considerable variation in the extent to which schools themselves *are* actively involved in the process of innovation in Western Europe. Alles's global survey of curriculum reform in developing countries draws attention to the dilemma of nation-wide efforts at curriculum change when time is a precious resource in short supply: 'If one limits oneself to winning participation, then the changes are more durable, but take a long time to be realized'. This makes it all the more necessary, as Dr Alles observes, to identify the formal and informal learning situations available as resources for basic educational provision in developing countries.

The rest of the papers in Part 2 relate to current problems in the administration of education in the United Kingdom, though they also exemplify principles of wider significance. Of the several issues presented by Joselyn Owen and Dr Tom Bone in Chapters 9 and 10, the interest of IIP participants centred especially on the problems and opportunities that are involved in *participation* (whether of staff, students or community) and in *corporate management*. The extracts in Chapter 11 from papers by Dr W. A. Gatherer, Trevor Morgan and James Miller give a brief indication of some other topics considered. Dr Eric Briault in Chapter 12 draws on his unique knowledge of London's educational problems to develop the theme of 'Educational Administration and the Contemporary City'. For him a key aspect of the role of the central administration is to provide resources and support for the individual institution of learning, which is then encouraged to use its comparative freedom from restrictive controls to work towards a 'creative consensus' concerning problems and innovation. This implies participative processes of decision-making, and also requires some means of evaluating both the problems and the outcome of the decision-making process. Briault thus returns from a rather different standpoint to the themes of participation and accountability discussed in previous chapters.

In Part 3 the contributors present us with the ubiquitous challenge to relate theory to practice, which may be seen as the basic justification of the whole IIP enterprise. Dr William Taylor provides a penetrating analysis of the contribution of research, and cautiously advocates a 'sociology of knowledge' perspective to elucidate the research-study-practice relationship. This is followed in Chapter 14 by appraisals, by Professors Gibson and Holdaway respectively, of trends in educational administration research and its application in the United States and Canada, two countries which have made notable advances in this field.

The next three chapters are concerned from different viewpoints with teaching in educational administration. Gordon Wheeler invites us in Chapter 15 to think critically about current teaching practices, and provides a rich store of hypotheses for future research. In Chapter 16 Per Dalin describes a current, and developing, international training project in educational management. The standpoint taken is that educational change is best regarded, not as the responsibility of an exclusive cadre of 'change agents', but as a *function* penetrating the educational enterprise at all levels, to which many individuals contribute. Professor James Lipham provides an authoritative study in Chapter 17 of a new emphasis in the teaching of educational administration in the United States (C/PBAE), which seeks to meet the requirement of accountability to the community by adopting an elaborate and highly sophisticated systems approach to administrator education. Lipham identifies both the strengths and the limitations of the new movement; it could be that the 'new humanistic approach' which the writer prophesies as a further development might emerge sooner rather than later, as the competency/performance-based trend interacts with and is modified by other approaches, some of which may be found in this book.[13] At

[13] In this contéxt see Ron Glatter in Appendix 1 (p. 306) on possible alternative strategies, based on Organizational Development and 'phenomenological' perspectives.

the present time the utility of the C/PBAE paradigm, as a powerful manifestation of the quest for 'acceptability' to which Lord Morris draws attention, is strongly urged (Craigmile and Kerr, 1974) and vigorously contested (Andrews, 1974) in the United States.

The final chapter by Professor William Walker appropriately looks to the future, and brings together many points that are relevant to the growing professionalization of educational administration as a domain of research, teaching and practice. As Professor Walker came to the end of his address on the last day of the third IIP, it was clear that the participants from twenty-one nations had not only come to recognize an *international challenge* in the administration of education, but that they also viewed the occasion itself, like its two predecessors, as a significant *international response* to the complex and daunting problems associated with administering education in the modern world. That this particular mode of response would be continued and developed further was assured at the close of the conference by a joint announcement by H. R. Thompson on behalf of the Canadian Association of School Administrators and Professor L. R. Gue on behalf of the Canadian Association for the Study of Educational Administration that the *fourth* International Intervisitation Programme will take place in Canada in 1978. As the proceedings of IIP 1974 go to press, plans for IIP 1978 are being prepared by a joint CASA/CASEA Steering Committee, under the chairmanship of Dr Robin Farquhar, Assistant Director of OISE and Vice-President of CCEA.

In concluding this Introduction the warm thanks of the Editor are expressed to a number of people: to the contributors of the papers for their cooperation and forbearance, to the sponsors of the Programme, and particularly to the officers of UCEA, CCEA and BEAS, for the essential part which they played in making IIP 1974 possible, to the Programme Secretary, Mrs Eleanor Wheeler, and members of the Steering Committee for assistance and encouragement, to the Athlone Press through its Secretary A. M. Wood, and most notably to George Baron, Steering Committee Chairman and CCEA Vice-President, who was truly the 'Moving Spirit' of IIP 1974.

December 1974

M.G.H.

BIBLIOGRAPHY

Andrews, R. L. (1974), 'Lethal Assumptions of Competency-Based Programs', *UCEA Review*, 16(1), September 1974.

Baron, G., Cooper, D. H. and Walker, W. G. (1969), *Educational Administration: International Perspectives*, Rand McNally, Chicago.

Craigmile, J. and Kerr, R. D. (1974), 'Improved Preparation of Educational Administrators through Competency-Based Programming', *UCEA Review*, 16(1), September 1974.

Hills, J. (1974), 'Some comments on T. B. Greenfield's "Theory in the Study of Organizations and Administrative Structures"', unpublished paper.

Thomas, A. R., Farquhar, R. H. and Taylor, W. (1974), *Educational Administration in Australia and Abroad: Analyses and Challenges*, University of Queensland Press, St Lucia, Queensland.

Thomas, E. B. (ed) (1975), *Education in Papua New Guinea*, Oxford University Press, Melbourne, Australia, forthcoming.

Walker, W. G., Mumford, J. E., and Steel, C. (1973), *A Glossary of Educational Terms: Usage in Five English-Speaking Countries*, University of Queensland Press, St Lucia, Queensland.

PART ONE

Perspectives

1 Acceptability: The New Emphasis in Educational Administration

LORD MORRIS OF GRASMERE

It seems to me that if free institutions and some form of democracy are going to survive in the coming age, a very great deal will have to be demanded of the administrator. Half a century ago we thought that all problems were going to be solved by the economists and the technocrats. Problems would be broken down into their component parts, and the solution in each case would be ground out inexorably because analysis, if it was thorough enough and persistent enough, would show that there was only one right answer. There might of course be time-lags, whenever technology could not keep up to the pace of what was demanded; but time-lags would be of limited duration and reasonably predictable, and so they would in general be quite acceptable. And the forward march of an improving society would go on.

Under this pattern of government, economists and technocrats would be of the first order of importance. Indeed in the hierarchy of power, they would be first and the rest nowhere. Politicians would drop into the background, with a role to play which was partly formality, and partly public relations. Somebody would have formally to decide to do what the economists and the technocrats had shown to be demonstrably the right thing. And somebody would have to explain things to the public in terms which would appeal to them and which enough of them would understand. Administrators, who would of course remain in the background as before, would comprehend what the economists and technocrats were commanding, and would adjust the laws, regulations and procedures of society, including industry and commerce, to execute the policies handed down to them. These policies would commend themselves to the administrators, who, though not technocrats, would be highly educated persons, by the light of pure reason. The functions of both the politicians and the administrators would be of a subordinate order as compared with those of the economists and technocrats. But inevitably the functions of the administrators would be accepted as of the second order, and those of the politicians—with the exception of the occasional Prime-Minister or Leader—as of the third order.

In the light of history, this kind of government seems pretty well to have established itself as a going concern during the second world war. In war-time the whole economy and the whole of society were rigorously geared to management by objectives, or rather one objective 'surviving the war'. The technocrats played their parts, though the economists, even including Keynes, did not count for very much. So long as the war economy lasted, the administrators did pretty well on balance, though once or twice their plans had to be torn up because they were further outside human nature than the public would take even in war-time; and the politicians who did not have very much to do— except for a few Ministers who were brought in from business and the public service to provide an additional tier of administrators—did it quite well. Only the great leaders, Roosevelt, Stalin and Churchill, in that order, were in addition concerning themselves with the funda- mental matters of politics. Only they were already fighting out, in their own minds, and as against one another, policies for a post-war world. And even they, as we should now judge, did not do very much good, though they set the main lines of post-war history.

In this country the massive rejection of Churchill in the general election of 1945 gave immediate warning that peace-time government was to be a very different affair. Clearly there could be no management by objectives, because once war stopped there could be no clear objectives. And for any practical purpose of management, objectives have to be very clear indeed. From 1946 on, as we can now see, the centre of the field has been taken, not by technocracy or economics, but by politics. And it is a new kind of politics. The new Machiavelli can no longer make up his mind what he wants to do, and then bring the people round to putting up with it. His primary problem, almost it seems his *whole* problem, is to find some act of government, or *any* act of government, which is acceptable. The peoples do not want to be governed, and clearly they do not believe that there is any real and final necessity to be governed. Their political posture is no longer very far removed from that of the hippies and the flower people; and the signs are that it is getting not further away but nearer to it. Hence govern- ments which eschew the determined use of force in internal affairs find themselves in apparently insuperable difficulties. And any successful government will be some kind of *tour de force*.

Yet governments must clearly go on trying to govern. And it is against this background that administrators will have to live and work. It is hardly an exaggeration to say that, outside war-time, no democratic leader nowadays wastes much time on seeking to determine what is 'best' for his country or for humanity, certainly not in economic or technocratic or 'equity' terms. He does not even bother himself about the lessons of history—he confines his thoughts and plans within what he takes to be realism, and simply tries to work out some kind of action which will prove to be 'acceptable'; acceptable in the short run within the requirement of maintaining unity among his supporters, and acceptable for the next two or three years in the wider field of the community where the proposed line of action has to be effectively carried out, and of course defended.

It could possibly be true that a great leader, even now, with sufficient charisma to illuminate a personal influence, could get away with going his own way in his policies for a time, but long enough to show that his policies looked promising. But it seems hardly believable that the present state of society could throw up such a leader under free institutions. The most that is likely to emerge is a leader who is a genius at forecasting what is practical in government, which means fundamentally, and perhaps exclusively, what is 'acceptable'.

This will not be an easy world in which to be an administrator: not only because government policies arrived at on these principles will be apt to be highly changeable, but also because the same causes which make statesmanship so very difficult will have similar effects and influences in the sphere of administration. The administrator too will have to see that his methods are 'acceptable' and it will be for him a far more complicated and never-ending business to make everything that he does comprehensible, as it will have to be if it is to be acceptable. Also a plan which has been acceptable and accepted at the level of national statesmanship will commonly look very different in the detail of implementation; and perhaps the most difficult part of defending the whole basic policy as the months go on will inevitably fall among the tasks of administration. It is not surprising that there is now a demand for civil servants to enter the public relations field and even to come right out into controversial discussions. For some time now chief education officers have had personally to conduct or organize explanations and defence of their authorities' decisions at town meetings and other public assemblies. And clearly there will be more and more of this: and in addition the same kind of exercise is going to have to be conducted, almost as a matter of course, before ever decisions are made. This is going to require skills of a very high order indeed in the administrator. Not indeed skills which are *entirely* different from his skills of the past; but skills which are different enough in complexity and degree to be *almost* different in kind.

Then too there are the tasks and the problems which will fall upon the administration of education in particular. Can the education system as we have known it in rece nt generations produce and sustain a general public of voters, not to mention potential protesters and activists, who will be able to live with the strains and stresses of the new order? And in any case are parents, and pupils themselves, demanding and going to continue to demand changes in schools and colleges which are really radical and fundamental? Are we going to have to try out a system under which they are governed and managed by pupils? Or by the parents? Or by both together, notwithstanding the generation gap? Are all appointments to be made by promotion in accordance with trade union rules, ultimately enforceable in the courts? Is all instruction to be forbidden, so that learning is acquired only by discussion and dialectic? Most of these things have been tried somewhere in the world in the last twenty or thirty years, so that the questions are more than fantasies. Indeed very basic changes indeed are at this moment being pressed for in the younger generation; and it is noticeable that the establishment comes along much faster in many of the directions advocated than would have been thought conceivable a few years ago, or than would be commonly admitted today.

So where does the administrator stand? Let us ask the big question first; just what does he think the education system can achieve? A lot, or only quite a little? Could the battle of Waterloo have been won on the playing fields of Eton? Was the British Empire built and sustained by the public schools and ancient universities of the nineteenth century? Was the American nation produced out of an amalgam of races by the American schools and colleges? And could such things be done again today? Or is nothing really at issue but the organization and maintenance of certain practical arrangements, and a convenient control of the allocation of scarce resources? These questions must surely be asked again at the present day. As never before we need to know what we are trying to make the educational system achieve. The young must be right in thinking that we have for too long concentrated our efforts on the improvement here and there of means, without any clear conception of a modern objective.

The administrator must necessarily ask himself, what should the nation *expect* of the schools and colleges, and of the education system in the coming years. As to what in fact it *does* expect, perhaps the answer is that it does not really any longer expect very much—as compared with its expectations fifty years ago, at about the time of the end of the first war. For a long time since the second war, people in this country mainly concentrated their interest on the need for technologists and scientists, and the whole education system had a very considerable success in organizing itself to produce them, on a new pattern and in very large numbers. As I have said, this was a success, both in quantity and quality. British trained technologists and engineers are very well thought of in the world at large, not only in the new countries but also in America. And numbers have increased so much that there is a tendency at large to think that there are now too many in these fields, and forward-looking educationists have lost interest in this once all absorbing problem.

They have turned their attention to problems of 'motivation' and 'incentives'. In the narrower sphere this means concentration on management and in the wider sphere on social and moral attitudes, and also perhaps on 'political maturity', in the encouragement of which nineteenth century English education was widely thought to be so good. Almost everybody has in effect now succumbed to Dean Acheson's famous dictum, about which everyone was so angry years ago when it was first spoken—'England has lost an Empire and has not found a role'. But the dictum has become widened. It no longer refers only to Britain's role in international affairs. The broader and deeper question is whether to move over from being a country of national ambitions and enterprises to a community concentrated on the enjoyment of the art of living. Are we going to abandon 'growth' and devote ourselves to 'environment'? In the great days of the public schools and of 'Greats' at Oxford, it would have been taken for granted that education had a great part to play in answering these questions. But nowadays it seems nobody expects very much of the schools and colleges. Nobody any longer looks to the playing fields of Eton, or even of the grammar schools which were credited with the heroes of the Battle of Britain, only a little more than thirty years ago. Eyes are turned rather to the factory floor, or to the back rooms of the great office buildings. The set of a young man's character and competence, and his ambitions, is thought to be fixed for life much more by his first ten years of working for his living than by his ten years at school. And his health matters much more than his schooling. And above all there is the family. The family, like marriage, has surprised everybody by surviving, and indeed become stronger and stronger, taking the nation as a whole. The courts take their advice and guidance no longer from the schoolmaster, but from the social worker who knows the family; and remedial action is in the same hands. The schools are no longer blamed much for juvenile delinquency, but equally they are no longer looked to for its elimination. And this is significant of a public attitude of mind.

So in this matter of the objectives of education the administrator has only restricted expectations to face. He need not aim to compete with Arnold, or with Jowett. And he may have to do without such satisfactions as these great men may have felt. But in another direction neither the public, nor perhaps anyone else, has yet recognized how very exacting his problems are going to be. Administration in the public services has already become much more difficult than it used to be, and it seems clear that it will go through a phase—if it is only a phase—of becoming progressively more difficult still. As a function it is going to move more towards the activities of politics, not in the party sense but in fundamental approach. Its practitioners will have to show more of the arts and skills of politics. People are going to be more difficult to govern; or if you like, the public are going to be much more difficult to manage. The welfare state, which is throughout aimed at the interests of the public, is going to be very much more difficult to administer. This was not, I think, really anticipated; but it is by now clearly the fact.

All sections of the community, divided up and organizing themselves in very crisscross and elaborate ways, are going to speak up for themselves without apology and if necessary with vigour. The time is now upon us when it is necessary to ensure that decisions are acceptable before they are ever made; and this means among other things that many and varied sections of the community will have to feel that they have been able to play some part in actually making the decisions.

This will seem to many administrators to present them with a quite impossible task; though of course much public administration has moved a long way in this direction for quite a long time. Still, many administrators will tend to resent the modern situation, though experience suggests that they will not resent it half as much as the elected representatives will, both in central and in local government. And this will not make the task of administration any easier.

But the important point is that the problem cannot be solved without the administrator. If he does not devise the solution nobody else will. It is not the job of the politician—and all elected representatives are now politicians—to find solutions or design systems. Whenever there is a public task to be performed, administration must work out a scheme. Without this the politician is helpless. He can choose between well-prepared schemes, and even sometimes amend them. But the professional administrator must research the facts and devise an operable scheme. And by the same token it is his task to present an *acceptable* scheme; for today only acceptable schemes are operable. In all parts of the world this is a task which is likely to prove a formidable and exacting challenge to the educational administrator in the years ahead.

2 Approaches to Educational Administration as a Field of Study, Research and Application

GEORGE BARON

One of the most significant features of educational thinking at the present time is that it is at last being realized that administration is an integral part of the learning situation and not extrinsic to it. In an age of rapid change it is necessarily dynamic and innovatory. Most important of all, administration can be studied and overall performance improved with the help of the social and managerial sciences developed during the present century.

This development is, of course, in line with the expanding role of education in a technological society. I do not mean expansion in terms of student numbers and mounting costs, but in terms of the realization that more and more of the activities of human beings can be brought within the realms of study, training and research. In particular, this realization has been reflected in new studies of how men may rationally construct, provide resources for and behave within the organizational society in which education at all levels and of all kinds plays an essential part.

In taking account of the wider context of the study of educational administration, I suggest that we structure our thinking in terms of four main approaches: the behavioural, the economic, the managerial and the political. I am well aware of the untidiness of this classification and of the extent of the overlap which must exist. Any behavioural approach must necessarily be concerned with political attitudes and action and any economic approach with managerial techniques for resource allocation and control. Similarly, managerial techniques may have highly political overtones and the behavioural sciences of sociology and social psychology fuse in organization theory and analysis.

I shall deal first with the behavioural approach, because it provided the starting point for the emergence of what came to be known as the New Movement in the United States in the fifties and sixties. Hitherto, interest in administration had been largely restricted to legal, financial and regulatory matters relating to the management of school systems on the one hand and to curriculum control and supervisory practices on the other. But newer approaches in business management, earlier disseminated through the work of Chester Barnard and Herbert Simon, opened the way for the insights of the social sciences (Culbertson *et al.*, 1973). Attention was diverted from the definition of the administrator's task to his behaviour in relation to his environment. Concern for the establishment of universal principles characteristic of the Scientific Management School, so exhaustively and entertainingly described by Callahan (1962), gave way to concern for the nature of leadership, the processes of decision-making, the problems of human interaction and means for defining and re-defining purposes and goals. The limitations of a purely pragmatic approach were stressed and the search began for theories which would sustain programmes of empirical research modelled on the methods of the exact sciences. The New Movement spread to Canada and Australia and more recently to Britain, and its general influence has been felt in all English-speaking countries in which study and research in educational administration have taken root. It has brought social scientists into the field and it has paved the way for the application to educational systems and their institutions of disciplined modes of study and research. Moreover, because the interests of the social sciences are so wide-reaching, the practice of educational administration is being seen as necessarily liberal and humane rather than, as so often in the popular imagination, narrow and restrictive.

During the same period, another kind of activity was gaining momentum in countries, whether developed or developing, in which governments were repairing the damages of war or building up new nations in former colonial territories. This was the activity of the planner, linking together the concepts of social development with the increasingly sophisticated tools of the demographer and the economist. Such activity has found its place in the great international agencies, such as UNESCO with its International Institute of Educational Planning. It has been especially closely linked with developing countries. But it has also been a feature of the restructuring of educational systems in France, Norway, Sweden and to a lesser degree in Britain, since in these countries planned change and innovation, in curricular as well as in administrative terms, has become increasingly necessary in view of mounting demands on scarce resources.

Planning is an integral part of any form of administration but it also has an identity of its own, expressed through its own distinctive institutions, literature, conferences and programmes. Our concern is with the demands which the translation of plans into practice make on the administrator. As Beeby (1967) has pointed out in his illuminating essay on *Planning and the Educational Administrator*, the expert costing of policy recommendations is a new dimension which the economist as planner has brought to educational administration. Moreover, planning implies social change leading to a future different from the present. The administrator can no longer view his task, whether it be that of official, inspector, principal or head as being simply the implementation of policy and the maintenance of the system for which he is responsible. He now needs to have a very lively awareness of the environment within which he works, a capacity for devising appropriate strategies and the command of a wide range of evaluative techniques. In short, the administrator (and the term embraces all who perform administrative functions, whether styled administrators or not) is concerned with objectives and their attainment, rather than with adherence to detailed regulations and procedures, important though the latter must inevitably be.

Concern with planning, whether at the international, national, regional, local or institutional level must, for the administrator, be a matter not only of producing blueprints but also of devising strategies by which they may become realities. Hence the importance attached to innovation: it is the need to change and to innovate which has made the study of educational administration and preparatory and in-service programmes for administrators so urgent a matter.

Perhaps the most dominant approach at the present time and one which is much influencing developments in Britain is the management approach.[1] It embraces the concern for the efficient use of resources for specified ends shared by the planner and the economist and the interest in individual and collective behaviour characteristic of the social scientist and the organization analyst. But above all it emphasizes the need for the clear statement of objectives, for a rational sequence of operations, for the measurement of 'inputs' and 'outputs' and for built-in feedback mechanisms.[2] In its crudest forms it works on the assumption that operational theories developed in industry, in the public services

---

[1] See, for example, Taylor (1970), Fielden and Lockwood (1973) and Hughes (1974).
[2] See Davies (1973) and Webb (1973).

and the armed forces can be generalized and applied to educational systems and educational institutions. There is little evidence, as Glatter (1972, p. 9) has shown, that this can be done but, he argues:

... it is scarcely possible to conceive of administrative training without substantial borrowing from studies of management in other contexts—particularly the industrial, since this is where most of the research work has been done. This work must be reinterpreted for its relevance to education and, where appropriate, studies to test such relevance should be mounted.

There is, he is saying, no substitute for the painstaking study of how educational systems and institutions work. Such study is now taking place in Britain as well as in the United States and efforts are being made to adapt management by objectives, planning-programming-budgeting systems, cost-benefit analysis and such techniques as critical path analysis and job evaluation to the administration of school systems and schools themselves. Perhaps the most valuable outcome so far of such efforts has been a more imaginative approach to resource allocation and a breaking away from financial control exercised through regulations drafted with little regard for the needs and realities of the tasks of education.

The management approach is also attractive because it offers hope of means being found to assess the effectiveness and efficiency of educational systems, institutions and methods. 'Accountability' has become a major preoccupation, both in developing countries where, as education develops, its products come under close scrutiny and in developed countries where the worthwhileness of what goes on in schools and universities is being questioned by both traditionalists and radicals. 'Accountability' does not, of course, only refer to the measurement of end products. It also calls for the definition within a system of who is responsible to whom for what. The struggle to resolve this problem, especially in universities, is worldwide.

Finally, it is possible to identify a political approach to educational administration which is interested in the power relationships within educational systems and also in their relationships with their total social environments. Indeed, education and the ways in which it is administered is an element in most of the major political issues of our time. Provisions for the Maori population in New Zealand, the place of separate school systems in Australia, the Public School question in England, the potential threat posed by universal primary education to traditional society in Northern Nigeria, the significance of English in higher education in India, the just distribution of resources between the Greek and Turkish populations of Cyprus and the coordination of the efforts of the scattered peoples of the Carribean and the South Pacific are administrative-political problems requiring skills and insights of a different order from those furnished by the management approach.

Apart from such specific political issues there are two other main areas of concern:

the distribution of responsibilities for decision-making throughout political, administrative and institutional structures both in terms of their centralisation or their diffusion and in terms of the relative strengths of lay, administrative, professional and 'consumer' authority and influence; the internal politics of education, in the sense of the power-relationships existing between teacher associations, parent and other community groups, church bodies and student associations; and, within schools and colleges themselves, the clash and interactions of status levels and departmental rivalries.

It is important to recognize the political content of educational administration since education is conditioned by and conditions, in Easton's well-known phrase, the 'authoritative allocation of values' in all our societies.

I wish in the second half of this paper, to turn to issues of a different order, and to raise three questions of importance both for those who teach educational administration and those who are first and foremost practitioners. These questions are:

Where in the institutional structures of higher and professional education should the study of educational administration and the training of administrators be situated?
How does educational administration as a field of study and research relate to educational administration as a practical activity?
To what extent is educational administration 'culture-bound' and to what extent can our studies and our experience be effectively shared?

These are very large questions and I can only draw attention to them briefly.

WHERE IN THE INSTITUTIONAL STRUCTURES OF HIGHER AND PROFESSIONAL EDUCATION SHOULD THE STUDY OF EDUCATIONAL ADMINISTRATION AND THE TRAINING OF ADMINISTRATORS BE SITUATED?

In the United States and Canada educational administration is firmly established as a field of study in the vast university worlds of those countries. In the United States alone the staggering total of 362 institutions were offering preparation programmes in 1972 and of these 130 were offering doctoral programmes (UCEA Commission Report, 1973). Nothing like this is the case elsewhere, although great progress has been made in some Canadian centres. Yet it would be quite untrue to suggest that those who administer education receive no systematic training in general, as distinct from educational, administration. For example, officials of the Department of Education and Science for England and Wales and the Scottish Education Department follow courses at the Civil Service College. For local education authority officers there is the University of Birmingham Institute of Local Government Studies and also courses in polytechnics and further education institutions. In developing Commonwealth countries the preparation of those who administer education is done under the auspices of university Institutes of Public Administration and government Staff Colleges. For example, universities in Ghana, Kenya, Malawi, Malaysia, Singapore, Tanzania and the West Indies, all have Institutes of Public Administration which award in most cases post-graduate Diplomas. A common pattern of administration, including organizational, accounting, establishment and reporting procedures runs through all public services. Hence the training of educational personnel in the practice of administration naturally takes place alongside that of other government employees.

A clear need at the present time, in my view, is the firm establishment of educational administration within the universities not merely as an aspect of public administration or social administration but as a field of study in its own right. This is not to say that there should be a diminution of the bringing together for study and training of public officials with varied responsibilities, but rather that the special task of educational administration should have its own centres for study and research. These would offer their facilities not only to those working within education but to others who, as finance officers, planners and social workers need to strengthen their links with the most widespread service of all.

Whilst in many countries the universities, and within the universities schools or departments of education would appear to provide the proper setting for development, this does not mean that there is not an important role to be played by the specialized Staff College, of which in this country the Further Education Staff College is the only, but a highly successful, example. Especially for senior practitioners the Staff College with its emphasis on intensive training has much to offer.

HOW DOES EDUCATIONAL ADMINISTRATION AS A FIELD OF STUDY AND RESEARCH RELATE TO EDUCATIONAL ADMINISTRATION AS A PRACTICAL ACTIVITY?

Any consideration of the place of educational administration in higher and professional education immediately brings to the surface the constantly present tensions between the teacher and the practitioner, between 'theory' and 'practice', between academic respectability and vocational relevance. For my own part I think that the tensions are, as Dr Taylor has indicated in a recent book, *Research Perspectives in Education* (1973), inherent in the way in which knowledge is acquired and organized by those occupying different roles in our society. The academic worker abstracts from his reading and experience that which he needs to create, maintain and elaborate a coherent pattern of understanding and explanation. The practitioner, on the other hand, selects from *his* reading and experience that which he needs to solve quite specific problems. Put otherwise, the academic, by the very nature of his task, fashions constructs and models which cannot prescribe all the procedures the practitioner may need to use in particular situations: his thinking may, indeed, appear to throw doubt on expedients which indubitably work well in skilled hands. On his side the practitioner threatens the academic because he can draw on a store of specific instances which may all too often appear to destroy the generalizations of the latter.

Can research bridge the gap, through the testing by rigorously designed experiments of carefully formulated hypotheses relating to the behaviour of individuals and organizations? The results so far are not encouraging and in recent years the transferability of methodologies applicable in the natural world to the world of social action has been searchingly questioned (Walsh, 1972).

Teaching in any field of administration is certainly no light task, either for the academic or the practitioner; and the transition from one role to the other is one which merits more consideration than it generally receives. The most commonly suggested solution is that teachers and practitioners of administration should exchange positions, so that teaching becomes a shared activity. Indeed, this is the basis of the staff college concept, whether in the armed forces, business management or public administration. But in each case the prerequisite is a very well comprehended body of custom, theory and practice. In educational administration this is now beginning to emerge.

TO WHAT EXTENT IS EDUCATIONAL ADMINISTRATION 'CULTURE-BOUND' AND TO WHAT EXTENT CAN OUR STUDIES AND OUR EXPERIENCES BE EFFECTIVELY SHARED?

The administration of education inevitably takes a different form in Ghana from the administration of education in Sri Lanka or New Zealand or Papua New Guinea or Guyana. Yet the school and the college and the educational system are universals now throughout the whole world. We are therefore challenged to develop frames of reference through which both the general and the specific in the experiences of our different countries can be identified and interpreted.

For myself, I find a developmental frame of reference helpful. It seems to me that in all our countries we can detect three strata. There is, first of all, the stratum dating from pre-industrial times. It is from deep in this level that emerged our differing languages, religions, customs and traditions and our sense of local-regional and national identities. Then there is the industrial stratum, where there emerged new forms of relationships between human beings, expressed through large-scale industrial enterprises, highly organized political parties, powerful trade unions and all-embracing national educational systems. Finally there is the technological stratum in which we are now living, with its great international governmental, industrial and commercial agencies, its facilities for incredibly rapid travel and its massive network of communications, including world wide telephone, cable, radio and television systems and stores of computerized information.

It is at this third level that has arisen our present concern with the administration of organizations and with the behaviour of human beings in them; with planning and resource allocation and with new forms of decision-making and participation. At this level it is not too difficult to share our knowledge and our understanding, because so much is new to all of us, no matter how distinctive our cultural histories or the routes by which we have arrived at the present day. Our ways of thinking and writing about organizations and the ways in which they are administered constitutes (despite obvious problems of terminology) an international idiom, not least significant in what concerns our educational systems.

Yet caution is needed. The very ease of communication within the technological stratum can lead to an over-generalization which obscures major and persisting differences and perceptions stemming from the pre-industrial and the industrial strata. Study and research in educational administration must continue, the more it becomes international in its scope, to be sensitive to these differences and, as Farquhar (1970) has argued, be ready to draw on the study of history and literature to interpret them.

Occasions such as the 1974 International Intervisitation Programme provide an opportunity to clarify thinking on issues such as those I have raised. In response to the challenge, we can, I think, reasonably hope:

to establish common ground where none may have existed before, without minimizing real differences of opinion and conviction; as individuals, to establish a framework for the identification and satisfaction of specific interests;
to promote and stimulate action and interest in our various countries in the Commonwealth Council for Educational Administration and the University Council for Educational Administration;
perhaps most important of all, to make those personal contacts which will enable us to achieve the three objectives I have listed and which will serve as a solid basis for further efforts during the coming years.

BIBLIOGRAPHY

Beeby, C. E. (1967), *Planning and the educational administrator*, Fundamentals of Educational Planning No. 4, International Institute of Educational Planning, Unesco, Paris.
Callahan, Raymond E. (1962), *Education and the Cult of Efficiency*, University of Chicago Press, Chicago.

Culbertson, Jack, Farquhar, R. H., Fogarty, B. M. and Shibles, M. R. (eds) (1973) *Social Science Content for Preparing Educational Leaders,* Merrill Publishing Co, Columbus, Ohio.

Davies, J. L. (1973), 'Management by Objectives in Local Education Authorities and Educational Institutions', *Educational Administration Bulletin,* 2(1), 38–54.

Farquhar, R. H. (1970), *The Humanities in Preparing Educational Administrators,* ERIC Clearinghouse on Educational Administration, University of Oregon, Eugene, Oregon.

Fielden, J. and Lockwood, T. G. (1973), *Planning and Management in Universities,* Chatto and Windus, London.

Glatter, Ron (1972), *Management Development for the Education Profession,* Harrap, for the University of London Institute of Education, London.

Hughes, Meredydd G. (ed) (1974), *Secondary School Administration: A Management Approach,* 2nd edn, Pergamon, Oxford.

Taylor, G. (ed) (1970), *The Teacher as Manager,* Councils and Education Press, London.

Taylor, William (ed) (1973), *Research Perspectives in Education,* Routledge & Kegan Paul, London. Ch. 8, Knowledge and Research.

University Council for Educational Administration (1973), *The Preparation and Certification of Educational Administrators,* Columbus, Ohio.

Walsh, David (1972), 'Sociology and the Social World', Ch. 2 in Filmer, Paul, Phillipson, Michael, Silverman, David, Walsh, David, *New Directions in Sociological Theory,* Collier-Macmillan, London.

Webb, P. C. (1973), 'Staff Development in large secondary schools', *Educational Administration Bulletin,* 2(1), 24–37.

3 Leadership and Decision-Making in Education

ERIC HOYLE

Leadership and decision-making are two closely linked issues which together constitute a massive topic for a short paper. In defining my areas of discussion I have chosen to indulge my own interests as a sociologist concerned with the application of organizational theory, and particularly theories of planned organizational change to schools. As a result leadership and decision-making are set in the context of the organization as a whole and also in the broader context of organization-in-environment.

The basic argument of the paper is as follows: Theorists of organization, management and administration have identified two fundamental models of organization. The more 'open' of these two models has provided the guiding metaphor for those who would seek to democratize the processes of leadership and decision-making and improve the functioning of organizations. However, in recent years some of the limitations of this model have become more obvious. This has consequently led to a more cautious and pragmatic approach to organizational change.

The paper falls into three main parts. In the first part the two basic models of organization will be outlined and considered in relation to a number of theoretical and substantive problems. The second part will examine the implications of these models in the context of the school. The third part will summarize recent trends in the field of organizational study and indicate what implications this has for theory, research and action.

TWO MODELS OF ORGANIZATION

There is a degree of consensus amongst students of organization that two fundamental models of organization can be identified. They have been given different names by different writers who have also focused upon different characteristics according to their interests and perspectives. They are, of course, 'ideal types'. The different attributes ascribed to these models are not always logically consistent, but they are sufficiently interrelated to permit generalizations to be made for the purpose of discussion. We can refer to them as Model A and Model B and in summary form they can be represented as follows:[1]

	MODEL A	MODEL B
BOUNDARY RELATIONSHIPS	Closed	Open
INTERNAL RELATIONSHIPS	Mechanistic	Organismic
ROLE PRESCRIPTIONS	High Specificity	Low Specificity

Although the models have been labelled A and B, they would clearly incorporate respectively the relationships referred to by McGregor (1960) as Theory X and Theory Y. Model A incorporates the characteristics which Weber and others have identified as bureaucracy i.e. authority vested in office, hierarchy, specific rules, clearly defined responsibilities, routinization, etc. Whereas Model B incorporates elements of the 'human relations' model i.e. horizontal patterns of authority, low specialization, a minimum of general rules, an emphasis on personal relations, etc. (Litwak, 1961).

Clearly leadership and decision-making are conceptualized differently in each model. In Model A leadership is a function of formal position in the hierarchy with its prescribed range and scope of decision-making. In Model B leadership is seen as informal, achieved, and related to task, whilst decisions are made collaboratively by the group who will be affected by the decisions made. Generally speaking, greater moral value and practical efficacy has been attributed to concepts of organization which approximate to Model B—often implicitly, sometimes explicitly. This form of organization is held to have two great advantages. One is that it is characterized by a flexibility, adaptability and structural looseness which is regarded as 'functional' in a

[1] For a more extensive analysis see Hickson (1966-7) who draws attention to the distinction between high/low role specificity. The terms 'mechanical' and 'organismic' are used by Burns and Stalker (1961).

period of rapid change. The other is that its democratic structure and support for the self-actualization amongst participants is congruent with the prevailing Weltanschauung.[2]

Model B has provided the guiding metaphor for training experiences in management and administration, and the theoretical materials for a variety of change strategies. Initially the emphasis was on group techniques for improving interpersonal competence but latterly this has extended to a concern with the problem-solving capacities of the organization as a whole. A neat summary of the organizational pattern towards which many change strategies were directed has been provided by Bennis[3] (1970):

First of all, the key word will be temporary: organizations will become adaptive, rapidly changing temporary systems. Second, they will be organized around problems-to-be-solved. Third, these problems will be solved by relative groups of strangers who represent a diverse set of professional skills. Fourth, given the requirements of coordinating the various projects, articulating points or 'linking pin' personnel will be necessary who can speak the diverse languages of research and who can relay and mediate between various project groups. Fifth, the groups will be conducted on organic rather than on mechanical lines; they will emerge and adapt to the problems, and leadership and influence will fall to those who seem most able to solve the problems rather than to programmed role expectations. People will be differentiated, not according to rank or roles, but according to skills and training.

Adaptive, temporary systems of diverse specialists solving problems, co-ordinated organically via articulating points, will gradually replace the theory and practice of bureaucracy. Though no catchy phrase comes to mind, it might be called an organic-adaptive structure.

Organization theory in general, and in particular the two models outlined above, generate a number of theoretical and substantive problems. One basic difficulty arises from the conceptualization of organizations as entities which have 'goals', 'purposes', 'characters', etc. This reification has been under attack in recent years as part of a general critique of the 'system' paradigm in sociology by those whose approach is within an 'action' or 'phenomenological' framework.

The phenomenologists criticise those sociologists who take a social

[2] Needless to say organization theories are historically and culturally relative. See Mayntz (1964).

[3] Bennis has more recently come to question his own earlier views on these points. This work will be referred to later in the paper.

system as such (e.g. an organization) as the focus of enquiry and give it ontological priority as an object external to the actor and constraining him. The phenomenologists give priority to action and the focus of their enquiry is the meaning which actors impose upon the situation. Thus an organization is seen as having only an intersubjective rather than objective reality. The phenomenological perspective is illuminating the nature of organizations. In particular it draws our attention to the definitions of the situation held by different groups of participants in an organization and the manner in which some groups succeed in imposing their own definitions on others. While this is an important perspective which is beginning to throw fresh light on organizations and the behaviour of participants it is not the perspective adopted in this paper. It is my view that, at least at the present time, the 'phenomenological' and the 'systems' perspectives cannot be simultaneously adopted, just as one cannot look down both ends of a telescope at one and the same time. The argument of the paper will be presented from the 'systems' perspective with which the writer feels most comfortable.

One important substantive point is the relative neglect of the problems of power in Model B type organizations. Power is, in one sense, relatively unproblematical in Model A type organizations. It is legitimized through investing the organizational head with legal authority which he may then partially delegate through the hierarchical structure. Modifications come through *informal* power within the organization and through the power which trade unions can exercise. The legitimacy of legal authority becomes much more problematical as one moves toward organizations of Type B. Whilst heads of organizations have legal authority vested in them, there are obvious limits to the diffusion of power in organizations. Legal authority tends to be underplayed in Model B approaches. Many of the change strategies associated with Model B are concerned with the 'management' of conflict. Conflict is domesticated; it is seen as having a 'function', as stimulating creativity, as generating innovation—which, of course, may well be the case. In many organizations—especially those staffed by professionals—conflict has in the past been limited in scope since disputes have tended to be about means and therefore resolved by reference to the ends about which there is a general consensus.

However, two developments have occurred which are creating new problems of authority. One of these is the growing demand for participation in decision-making in organizations. Whilst legal authority is vested in the head of the institution there are limits to the extent to which other members can exercise ultimate power through the decision-making process. The problem here is that unless the limits are spelt out, involvement in decision-making can come to be seen as a sham. A further factor in the situation is the growing tendency to question the legitimacy of organizations which has been particularly evident in the universities. Here conflict has been about organizational goals which Model B type strategies are incapable of handling.

The second development is the growing impact of the environment of an organization upon its internal activities. Although lip service has long been paid to organizations as 'open systems', with some exceptions the impact of the environment has until recently been underestimated in organization theory. This may be due either to the mainly introspective approach of organizational theorists or to the fact that the environment is, in fact, becoming more 'turbulent', or perhaps to both. The following are some of the environmental changes which are likely to impinge upon the internal activities of many types of organization: the changing attitudes to authority which have already been mentioned, together with a greater reluctance to accept institutions as sacrosanct, the explosion of knowledge, technological developments, the growing interdependence of organizations, and the increase in rate of change. In this situation organizations may lose the capacity for self-determination.

ORGANIZATIONAL THEORY AND THE SCHOOL

The study of schools as complex organizations has followed general trends in the sociology of organizations.[4] Traditionally the focus has been upon the professional-in-organization. The tension between the requirements of coordination (control) and the requirements of the exercise of professionality (autonomy) has been a recurrent theme in the literature. Although some studies have characterized school as bureaucracies, i.e. Model A, most commentators have noted that the school approximates neither to Model A nor to Model B in their pure form, but contains elements of both (e.g. Bidwell, 1965, Lortie, 1969). They conform to what Litwak (1961) referred to as a 'professional' model which would be applicable to such organizations as universities

[4] See Hoyle (1965, 1969b, 1973b). For an alternative view from a phenomenological perspective see Dale (1973).

and hospitals which handle both uniform events (need for coordination) and non-uniform events (need for autonomy). Hence they are, in Litwak's terms, 'one part bureaucracy and one part human relations'.

This mixed model is generally applicable to the British school. Typically, the headmaster has been largely free from external control and has had a high degree of authority within the school. He has usually made the most of the crucial decisions regarding the goals and policies of the school, but he has had little control over the teacher in relation to the core professional act of teaching.

Conversely, the teacher has enjoyed a reasonable degree of autonomy over matters of teaching style, methods, the pacing of work and so on.[5] This has been supported by his physical isolation from other teachers and by the strong professional norm of non-interference. On the other hand, teachers have not in the past been extensively involved in decision-making in relation to the goals and curriculum of the schools as a whole. However, changes have recently been occurring in the nature of the relationship between the authority of the head and the autonomy of the teacher. Of particular significance have been changes in educational practice and the demand by teachers for greater participation in decision-making.

Table 1 summarizes some of the changes in educational practice.

Table 1

Dimension	From	To
CURRICULUM CONTENT	Monodisciplinary	Interdisciplinary
PEDAGOGY	Didactic teaching	Discovery learning
ORGANIZATION OF TEACHING/LEARNING	Rigid timetabling	Flexible timetabling
PUPIL GROUPING	Homogeneous	Heterogeneous
PUPIL CHOICE	Limited	Extensive
ASSESSMENT	Single mode	Multiple modes
BASIS OF PUPIL CONTROL	Positional	Personal
TEACHER ROLES	Independent	Interdependent
ARCHITECTURE	Closed	Open Plan
SCHOOL-COMMUNITY LINKS	Weak	Strong

[5] But one should not underestimate the constraints of the examination system, nor, in secondary schools, the degree to which the head of a subject department controls the syllabus.

Some of the implications of these changes have been explored in a most insightful way by Bernstein (1967, 1971) who has approached the sociology of the school from a Durkheimian rather than Weberian perspective and has emphasized the symbolic order rather than the structure of the school. The changes potentially involve an increased permeability of boundaries between subjects, between categories of pupils, between teachers, between school and home. The shift is along the continuum from closed system to open system. As Bernstein puts it, 'Roles are no longer made, but have to be made' and, significantly, he notes that in such a system 'problems of boundary, continuity, order and ambivalence are likely to arise'.

The teacher's demand for participation in decision-making has perhaps two sources. One source is the changes in educational practice described above; as boundaries are weakened and more collaborative teaching and curriculum planning occur, teachers need to extend the scope of the decisions which they take. The other source is the general movement towards the democratization of institutions. In England and Wales this demand has been recently pressed by the teacher unions (NAS, 1972; NUT, 1973) but it is important to note that schools have not been unionized according to the industrial pattern of management-worker dichotomy, although this is currently advocated by some younger teachers.

We can consider against this background issues relating to the authority and professionality. Changes in the school illustrate the dilemma of leadership in an organization moving towards Model B. It has often been argued that the most appropriate pattern of authority in an organization staffed by professionals is 'collegial' authority whereby professional equals govern their activities by means of democratic procedures. However, as long as legal authority is vested in the head, he is unlikely to relinquish final responsibility to his group of teachers. Thus it is probable that participation will be limited to consultation—although the degree of consultation can be extensive or minimal. The problem here is that in attempting to reconcile democratic expectations and legal responsibility the head is tempted to blur the boundaries of his authority in order to appear to satisfy demands for participation. As teachers seek a greater voice in the affairs of the school, the head may need to develop various strategies in order to defend his authority. These may include invoking external authority to legitimize his decisions ('the office wouldn't hear of it'), the absorption of protest by cooptation, playing off competing interest groups against each other, invoking consensus without taking a vote, etc. There is obviously a need to investigate these processes and also such aspects of collegiate or quasi-collegial authority as 'involuted hierarchies' and 'the receding locus of power' (Noble and Pym, 1970) wherein it is difficult to determine who actually makes a decision, when and how. Sub-committees claim that they pass recommendations up the line but do not make decisions; the main committee claims that the real decisions are made below and that it acts merely as a rubber stamp.

Analyses which have focussed upon the teacher as professional-in-organization tend not to have explored the nature of professionality. Yet differences in professionality have quite fundamental implications for the decisions which teachers take. To further the argument a tentative distinction can be made between two kinds of professionality, *extended* and *restricted*.

Table 2

Restricted Professionality	*Extended Professionality*
Skills derived from experience	Skills derived from a mediation between experience and theory
Perspective limited to the immediate in time and place	Perspective embraces the broader social context of education
Classroom events perceived in isolation	Classroom events perceived in relation to school policies and goals
Introspective with regard to methods	Methods compared with those of colleagues and with reports of practice
Value placed on autonomy	Value placed on professional collaboration
Limited involvement in non-teaching professional activities	High involvement in non-teaching professional activities (esp. teachers' centres, subject associations, research)
Infrequent reading of professional literature	Regular reading of professional literature
Involvement in in-service work limited and confined to practical courses	Involvement in in-service work considerable and includes courses of a theoretical nature
Teaching seen as an intuitive activity	Teaching seen as a rational activity

The boundary changes which were described earlier are loosening the structure of the school and creating areas of uncertainty. But teachers have an increased opportunity to exercise a greater collaborative control over their own work situation. As the decisions which they collectively take broaden in scope, effective participation in collaborative decision-making would appear to be associated with a movement towards extended professionality. However, there are some indications (Jackson, 1968; Lortie, 1969) that teachers place a very high value on autonomy and professional activities of a restricted form. This issue throws into relief an important paradox. If teachers wish to resist trends towards greater openness and hence limit uncertain situations, they need to have greater control over their work situation; but the form of control implies an increased degree of collaboration which is itself a component of the extended professionality which is being resisted.[6]

If one turns from organizational theory to the strategies of organizational change which have been employed in education, mainly in North America, one finds, perhaps not surprisingly, that there have been parallel developments in non-educational organizations. Action to improve the functioning of schools has hitherto been largely concerned with utilizing group techniques to improve inter-personal and decision-making skills. However, it has recently come to be appreciated that the improvement of leadership and decision-making skills must occur in the context of the management structure of the school as an organization, with due consideration given to legitimate authority. Current approaches begin with improving communication skills, move to changing norms, and thence to changing organizational structures. The application of these techniques of Organizational Development (OD) to schools has been pioneered by Schmuck and Miles. The objectives of Organizational Development are: clarifying communication, establishing goals, uncovering conflicts and interdependence, improving group procedures, solving problems, making decisions and assessing changes (Schmuck and Runkel, 1972). This approach appears to have considerable potential for improving leadership and decision-making in schools. However, two points need to be made. The first is that the assumptions about goal consensus which appear to be implicit in OD approaches cannot go unquestioned. The second is that in so far as OD is 'introspective'—in the sense of concentrating upon the internal

[6] See Hoyle (1974) for a more extended discussion of this point.

problem-solving capacities of the school—it may be that O D activities are overwhelmed by the press of changes in the school environment.

In sum, an examination of organizational theory and action in relation to the school again suggests two points: that both theory and action must increasingly take account of the organizational environment and that power needs to be given greater attention than has generally been the case in Model B type approaches. These problems are influencing recent trends in the field of organizational studies outside education.

RECENT TRENDS IN ORGANIZATIONAL THEORY

In this final section we can extend our immediate concern with educational organizations to a brief consideration of more general trends in organizational theory. Warren Bennis was earlier cited as a protagonist of the Model B approach. However, in his more recent works he has expressed some doubts about his earlier position.[7] He has recorded the following doubts (Bennis, 1970):

1. The organizations I had in mind then were of a single class: instrumental, large-scale, science-based, international bureaucracies, operating under rapid growth conditions. Service industries and public bureaucracies, as well as nonsalaried employees, were excluded from analysis.
2. Practically no attention was paid to the boundary transactions of the firm or to interinstitutional linkages.
3. The management of conflict was emphasized, while the strategy of conflict was ignored.
4. Power of all types was underplayed, while the role of the leader as facilitator—'linking pin'—using an 'agricultural model' of nurturance and climate building was stressed.
5. A theory of change was implied, based on gentle nudges from the environment coupled with a truth-love strategy; that is, with sufficient trust and collaboration along with valid data, organizations would progress monotonically along a democratic continuum.

[7] See Bennis (1966), Bennis and Slater (1968), Bennis (1970), Thomas and Bennis (1972) and Bennis (1973) for the elaboration of these ideas. Bennis's views have undoubtedly been influenced by his chastening experience as an administrator at the State University of New York at Buffalo where he faced serious student and faculty problems. In his account of this experience (Bennis, 1973) he notes that as an organizational theorist confronting this practical challenge he felt like the character in a poem by W. H. Auden 'who lectured on navigation as the ship was going down'!

Without switching to a Model A approach to contemporary organizations, Bennis draws attention to some of the shortcomings of Model B. In particular, the two neglected issues mentioned earlier in the paper—power and the influence of the environment. Model B is predicated upon the dispersal of power and the possibility of maintaining consensus or, at least, managing conflict. But doubts about the management of conflict need not be expressed only in terms of irreconcilable class interests or confined to industrial organizations. There is no doubt that some of the conflicts which are being brought into organizations—conflicts amongst professionals themselves or conflicts between professions and clients—arise from class interests, but others do not. Perhaps more important is the use of conflict as a strategy which, though usually linked with radical interests, is logically capable of separation from them. This raises enormous questions of power *vis à vis* both Model A and Model B. It arises from the more general question of the autonomy of institutions versus their politicisation.[8] Clearly the two problems of power and environment are, at one level, linked since it is change in the political environment which is leading to problems of authority, participation and conflict within organizations.

A number of organization analysts and students of management have recently drawn attention to the increasingly problematic nature of the environment with which future theory and practice will need to deal. In their recent book *Towards a Social Ecology*, Emery and Trist (1973) refer to environments as 'turbulent fields'. 'These are environments in which there are dynamic processes arising from the field itself which create significant variances for the component systems.' Similar points of view have been expressed by other writers e.g. Schon (1971), Vickers (1968), Terreberry (1968), Clark and Krone (1972). The turbulence arises from social, cultural, technological and practical trends in society and it should be particularly noted that turbulence for one organization is, increasingly, created by the activities of other organizations because of the trend towards inter-dependence.

One implication of the consideration of the organization-environment nexus is that the 'one right model' of organization must finally be discounted. Organizational theorists currently advocate a 'contingency model' (Lawrence and Lorsch, 1967) which points to the fact that structures are contingent upon the problems with which they have to deal, and that within one organization different sub units which deal

[8] On this question see Schelsky (1974), and Lowenthal (1974).

with different problems may vary in structure, style, time-perspective etc. Another implication is that organizations need a 'situational' perspective, that is, they need to make a careful diagnosis of their environmental context. This has significance for modes of achieving organizational change. It suggests, for example, that Organizational Development strategies perhaps need to take more cognizance of the context. This has been suggested by Clark and Krone (1972) who have mapped out an approach termed 'open system planning' which involves procedures which can:

1. Rapidly identify and map out the dynamic realities which are in their environment
2. Map out how the organization represented by the members of the group presently acts toward and hence values those realities
3. Map out how the organization wants to engage with those realities in the future (that is, to set value-goals)
4. Make plans to restructure the 'architecture' of the organization in order to influence the environmental realities in the valued directions.

They note that this does not constitute an alternative to existing patterns of organizational development but is an extension of them.

The growing salience of the organizational environment suggests that those who have decision-making responsibilities in any organization should be aware of the broader social, economic and political trends which, of course, have implications for their training. One example has already been mentioned, that is the relevance of current socio-political trends. The theme of 'participation' has been touched upon at several points in this paper. This demand raises some fundamental issues not only in the context of the micro-decision processes of an organization but more generally in relation to the nature of democracy. And yet, in the 'interdisciplinary' study of educational administration, political theory has been relatively neglected.[9] Another example is the relevance of inter-organizational analysis. This is particularly relevant to the area of curriculum development and welfare. The boundaries of the school are becoming much more open to the potential influence of a variety of outside agencies of curriculum development and of pupil welfare which are presenting the schools

[9] As it has been in this paper. It has been argued that in fact the relationship between participation and the political theory of democracy has been neglected by political theorists themselves (Pateman, 1970).

with the problem of taking advantage of the various external services whilst retaining their own identity.[10]

CONCLUSION

This paper has not dealt with the processes of leadership and decision-making in behavioural terms but has placed them in the broad context of organizational theory. It follows from the argument of this paper that one needs to be sceptical of overarching organization theories and that the more tentative 'contingency' perspective is appropriate. This is not to say, however, that organizational theorizing has no value. So long as it is balanced by a phenomenological approach to the study of organizational processes, the development of models of organization can sensitize one to key issues and permit tentative generalizations and comparisons. However, organizational theory and associated strategies of organizational development perhaps need to be more outward looking and take more account of the organizational environment and, beyond this, the salient changes in society. But this is not to deny the continuing importance of work with groups nor of current patterns of Organizational Development. It is simply to put the case for adding new levels of theory and action.

BIBLIOGRAPHY

Bennis, W. G. (1966), *Changing Organizations*, McGraw-Hill, New York.
Bennis, W. G. and Slater, B. E. (1968), *The Temporary Society*, Harper and Row, New York.
Bennis, W. G. (1970), 'A funny thing happened on the way to the future', *American Psychologist*, 25(7).
Bennis, W. G. (1973), *The Leaning Ivory Tower*, Jossey-Bass, New York.
Bernstein, B. (1967), 'Open schools, open society ?', *New Society*, 10.
Bernstein, B. (1971), 'On the classification and framing of educational knowledge', in Young, M. F. D. (ed) *Knowledge and Control*, Collier-Macmillan, London.
Bidwell, C. E. (1965), 'The school as a formal organization', in March, J. G. (ed) *Handbook of Organizations*, Rand McNally, Chicago.
Burns, T. and Stalker, G. M. (1961), *The Management of Innovation*, Tavistock, London.

[10] For the problem of the linkage between schools and agencies of welfare see Litwak and Meyer (1967).
For the problem of linkage between schools and agencies of research and curriculum development see Havelock (1971) and Hoyle (1967, 1969a, 1969b, 1970).

Clark, J. V. and Krone, C. G. (1972), 'Towards an overview of organizational development in the early seventies', in Thomas and Bennis, op. cit.

Dale, R. (1973), 'Phenomenological perspectives and the sociology of the school', Ed. Rev., 25(3).

Douglas, J. (ed) (1971), Understanding Everyday Life, Routledge & Kegal Paul, London.

Emery, F. E. and Trist, E. L. (1973), Towards a Social Ecology, Plenum Press, London.

Filmer, P. et al. (1972), New Directions in Sociological Theory, Collier-Macmillan, London.

Havelock, R. G. (1971), 'The utilization of educational research and development', British Journal of Education Technology, 2(2).

Hickson, D. J. (1966–7), 'A convergence in organization theory', Admin. Sci. Quart., 11.

Hoyle, E. (1965), 'Organizational Analysis in the field of education', Educ. Res., 7.

Hoyle, E. (1969a), 'Organizational Theory and educational administration', in Baron, G. and Taylor, W., Educational Administration and the Social Sciences, Athlone Press, London.

Hoyle, E. (1969b), 'How does the curriculum change? A proposal for enquiries', J. Curric. Stud., 1(3).

Hoyle, E. (1969c), 'How does the curriculum change? 1. Systems and strategies', J. Curr. Stud., 1(2).

Hoyle, E. (1970), 'Planned organizational change in education', Research in Education, 3.

Hoyle, E. (1973a), 'Strategies of curriculum change', in Watkins, R. (ed) In-Service Training: Structure and Content, Wark Lock, London.

Hoyle, E. (1973b), 'The study of schools as organizations' in Butcher, H. J. and Pont, H. (eds) Educ. Res. in Britain III, University of London Press, London.

Hoyle, E. (1974), 'Professionality, professionalism and control in teaching', London Ed. Rev., 3(2).

Jackson, P. (1968), Life in Classrooms, Holt, Rinehart and Winston, New York.

Lawrence, P. and Lorsch, J. W. (1967), Organizations and Environment, Harvard University Press, Cambridge, Mass.

Litwak, E. (1961), 'Models of bureaucracy which permit conflict', Am. J. Soc., 67.

Litwak, E. and Meyer, H. J. (1967), 'The school and the family: linking organisations and external primary groups', in Lazardsfeld, P. et al. The Uses of Sociology, Basic Books, New York.

Lortie, D. (1969), 'The balance of control and autonomy in elementary school teaching', in Etzioni, A. (ed), The Semi Professions, Free Press, New York.

Lowenthal (1974), 'The conservative utopia', Encounter, 62(6).

Mayntz, R. (1964), 'The study of organizations', Current Sociology, 13(3).

McGregor, D. (1960), The Human Side of Enterprise, McGraw-Hill, New York.

National Association of Schoolmasters (1972), Management, Organization and Discipline, N.A.S., Hemel Hempstead.

National Union of Teachers (1973), Teacher Participation. A statement of recommendations made to the Annual Conference.

Noble, T. and Pym, B. (1970), 'Collegial authority and the receding locus of power', *Brit. J. Soc.*, 21(4).

Pateman, C. (1970), *Participation and Democratic Theory*, Cambridge University Press, Cambridge.

Salaman, G. and Thompson, K. (1973), *People and Organizations*, Longmans/Open University Press, London.

Schelsky (1974), 'A German dilemma', *Encounter*, 62(2).

Schmuck, R. A. and Runkel, P. J. (1972), *Handbook of Organizational Development in Schools*, National Press Books.

Schon, D. (1971), *Beyond the Stable State*, Smith & Temple, London.

Silverman, D. (1970), *The Theory of Organizations*, Heinemann, London.

Terreberry, S. (1968), 'On the evolution of organizational environments', *Admin. Sci. Quart.*, 12.

Thomas, J. M. and Bennis, W. G. (eds) (1972), *The Management of Conflict*, Penguin Books, London.

Vickers, G. (1968), *Value Systems and Social Processes*, Tavistock, London.

4 Changing and Improving Educational Systems and Institutions

A. ROSS THOMAS

Nowadays it is extremely difficult to discuss education without mentioning change and innovation. That the social context of education is ever-changing—and at an increasing rate—there is no doubt. That education is changing also appears a valid conclusion but the speed with which it is changing is open to considerable debate. Certainly it is conventional wisdom to speak of widespread and spontaneous change and innovation in education as though the processes are self-evident. Yet when one asks if, in recent years, schools have changed at a rate and in a manner commensurate with that of society as a whole, the foregoing assumption appears, at the least, extremely tenuous. At times, one is forced to conclude that for many educators—and especially for many administrators—conversation and publication amply laced with the mention of 'innovations adopted' are *the* hallmarks of professional standing, the enhancers of peer group status and the symbols of the educator's plugged in, switched on, with it, modern image. Thelen (1961) expresses a not uncommon view of the contemporary situation:

In the face of all these changes ... the schools' society and culture seems largely undisturbed. Comparing classrooms now with the classrooms of 40 years ago, one notes that at both times there were numbers of students not much interested in what was being done; the typical teacher still presents material and quizzes the kids to see if they understand it; the amount of creativity and excitement is probably no greater now than then. The development of new materials and techniques has enabled us to spin our wheels in one place, to conduct business as usual in the face of dramatic changes in the society and in the clientele of the school.[1]

Accordingly, this paper has two purposes: first, to consider briefly

[1] See also Martin and Harrison (1972) and Fullan (1972) who lend emphasis to this perception of the amount of 'real' change that has taken place in contemporary education.

the contribution that research has made to an understanding of educational change; second, to offer a model which, it is hoped, will assist administrators in effecting beneficial educational change.

RESEARCH ON EDUCATIONAL CHANGE: THE MAIN THRUST

What is known about change in educational organizations? Most studies of educational change have been concerned primarily with the adoption of specific educational innovations. They have been conducted in the relatively decentralized milieu of education in the U.S.A. where research has largely focussed on the diffusion concept, namely the spread or permeation of an innovation from system to system or from school to school throughout a particular state or number of states. Attempts to answer such questions as why one innovation is adopted more readily than another or why one system of education is more innovative[2] than another, have all been contingent in one way or another on this approach. Most diffusion research has been directed towards the variables associated with innovativeness. Two distinct approaches are identifiable. The first has been concerned with identifying the intrinsic characteristics of an innovation that influence its adoption; the second has considered factors not directly related to the innovation itself.

(i) *Intrinsic Characteristics of the Innovation*

At first glance it might appear that adoption is dependent simply upon the 'nature' of the innovation itself, especially those intrinsic characteristics held to be preferable to those of other innovations. Miles (1964), for example, in an analysis of research findings, asserts that there are five characteristics of an innovation that influence its adoption, namely, (i) cost, (ii) technological factors, (iii) availability of associated support materials, (iv) simplicity of implementation, and (v) innovation-system congruence. Those most widely accepted as influencing adoption have been identified by Rogers (1962).[3] The characteristics, all of which are dependent upon the *perceptions* of the adopter, are (i) the relative advantage offered over any similar idea or process, (ii) the

[2] For some of the problems encountered (i) in defining school innovativeness see Fullan and Eastabrook (1970); (ii) in measuring innovativeness see Holdaway and Seger (1968).

[3] See also Rogers and Shoemaker (1971).

compatibility of the innovation with the adopting system, (iii) its complexity, (iv) its divisibility, i.e. the extent to which the innovation can be 'tried' on a partial or limited basis before adoption, and (v) communication, i.e. the ease with which an innovation can be described and explained.

The use of its intrinsic characteristics as a device to predict whether an innovation will be adopted (or whether a particular school or system will adopt that innovation) has not proved very revealing, however. It seems that the 'nature' of an innovation is not sufficient alone to predict whether (or when) an innovation will be adopted by an individual, a school or an education system.[4]

(ii) *Non-Intrinsic Factors Related to Adoption*

The second and more popular approach to the study of the adoption of educational innovations has been to investigate characteristics of the 'adopter unit', namely, communities, schools, systems, superintendents, principals and teachers. Again, the great majority of this research has been carried out in the U.S.A. To attempt to document the multitude of findings that have emerged is certainly beyond the ambit of this paper.[5] Generally, however, one finds a series of 'biographical' and demographic characteristics which distinguish between the more innovative and the less innovative adopter units. For example, relative to his less innovative counterpart, the innovative superintendent (i) is younger,[6] (ii) has attained a higher level of education,[7] (iii) has had more administrative experience,[8] (iv) has taught for fewer years,[9] (v) is better prepared professionally, through reading and through attendance at conferences and workshops,[10] (v) has belonged to and supported more professional organizations,[11] (vii) has come from the 'outside' into his current system,[12] (viii) remains in his current system

[4] See, for example, Carlson (1965); Kohl (1966); Spencer (1967); Oskamp (1968); Littleton (1970).

[5] For a detailed summary see Rogers and Shoemaker (1971).

[6] See, for example, Todd (1963); Jensen (1967); Hawkins (1968); Heisler (1968); Ramer (1968); Hearn (1969).

[7] Todd (1963); Jensen (1967); Spencer (1967); Hawkins (1968); Heisler (1968); Ramer (1968); Hearn (1969).

[8] Klingenberg (1966); Hearn (1969).   [9] Allen (1967).

[10] Nicholson (1965); Hearn (1969); Scott (1970).   [11] Heisler (1968).

[12] Carlson (1962); Reynolds (1965); Hall (1966); Knedlik (1967); Heisler (1968); Preising (1968).

for a comparatively shorter period of time,[13] (ix) has more extensive channels of communication,[14] and (x) enjoys a higher status in the social structure relative to other superintendents.[15] Nor does the description end there. Numerous additions could be made to the profile from findings that relate to differences in personality traits,[16] and leadership characteristics.[17] Characteristics of innovative principals and innovative teachers can also be combined to construct very similar profiles.

Factors relating to other than school administrative and teaching personnel have also been shown to have an influence on the adoption of educational innovations. Community factors have been identified, for example, the educational and social characteristics that reflect the level of faith or expectancy in education as a powerful instrument of society,[18] the attitude of school boards,[19] the location[20] and size of schools[21] and school districts.[22] Foremost among this category of studies, however, have been those that have revealed the apparent importance of an economic factor which, although defined in a variety of terms, has linked innovative schools and systems with 'wealthier' districts or communities,[23] higher per-pupil income or expenditure,[24] and the payment of higher salaries to administrative and/or teaching staff.[25]

[13] Todd (1963); Reynolds (1965); Hall (1966); Jensen (1967); Hawkins (1968); Ramer (1968); Hearn (1969).

[14] Carlson (1962); Klingenberg (1966); Heisler (1968); Scott (1970).

[15] Carlson (1965); Jensen (1967); Heisler (1968); Peets (1970).

[16] Nicholson (1965); Allen (1967); Reese (1967); Spencer (1967); Heisler (1968).

[17] Goetz (1965); Jacobs (1965); Sargent (1965); Klingenberg (1966); Jensen (1967); Spencer (1967); Santo (1968); Hearn (1969); Kuhn (1969); Scott (1970).

[18] Mort and Ross (1957).

[19] Currie (1966); La Plant (1966); Hawkins (1968); Heisler (1968); Kunzler (1968); Richland (1968); Scott (1970).

[20] Bergsma (1963); Mertz (1965); Spencer (1967); Richland (1968).

[21] Bergsma (1963); Kendig (1965); Kohl (1966); Allen (1967); Spencer (1967); Preising (1968); Gill (1970); Wright (1970).

[22] Spencer (1967); Lawrence (1968); Preising (1968).

[23] Mort and Ross (1957); Bergsma (1963); Kendig (1965); Nicholson (1965); Brievogel (1967); Spencer (1967); Pafford (1967); Hawkins (1968); Roosa (1968); Santo (1968).

[24] Storkel (1962); Nicholson (1965); Hanson (1966); La Plant (1966); Brievogel (1967); Spencer (1967); Hughes (1968); Marcum (1968); Preising (1968); Ramer (1968); Roosa (1968); Foster (1969).

[25] Carlson (1962); Goetz (1965); Nicholson (1965); Breivogel (1967); Spencer (1967); Johnson (1968); Richland (1968).

(iii) *Limitations of Diffusion Research*

In spite of the apparent wealth of generalizations that have emerged from diffusion-type studies the educational administrator must view such information with care for there are both methodological and applicational limitations that should be considered.

The most widely used method of ranking adopter units' innovativeness has been by means of an adoption scale. On this, the respondent is given a list of innovations that first became 'available' during a certain period of time. The respondent is asked to indicate which innovations he adopted and also *when* he adopted them.[26] In accord with the definition above the 'more innovative' unit will adopt more innovations and do so earlier than its less innovative counterpart. There have been many variations of this approach,[27] however.

The major weakness of adoption scale analysis is that it focusses on only a limited aspect of the total change process.[28] As such it assumes that innovations are developed elsewhere and 'imported' by the adopter unit. No allowance is thereby made for innovations developed *internally*, e.g. by the teachers in a particular school; no recognition is permitted to Thompson's (1952, p. 2) definition of innovation as ' ... the *generation*, acceptance and implementation of new ideas, processes, products or services. Innovation ... implies the *capacity* to change or adopt.' Further, the adoption scale assumes, in large measure, that its selected innovations are intrinsically 'valuable' and are implemented automatically by the commitment to adopt.

The adoption of a particular innovation by a school is usually reported by an administrator[29] (such as the principal or superintendent).[30]

---

[26] La Plant (1966); Allen (1967); Breivogel (1967); Carswell (1968).

[27] Adoption scales have included as few as one (Kindsvatter, 1966) and as many as 69 innovations (Carswell, 1968). Some are scored only in terms of the number of innovations adopted; (e.g. Addis, 1968; Lawrence, 1968; Peterson, 1968); in temporal terms some cover a wide span of years; others are concerned essentially with the short term. Some scales are used merely to distinguish between extreme groups such as 'most innovative' and 'least innovative'; others are used to place each adopter in any one of a number of categories.

[28] Havelock (1971) reported that adoption is an inadequate measure of educational change because it is the 'wrong' dependent variable. See also Fullan (1972) and Rogers and Shoemaker (1971).

[29] In Fullan's (1972, p. 6) terminology the adopter is, therefore, not necessarily the 'user' of the innovation.

[30] Information may also be gathered from (e.g.) central office records (Eibler,

Seldom, however, are other important details provided, for example, the nature and extent of the use of the innovation,[31] the degree of teacher acceptance (and, conversely, the degree of resistance) and the benefits and consequences of the outcome. A fundamental weakness, is that the diffusion research tradition is based largely on the adoption of innovations by *individuals*, e.g. farmers, medical practitioners. But, because of the nature of schools, educational innovations are *organizational* innovations. Consequently, *reported* adoption may give little if any indication as to the degree to which an innovation has been *institutionalized*, i.e. as to what extent it has become part of the regular day-by-day structure and/or process of the school *qua* organization. It is probably quite erroneous, therefore, to construct a profile—albeit hypothetical—of an innovative school or system by combining the results of findings such as those reported above.[32] Research on the factors associated with the adoption of innovations by schools in the relatively centralized Australian systems tends to confirm this belief.[33]

Undoubtedly studies of educational innovation conducted in the diffusion tradition tell something about educational change. Nevertheless, the value of such findings is limited. Obviously, the restrictions of the particular methodologies used impose necessary qualifications when interpreting results. The nature of the findings also appear somewhat discouraging for the practising administrator concerned with improving schools that are conservative, static and non-innovative. For example, how could such an administrator effect change in a school located in an indigent socio-economic area, staffed by a principal and teachers who are 'old', have neither read nor travelled extensively and have worked within the same system for a relatively long period? Perhaps he could replace the school staff with the 'hero innovator' whose characteristics match those of the research findings reported above. But this could only be done at the risk of denuding other schools in the system of the same qualities and certainly would not guarantee success

[31] Exceptions to this may be seen in the studies of Hinman (1966), Marcum (1968) and Ochitwa (1973).

[32] The author is guilty of such a practice. See Thomas (1972, p. 120).

[33] See Thomas (1972, pp. 128–9).

1965; Klingenberg, 1966; McGrath, 1971). *Ranking* of schools or personnel is also occasionally used. Although not a diffusion approach in the strict sense such a method usually aims at providing information and data of a similar kind. (Leas, 1965; Bickert, 1967; Jensen, 1967; Thomas, 1972).

in his objectives. Clearly, however, the socio-economic characteristics of the community are beyond his manipulation.

(iv) *Impediments to Change*

Thus far the approach of this paper has been to consider research that focussed essentially on factors related to school and system innovativeness, factors thought, therefore, to be the *facilitators* of educational change. The preceding sections have ignored what may paradoxically prove to be a more fruitful approach, namely the consideration of the factors that *inhibit* educational change.[34]

Again, although not as extensive as the output of diffusion research, an impressive volume of findings is emerging. Watson's (1966) comprehensive survey of inhibitors in the educational environment serves as an excellent summary of findings. Arguing along lines not unlike those in the Guba-Getzels nomothetic-idiographic model,[35] Watson indicates that a combination of inhibiting forces is at work—those within the individual personality, e.g. the principal and teacher, and those that operate within the social system.

In another significant analysis Abbott (1965, p. 47) argues that the bureaucratic ideology and related dysfunctions in U.S. schools impede educational change. He points out that the hierarchical ordering of power and authority imposes severe restrictions on the development and adoption of innovations at the lower levels.

Since the right to innovate represents a potent source of power in the organization ... innovation from below is difficult to achieve ... This is true for at least two reasons. First, ideas that originate at the lower levels in the hierarchy encounter difficulty in receiving an adequate hearing. Second, any individual in a subordinate position, who takes the lead in introducing new programs of action, runs the risk of having sanctions imposed by his superordinate to allow that superordinate to escape the blamability which is inherent in the monistic system.

Similarly, the hierarchical definition of roles impedes innovation. The superordinate has the 'rights' to veto (or to affirm), to receive deference, to decide the form of the organization, to determine the personnel to be employed, to initiate activities, to assign activities, to

[34] Lewin's (1951) crucial work in this area has, of course, always directed attention to the importance of *reducing resistance* if change is to be effected with minimal stress.

[35] See Lipham's discussion in Chapter 17, pp. 265–9.

settle conflicts, and, of particular importance, to control communication.[36] Abbott also argues that the bureaucratic structure of the school impedes the professional development of the teaching role.

Abbott's argument is supported by Miles (1965) who characterizes schools in terms of their 'output ambiguity', i.e. their goals are inadequately expressed and uncertain. Teachers have come to rely on the ritual application of rules. Rules have, in turn, become ends in themselves. Miles also believes that in these changing times schools are subject to high 'input variability' from their environments. There is, therefore, a high level of uncertainty associated with school procedures which also tends to consolidate the reliance on rules and prescribed procedures.[37]

RESEARCH: THE DEVELOPING THRUST

It is probably accurate to state that the studies collected and edited by Miles (1964) in *Innovation in Education* collectively represent the first concerted effort to break out of the constrictions of the traditional approach to the study of educational change. Further studies that have appeared in the 1970s have consolidated this movement by concentrating more on the internal operational aspects of schools undergoing change. Increasingly, attempts are being made 'to analyze the structure and function of the innovation-receiving system as a context for innovation' (Miles, 1965, pp. 55–6) or, as Fullan (1972, p. 7) interprets the movement, to study the use of innovations and 'the users' role in the process of school change'. In many ways these studies increase understanding of the resistance process.

Smith and Keith's (1971) *Anatomy of Educational Innovation* is a most intensive study whose purpose was to describe 'the events that make up the beginning of an innovative school'. The particular innovation studied was basically one of school design in which all facilities were especially planned to facilitate individualized learning. The innovation was, in effect, a totally new environment catering for team teaching and all of its varying organizational possibilities—ungradedness, total

[36] See, however, Shephard (1967) who points out that the 'underworld of technique and technology' (i.e. the informal organization) may also be very powerful in this regard.

[37] For further detailed commentaries on the nature of change resistance in organizations see, for example, Coch and French (1948), Zander (1950), Lawrence (1954), Lippitt, Watson and Westley (1958).

democratic pupil-teacher decision making and a learner-centred environment. Information for the study was provided by participant observation interview, analysis of documents, meetings and field notes that recorded in precise detail events that took place within the first year of life of Kensington school. As conceived by the local school superintendent and administered by the principal, the objectives of Kensington were not unlike those of Summerhill. But the incongruity of an innovative school and the resistances that developed among its teachers and a conservative, dissatisfied, political community, reduced the school within a year to much the same status as Risinghill.

Smith and Keith identified many change inhibitors in Kensington. For example, too much was expected of his teachers by the principal. Although a visionary with a detailed plan for the growth of his new born school the principal did not adequately communicate with his teachers. The developing organizational climate which he saw as conducive to change because it provided teachers with freedom to innovate was perceived by them as *laissez-faire*, unconcerned and unhelpful leadership. Unfortunately, it was not realized that to be successful Kensington required very significant role changes in its teachers. The study shows quite clearly, however, that teachers encountered great difficulty in coordinating staff and student schedules and team-teaching activities. A third unanticipated problem arose from the apparent inability of students to work in a programme so dependent upon a high degree of self responsibility. Again, inadequate provision was made for the additional demands on teachers' time and energy that the nature of the school's operation demanded.

It is relevant to report Gross, Giacquinta and Bernstein's (1971) findings. Their study, also conducted in a single school, analyzed the process of implementation and focussed, in particular, on 'the extent to which organizational members have changed their behaviour patterns required by the innovation'. Gross *et al.* explain the failure of the change in terms of teachers' (i) lack of a clear understanding of the details and purposes of the change; (ii) inability to play the new roles demanded of them; (iii) unwillingness to participate—or to continue to participate—in the innovation; and (iv) the lack of the necessary supporting instructional materials.

One important finding that emerges consistently from studies such as the two cited above is that 'successful' innovation is directly related to the extent and nature of teacher involvement in the total process of change. For example, the unsuccessful innovation in the Gross *et al.* study was introduced to teachers as a *fait accompli*. Similarly, in his extensive summary of school change attempts, Sarason (1971) defines a 'modal process of change', illustrating the concept with the development of 'new math'. The innovation, developed outside the schools, was introduced to teachers also as a *fait accompli* and with many faulty assumptions about teachers' ability to accept the innovation easily and without major doubts as to its efficacy. Speaking of the modal process of change in récent years Silberman (1970, p. 182) states that 'the failure to involve ordinary classroom teachers in the creation and modification of the new curricula—tended to destroy or at least inhibit the very spirit of inquiry the new courses were designed to create.'

A STRATEGY OF CHANGE MODEL

The foregoing sections have been presented in the belief that *knowledge* of the change process is of value to the educational leader since it provides him with a better information base on which to develop administrative action. Accordingly, attempts have been made (i) to describe what have been—and what are emerging as—the main methodological approaches to the study of educational change, and (ii) to identify what appear to be the important findings that emerge repeatedly from these studies. In this section attention is now turned to a particular strategy which, hopefully, in conjunction with the findings reported previously, will assist the practising administrator in more successfully effecting change.[38] This intention is based on the assumption that educational innovations are usually—although not exclusively—introduced by superordinate members of the organizational hierarchy.

Implicit in the concept of planned educational change is the process of innovation, i.e. the systematic introduction of 'a new or different concept, methodology, organization or programme ... into the classroom' (Miller, 1967, p. iv). Since most innovations initially are introduced into an education system 'from above' the nature of the administrator (change agent)—teacher (adopter) relationship assumes considerable importance during the adoption process. The manner in which the change-agent seeks to implement change will subsume a number of important elements of administrative behaviour. Egon Guba (1967, p. 4) argues that:

[38] For an excellent treatment of strategies of change see Dalin (1973).

the most potent solutions that man can devise to overcome his problems have little utility if practitioners are not informed about them, or if they have little opportunity to discover that which they need to know about how the solutions work.

It therefore becomes part of the administrator's behaviour

to create awareness and to provide opportunities for the assessment of the invention along whatever dimensions the potential adopter may feel necessary ... (this), in short, makes the invention available and understandable to the practitioner.

Guba states that basically the foregoing can be achieved through the use of one or more of six *techniques*:

A. *Telling*, a form of communication which involves the word, written as in newsletters, monographs, books, articles, or spoken as in conferences, speeches, conversations.

B. *Showing*, a form of communication which involves a direct confrontation with the phenomena of interest. It may involve structured experiences such as pictures, slides, films, videotapes.

C. *Helping*, consists of a direct involvement of the change agent in the affairs of the adopter *on the adopter's terms*. It may take the form of consultation, in-service trouble-shooting, and the like.

D. *Involving*, takes the form of an inclusion or cooptation of the adopter. It may enlist the adopter in assisting with the development, testing, or packaging of an innovation or in contributing the problems to which innovative solutions are to be sought.

E. *Training*, takes the form of familiarizing adopters with features of a proposed innovation, or of assisting them to increase their skills and competencies or to alter their attitudes. It may be accomplished through formal university credit courses, institutes, workshops, internships, apprenticeships, extension courses, local in-service training, T-group sessions and similar experiences. Training may involve telling, showing, helping, or involving, but differs from these other techniques in that the adopter makes a formal commitment to learn by allowing himself to become involved in the training.

F. *Intervening*, consists in the direct involvement of the change agent on his own terms, not those of the adopter. It may take the form of mandating certain actions, e.g. adopting a statewide textbook, or inserting certain control mechanisms, e.g. instituting a statewide testing programme.[39]

Hence the change agent

has the task of building awareness and understanding of an innovation and causing potential adopters to consider its features with a view to possible adoption. To discharge this function he has essentially six techniques at his disposal. He will use any combination of these techniques to cause favourable consideration without resorting to hucksterism or unethical manipulation. He sees himself as a person opening viable professional alternatives to the potential adopter with a problem to solve.

In large measure it seems likely that the techniques used by an administrator in introducing change are related to the implicit or explicit assumptions which he holds as to the nature of the adopter. Guba suggests seven basic assumptions[40] which may be held:

A. *Value assumption.* The adopter is viewed as a professionally oriented entity that can be *obligated* to adopt through an appeal to his values, e.g. on behalf of 'what is best for the children'.
B. *Rational assumption.* The adopter is viewed as a rational entity who can be *convinced*, on the basis of hard data and logical argument, of the utility (i.e. the feasibility, effectiveness, and efficiency) of the innovation.
C. *Didactic assumption.* The adopter is viewed as a willing but untrained entity, that is, as having the appropriate values, motivations and the necessary resources, but as not knowing how to perform. He can therefore be *taught* what is needed to achieve adoption.
D. *Psychological assumption.* The adopter is viewed as a psychological entity whose needs for acceptance, involvement and inclusion can be employed to *persuade* him to adopt.
E. *Economic assumption.* The adopter is viewed as an economic entity

---

[39] On closer examination these techniques have many similarities with Greiner's (1964) classification of the power resources most frequently practised by managers. A. *Unilateral Power*—decree, replacement, structural, B. *Shared Power*—group decision, group problem solving, C. *Delegated Power*—data discussion, sensitivity training.

[40] In his original presentation of this model (1967) Guba referred to the following seven concepts as 'strategies'. In a later treatment of this theme (1968) he uses the term 'assumptions'. I am still undecided about the utility of the latter term. 'Perceptions' may be more relevant.

who can be *compensated* for agreeing to adopt or *deprived* of resources or other possible rewards for refusing to adopt.

F. *Political assumption.* The adopter is viewed as a political entity who can be *influenced* to adopt. For example, schools may not be accredited unless they adopt a particular innovation.

G. *Authority assumption.* The adopter is viewed as an entity in a bureaucratic system who can be *compelled* to adopt by virtue of his relationships to an authority hierarchy.

By combining these techniques and assumptions, represented by intervals along adjacent sides of a rectangle, a simple two-dimensional

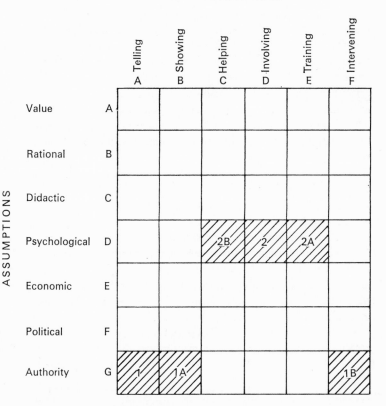

Figure 1. Two-dimensional Change Strategy Model

model of change strategies may be developed. Figure 1 displays forty-two strategy cells each of which represents a combination of assumption and technique. The shaded cells serve as examples. Cell 1 represents an authority-telling strategy, i.e. one in which the administrator assumes his teachers (adopters) are entities in a bureaucratic system. As such, change is effected 'simply' by telling teachers of a particular innovation which the administrator has determined will be introduced. In such a strategy the process of telling of an innovation carries with it the clear implication that the innovation will be adopted. (Educational history is, of course, rich with such examples!) Common variations in this authority-based strategy are represented by cells 1A and 1B. Cell 2 represents a psychological-involving strategy, one in which the administrator identifies and values his subordinates' needs for acceptance and inclusion in the day-by-day life of the organization and thus enlists the potential adopter in identifying problems and providing innovative solutions. Cells 2A and 2B represent common variations.

Experience with the model—both as a practical and an heuristic device—suggests, however, that it should be supplemented. Much greater relevance and applicability is obtained by the addition of a third dimension to take into account the immediate *targets* of the administrator's endeavours to bring about organizational change, i.e. organizational and/or environmental members who will be concerned with the innovation. Accordingly, Figure 2 displays a three-dimensional lattice structure,[41] intervals along the *target* axis representing:

A. Individual(s);

B. Group(s), both formal and informal;

C. Organization;

D. Environment, e.g. the community.

As with all classificatory schemes of this nature, overlap within the respective categories of assumption, technique and target is unavoidable. The three sets of categories are used, nevertheless, in the belief that such a model will help clarify and systematize an administrator's attempts to bring about change.[42] Nor is it intended to suggest that only

[41] One could, of course, readily conceptualize a number of relevant dimensions, each of them associated with a set of categories. Guba (1968, pp. 54–6), for example, suggests considerations such as 'the end state' of the change endeavours and the 'nature' of the innovation.

[42] This model, it must be stressed, is of the analogue kind. Its purpose is to aid the understanding of difficult and abstract ideas. As my colleague Keith Ross has pointed out, it is not of the iconic or symbolic kind.

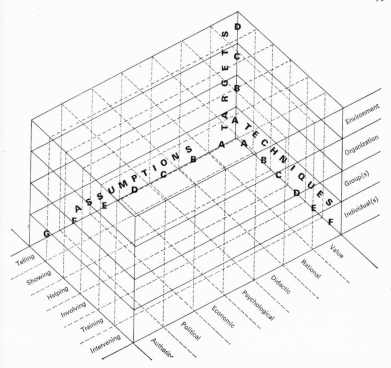

Figure 2. Three-dimensional Change Strategy Model

one strategy can be employed—or should be employed—by an administrator. The model allows for a variety of strategic approaches.

It should be stressed at this juncture (as the title of the paper suggests) that my concern is with *organizational change*. As the systems theorist would be quick to point out, an innovation introduced only in one classroom of a school affects (in some way or other) all other aspects of that organization's operation. Realistically, any attempt to adopt an educational innovation must be seen as an attempt *to change an organization*. Target refers in this sense,. therefore, to the particular *avenue* an administrator selects through which he works to effect organizational change.

The addition of a target dimension to the change model enables one now to conceptualize strategies more specifically. For example, the administrator referred to previously who used an authority-telling strategy may choose to direct such an approach at the organization as a whole, e.g. 'telling' his teachers at a staff meeting that they will adopt a particular innovation. His strategy is then represented by the element (G, A, C) of the lattice structure, the three 'co-ordinates' being given in the order: assumption, technique, target. It may be, however, that his immediate target is the subject or department heads in the school, in which case his strategy corresponds in the model to the element (G, A, B). At a later stage he may 'tell' certain individuals that they will adopt the innovation, the corresponding representation being now (G, A, A).

On the other hand, the strategy of the administrator who perceives his teachers' needs for inclusion and acceptance in the organization may be represented first by (D, D, B) as he encourages group problem identification and solving and, second, perhaps by (D, D, A) as he encourages contributions to the change process from specific individuals in his school.

It will be obvious that the three-dimensional model suggests a great number of possible change strategies. Seemingly, however, a number of these are unlikely in practice and, as such, appear to be hypothetical artifacts only. For example, in terms of the Guba definitions, authority and involving seem incompatible bases for a change strategy. Nevertheless, the model would appear to offer the administrator some useful guidelines in introducing change and, perhaps, some advantages over most other models: *First*, it is simply stated.[43] *Second*, the model does serve to add to the administrator's awareness of three vitally important components in the change process. *Third*, the model provides a means of retrospective analysis of previous (successful and unsuccessful) innovations. Generally, given the advantage of hindsight, the classification of such changes in terms of the three dimensions is not difficult.[44] *Fourth*, it provides a framework within which administrators may apply the research findings that have accumulated to date. For example, diffusion research in the U.S. provides the administrator there (and, perhaps, those in other relatively decentralized education systems) with a number of generally accepted dimensions characteristic of innovation-supporting communities (environment), schools (organization),

[43] See Lippitt's (1973, pp. 328–9) model as an example of the complicated structure which this paper tries to avoid.
[44] See, for example, Thomas and Bourne (1974). The model was used to analyse a major innovation introduced into one of the large Australian state systems.

intra-organizational dynamics (groups) and teachers (individuals). In spite of the limitations of these findings, especially in terms of their *causal* relationships with innovativeness, they may well serve as a means by which administrators may identify *potentially* innovative (or resistant) organizational members. Similarly, the relevant findings of the emerging studies, e.g. Smith and Keith (1971), may also be applied. Strategies may then be adjusted accordingly. The application of the model under these circumstances may well lead administrators attempting to introduce change to include—in varying degrees and at different times—all four targets in their strategies. *Fifth*, a significant feature of the model is the assumptions axis. The model cannot guarantee an administrator 'success' in effecting change, but it does serve to challenge the assumptions he holds about the nature of his subordinates and the basic administrative stance he adopts toward them. Hopefully, familiarity with organizational theory will cause him to ask, for example, 'Am I a "Theory X" or a "Theory Y" man?' or 'Do I prefer a Likert "system 1" or "system 4" organization?'[45]

THE THREE-DIMENSIONAL MODEL:
A NORMATIVE GUIDE FOR ACTION

It was hinted above that traditionally superordinates have adopted an authority-telling strategy base for introducing change. (The dismay and pessimism expressed in Thelen's quotation at the beginning of this paper may well be an outcome of this customary approach to change.) The model offers many alternatives to this particular strategy, however. In particular, one of these—the psychological-involving based strategy—seems to provide a foundation on which educational organizations may be successfully changed and also *improved*. This is, in fact, the strategy on which the most significant contemporary approach to change and improvement is founded—Organizational Development (OD).

As defined by Schmuck and Miles (1971, p. 2) OD is 'a planned and sustained effort to apply behavioural science for system improvement, using reflexive, self-analytic elements.' The writers stress that the emphasis of OD is on both the ability of a *system* to cope with change

[45] Ladouceur's (1973) study has revealed significant relationships between the Likert management profile of a school and its climate and capacity to change, teachers' innovative orientation and activity. The management profile accounted for 29 per cent of variance in change climate.

and the relationships of the system with its subsystems and the environment. Although individuals gain insights and new attitudes during the process, O D concentrates primarily on the adequacy of organizational communication, the integration of individual and system goals, the development of a climate of trust in decision-making and the effect of the reward system on morale. O D involves system members themselves in assessing, diagnosing and transforming their own organization. Organization members, with the *aid* of outside consultants, examine current problems, try to identify their causes and then actively participate in the reformulation of goals, the development of new group processes, the redesign of structures and procedures for achieving goals, the alteration of the working climate of the system and the assessment of results. O D is a planned and sustained effort.[46] Runkel (1970, p. 2) further elaborates the concept:

(O D) ... doesn't mean any particular technology ... (it) means any manner of help that enables an organization to achieve change deliberately and effectively and with minimal hurtful strain. The key idea is not to start thinking about the organization after someone has committed it to a particular innovation, but to be always ready to cope judiciously and flexibly with any new input from the environment.

In an excellent analysis of the movement Hall (1974) indicates that efforts at organizational development have focussed on the individual, the group and the total organization. In terms of the model O D attempts can, therefore, be identified as the (4, 4, 1), (4, 4, 2) and (4, 4, 3) elements.

By definition, some doubt attaches to the application of O D to the individual target. Beneath this rubric Hall places 'management training' and 'sensitivity training', both of which are generally regarded as forerunners of organizational development.[47] The group approach[48] to O D uses actual work groups composed of functionally and/or hierarchically related members of the organization. The approach focusses on the dynamics of group behaviour, tends to use a problem-centred approach and deals with relevant problems, processes and relationships affecting actual performance in the organization. System-

---

[46] As an example of O D in action see Croft and Barker (1973).

[47] See, for example, Schein (1963), Bass (1967), Dunnette and Campbell (1968).

[48] See, for example, Kuriloff and Atkins (1966), Blake, Mouton, Barnes and Griener (1963).

wide O D[49] involves the total organizational complement, usually over an extended period of time. The approach seeks to develop interdependence and linkage of individuals and groups in the organization. Multi-faceted approaches (rather than a single technique) are used in translating the specific goals of the O D programme into specific change objectives. O D becomes an integral part of an organization, interwoven into its goals and philosophy.

CONCLUSION

In presenting a brief yet relatively comprehensive summary of research on educational change and in proposing a change strategy model this paper has been an attempt (to use the jargon of the contemporary campus) to 'put it all together'. Undoubtedly, acknowledgement of other important change studies should have been made; more detailed examples of change strategies might well have been included.

Again, although mentioned in its title, the text of this paper has scarcely mentioned the *improvement* of educational organizations. Such an omission does not mean that I regard change and improvement as synonymous. The widespread disillusionment with much educational change in recent years makes such an assumption unlikely. And yet, there have been many attempts to change education. But, as Fullan (1972, p. 14) suggests 'The introduction of more and more innovations to reform the system add up to so many piecemeal attempts that can never get to the root of the problem.' To Miles (1965, p. 61) there are two avenues to improvement, the second of which he advocates (as I also do):

(a) altering the school's properties in some basic way so traditional bureaucratic approaches will be more congruent with them; or (b) developing alternative models of organization which are a better fit and give guidelines for improving school functioning.

In my development of a three-dimensional model I have combined the three sets of categories that I perceive to be the most important components of any change strategy. The application of the

---

[49] See, for example, Winn (1966), Dayal and Thomas (1968), Beer (1971), Pieters (1971), Hundert (1971) and Marcus (1971). For an excellent report on the application of system-wide O D to a high-school faculty see Schmuck, Runkel and Langmeyer (1969).

model to effect change depends to a large extent on the administrator's knowledge of organizations and change theory. The assumptions set from which an administrator launches his change strategy will, hopefully, have been influenced by the work of an increasing number of scholars who have conducted relevant research and who have developed models of effective and ineffective organizations. There is, for example, an obvious convergence of ideas[50] of men such as Shepard (1959), Bennis (1959), Barnes (1960), McGregor (1960), Likert (1961), Blake and Mouton (1961), Burns and Stalker (1961), Litwak (1961), and Argyris (1964). Each seems to have found it useful to develop at least two 'ideal types' of organizations in order to categorize his data. The categories are not mutually exclusive, nor do they exhaust all the possibilities. A summary of the preferred, more effective organization described by the foregoing scholars supports the psychological segment of the assumptions dimension. It assumes that people are capable of being responsible, committed, productive, and that they desire a world in which the rationality of feelings and inter-personal relationship is as valued as cognitive rationality. Improvement of an organization is effected by achieving these measures. Organizational Development, categorized in this paper as involving, is the most recently proposed change technique and, seemingly, that most compatible with the psychological assumption.

There seems some justification, therefore, in advocating the strategies represented by (D, D, A), (D, D, B), (D, D, C) and (D, D, D). Given the present state of knowledge, these appear to provide the best approach to effecting change and improvement in educational institutions.

BIBLIOGRAPHY

Abbott, M. G. (1965), 'Hierarchical Impediments to Innovation in Educational Organizations' in Abbott, M. G. and Lovell, J. T. (eds), *Change Perspectives in Educational Administration,* Auburn, Alabama, School of Education and U C E A, pp. 40–53.

Addis, W. C. (1968), 'An Analysis of the Perceptions of Principals of High and Low Innovative Schools', University of Iowa, dissertation.

Allen, J. E. (1967), 'The Adoption of Innovations and the Personality of the Superintendent of Schools', Ohio State University, dissertation.

[50] I am indebted to Ladouceur (1973) for an excellent summary of the work of these scholars.

Argyris, C. (1964), *Integrating the Individual and the Organization*, Wiley, New York.

Barnes, L. B. (1960), *Organizational Systems and Engineering Groups*, Graduate School of Business, Harvard University, Cambridge, Mass.

Bass, B. M. (1967), 'The Anarchist Movement and the T Group: Some Possible Lessons for Organizational Development', *Journal of Applied Behavioral Science*, 3(2), 211–27.

Beer, M. (1971), 'Organizational Diagnosis: An Anatomy of Poor Integration', paper presented to Division of Industrial and Organizational Psychology, American Psychological Association, Washington, D.C.

Bennis, W. (1959), 'Leadership Theory and Administrative Behavior', *Administrative Science Quarterly*, 4(3), 259–301.

Bergsma, S. K. (1963), 'The Relationship of Selected School District Characteristics to the Use of Educational Television in Michigan High School Districts', Michigan State University, dissertation.

Bickert, R. N. (1967), 'Selected Organizational Values and Characteristics of Innovative and Non-Innovative School Systems', University of Iowa, dissertation.

Blake, R. R. and Mouton, J. S. (1961), *The Managerial Grid*, H R T L Laboratory in Management Method, Jeniz Springs, New Mexico.

Blake, R. R., Mouton, J. S., Barnes, L. B. and Greiner, L. E. (1964), 'Breakthrough in Organizational Development', *Harvard Business Review*, 42, 133–55.

Breivogel, W. F. (1967), 'The Relationship of Selected Variables to the Introduction of Educational Innovations in New Jersey Public School Districts', Rutgers State University, dissertation.

Burns, T. and Stalker, G. M. (1961), *The Management of Innovation*, Tavistock, London.

Carlson, R. O. (1962), *Executive Succession and Organizational Change*, Midwest Administration Center, University of Chicago.

Carlson, R. O. (1965), *Adoption of Educational Innovations*, Center for the Advanced Study of Educational Administration, University of Oregon, Eugene, Oregon.

Carswell, E. M. (1968), 'Trends in Educational Innovation in Arizona Elementary Schools between 1960 and 1966', University of Arizona, dissertation.

Coch, L. and French, J. R. P. (1948), 'Overcoming Resistance to Change', *Human Relations*, 1, 512–32.

Croft, J. C. and Barker, C. (1973), 'The Organizational Inventory Meeting: Gaining and Integrating Administrative Commitment', *Journal of Educational Administration*, XI(2), 254–71.

Currie, C. H. (1966), 'Secondary School Principals' Assessment of the Importance of Personal and Situational Factors in the Adoption of Innovations', University of Oregon, dissertation.

Dalin, P. (1973), *Strategies for Innovation in Education*, Centre for Educational Research and Innovation, O.E.C.D., Paris.

Dayal, I. and Thomas, J. M. (1968), 'Operation K P E: Developing a New Organization', *Journal of Applied Behavioral Science*, 4(4), 473–506.

Dunnette, M. D. and Campbell, J. P. (1968), 'Laboratory Education: Impact on People and Organizations', *Industrial Relations*, 8(1), 1–27.

Eibler, H. J. (1965), 'A Comparison of the Relationship Between Certain Aspects of Characteristics of the Structure of the High School Faculty and the Amount of Curriculum Innovation', University of Michigan, dissertation.

Foster, W. R. (1969), 'The Elementary School Principal and his Relationship to Reading Curriculum Change', Wayne State University, dissertation.

Fullan, M. (1972), 'Overview of the Innovative Process and the User', *Interchange*, 3(2–3), 1–46.

Fullan, M. and Eastabrook, G. (1973), *School Change Project: Interim Report of Findings*, OISE, Toronto.

Gill, D. G. (1969), 'The Relationship of Innovation and Complexity in Public School Systems', University of Illinois, dissertation.

Goetz, F. R. (1965), 'Innovation and the Public Elementary School Principal', Wayne State University, dissertation.

Greiner, L. E. (1964), in Blake, R. R., Mouton, J. S., Barnes, L. B. and Greiner, L. E. (1964), op. cit.

Gross, N.. Giacquinta, J. and Bernstein, M. (1971), *Implementing Organizational Innovations: A Sociological Analysis of Planned Educational Change*, Basic Books, New York.

Guba, E. G. (1967), 'The Basis for Educational Improvement', unpublished address to the Kettering Foundation—U.S. Office of Education, National Seminar on Innovation, Honolulu.

Guba, E. G. (1968), 'Development, Diffusion and Evaluation', in Eidell, T. L. and Kitchel, J. M. (eds), *Knowledge Production and Utilization in Educational Administration*, UCEA and CASEA.

Hall, C. L. (1966), 'Relationship of Origin and Tenure of Superintendents to the Organizational Climate and Adaptability of Schools', Stanford University, dissertation.

Hall, F. S. (1974), *Organization Development and Intervention: An Introduction*, submitted manuscript.

Hanson, J. O. (1966), 'A Descriptive Study of Basic Data and the Educational Innovations Found in 22 Selected North Dakota Small Schools', University of North Dakota, dissertation.

Havelock, R. (1970), *A Guide to Innovation in Education*, University of Michigan, Ann Arbor.

Hawkins, W. D. (1968), 'Some Factors Which Contribute to Successful Educational Innovation', University of Southern California, dissertation.

Hearn, N. E. (1969), 'Innovative Educational Programs: A Study of the Influence of Selected Variables upon their Continuation Following the Termination of Three-Year ESEA Title III Grants', George Washington University, dissertation.

Heisler, D. P. (1968), 'A Study of Factors that Affect Change in Educational Systems', Ohio State University, dissertation.

Hinman, E. F. (1966), 'Personality Characteristics of School Principals who Implement Innovation in the Public Schools', Utah State University, dissertation.

Holdaway, E. A. and Seger, J. E. (1968), 'The Development of Indices of Innovativeness', *Canadian Education and Research Digest*, 8(4), 366–79.

Hughes, L. W. (1968), 'Organizational Climate—Another Dimension to the Process of Innovation?', *Educational Administration Quarterly*, 4(3), 16–28.

Hundert, A. T. (1971), 'Problems and Prospects for Project Teams in a Large Bureaucracy', paper presented to the Division of Industrial and Organizational Psychology, American Psychological Association, Washington, D.C.

Jacobs, J. W. (1965), 'Leadership, Size and Wealth as Related to Curriculum Innovations in the Junior High School', University of Michigan, dissertation.

Jensen, Le R. N. (1967), 'Characteristics of Superintendents in Innovative and Non-Innovative School Systems and Interaction with the Iowa Department of Public Instruction', University of Iowa, dissertation.

Johnson, C. H. (1968), 'The Identification of Teacher Opinion Leaders: An Element in the Change Strategy for Agricultural Education', Ohio State University, dissertation.

Kendig, T. E. (1965), 'An Analysis of the Relationship of Certain Educational Conditions to Curriculum Breadth and Innovation in Selected Pennsylvania School Systems', Pennsylvania State University, dissertation.

Kindsvatter, R. H. (1966), 'The Dynamics of Change in Marking Systems in Selected Innovative and Non-Innovative High Schools in Ohio', Ohio State University, dissertation.

Klingenberg, A. J. (1966), 'A Study of Selected Administrative Behaviors Among Administrators from Innovative and Non-Innovative Public School Districts', Michigan State University, dissertation.

Knedlik, S. M. (1967), 'The Effect of Administrative Succession Pattern Upon Educational Innovation in Selected Secondary Schools', New York University, dissertation.

Kohl, J. W. (1966), 'Adoption Stages and Perceptions of Characteristics of Educational Innovations', University of Oregon, dissertation.

Kuhn, J. A. (1969), 'Corporate Pressures on Educational Innovators', University of Wisconsin, dissertation.

Kunzler, W. J. (1968), 'A Study of Factors that Facilitate and Inhibit Instructional Change as Perceived by Principals', University of Iowa, dissertation.

Kuriloff, A. H. and Atkins, S. (1966), 'T Group for a Work Team', *Journal of Applied Behavioral Science*, 2(1), 63–93.

Ladouceur, J. (1973), 'School Management Profile and Capacity for Change', unpublished doctoral dissertation, University of Toronto.

La Plant, J. C. (1966), 'School District Innovativeness and Expectations for the School Board Role', University of Wisconsin, dissertation.

Lawrence, C. J. (1968), 'Personality Characteristics of School Superintendents Who Implement Innovation in the Public Schools', Utah State University, dissertation.

Lawrence, P. R. (1954), 'How to Deal with Resistance to Change', *Harvard Business Review*, 32(3), 49–57.

Leas, A. (1965), 'A Study to Determine the Characteristic of Innovative and Traditional Educators', Indiana University, dissertation.

Lewin, K. (1951), *Field Theory in Social Science*, Harper and Row, New York.

Likert, R. and Likert, G. J. (1969), 'Profile of a School' adapted from Likert, R. (1967), *The Human Organization: Its Management and Value*, McGraw-Hill, New York.

Lippitt, G. L. (1973), *Visualizing Change,* N T L-Learning Resources Corporation, Fairfax, Va.

Lippitt, R., Watson, J. and Westley, B. (1958), *The Dynamics of Planned Change,* Harcourt, Brace and World, New York.

Littleton, V. C. (1970), 'A Study of the Factors Contributing to the Predisposition of Elementary Principals to Try Selected Innovations', University of Texas, dissertation.

Litwak, E. (1961), 'Models of Bureaucracy which Permit Conflict', *American Journal of Sociology,* 67, 177–184.

Marcum, R. L (1968), 'Organizational Climate and the Adoption of Innovations' Utah State University, dissertation.

Marcus, S. H. (1971), 'Findings: The Effects of Structural, Cultural and Role Changes on Integration', paper presented to the Division of Industrial and Organizational Psychology, American Psychological Association, Washington, D.C.

Martin, J. and Harrison, C. (1972), *Free to Learn: Unlocking and Ungrading American Education,* Prentice-Hall, Englewood Cliffs, N.J.

McGrath, H. M. (1971), 'Innovation in Catholic Education', University of New England, dissertation.

McGregor, D. (1960), *The Human Side of Enterprise,* McGraw-Hill, New York.

Mertz, R. L. (1965), 'The Relationship of Selected Variables to the Adoption and Implementation of Recommendations of Educational Surveys of Public School Corporations', Purdue University, dissertation.

Miles, M. B. (1964), *Innovation in Education,* Teachers College, Columbia University, Bureau of Publications, New York.

Miles, M. B. (1965), 'Education and Innovation: The Organization as Context', in Abbott, M. G. and Lovell, J. T. (eds) (1965), *Change Perspectives in Educational Administration,* Auburn, Alabama, School of Education and U C E A, pp. 54–72.

Miller, R. I. (1967) (ed), *Perspectives on Educational Change,* Appleton-Century-Crofts, New York.

Mort, P. R. and Ross, D. M. (1957), *Principles of School Administration: A Synthesis of Basic Concepts,* McGraw-Hill, New York

Nicholson, E.W. (1965), 'Selected School District and Administrative Variables Related to the Adoption of Instructional Television', Purdue University, dissertation.

Ochitwa, O. P. (1973), 'Organizational Climate and Adoption of Educational, Innovations', *Saskatchewan Journal of Educational Research and Development,* 3(2) 38–44.

Oskamp, E. (1968), 'An Investigation of the Determiners of the Curriculum in Three Elementary Schools in West Milford Township', Columbia University, dissertation.

Pafford, W. N. (1967), 'Relationships Between Innovation and Selected School Factors', University of Kentucky, dissertation.

Peets, E. F. (1970), 'A Comparative Study of Factors Related to Innovation in Selected Public School Districts of Southern Lower Michigan', Western Michigan University, dissertation.

Peterson, I. M. (1968), 'Relationships Between School Superintendents' Personality Orientations, Perceived Situational Pressures, and Innovativeness', Rutgers University, dissertation.

Pieters, G. R. (1971), 'Changing Organizational Structures, Roles and Processes to Enhance Integration: The Implementation of a Change Program', paper presented to Division of Industrial and Organizational Psychology, American Psychological Association, Washington, D.C.

Preising, P. P. (1968), 'The Relationship of Staff Tenure and Administrative Succession to Structural Innovation', Stanford University, dissertation.

Ramer, B. (1968), 'The Relationship of Belief Systems and Personal Characteristics of Chief School Administrators and Attitudes Toward Educational Innovation', State University of New York, Buffalo, dissertation.

Reese, W. M. (1967), 'A Study in the Differences in Role Perception of Educators in Highly Innovative Educational Environments as Compared with Educators in Less Innovative Educational Environments', University of Utah, dissertation.

Reynolds, J. A. (1965), 'Innovation Related to Administrative Tenure, Succession and Orientation. A Study of the Adoption of New Practices by School Systems', Washington University, dissertation.

Richlands, M. (1968), 'A Study to Define an Operational Index of Innovation for School Administrators', University of Southern California, dissertation.

Rogers, E. M. (1962), *Diffusion of Innovations*, Free Press, New York.

Rogers, E. M. and Shoemaker, F. F. (1971), *Communication of Innovations*, Free Press, New York.

Roosa, J. L. (1968), 'A Study of Organizational Climate, Leader Behavior, and their Relation to the Rate of Adoption of Educational Innovations in Selected School Districts', State University of New York at Albany, dissertation.

Runkel, P. J. (1970), 'Linking Organizations to Maintain Organizational Development and Transmit Innovation', CASEA, University of Oregon, mimeo.

Santo, J. D. (1968), 'School Administrators' Perception of Critical Factors of Planned Change in Selected Illinois School Districts', Illinois State University, dissertation.

Sarason, S. (1971), *The Culture of the School and the Problem of Change*, Allyn and Bacon, Boston.

Sargent, R. R. (1965). 'A Test of Motivational Appeals Judged Effective by Chief School Administrators to Induce Teacher Acceptance of Educational Innovation', Pennsylvania State University, dissertation.

Schein, E. H. (1963), 'Forces which Undermine Management Development', *California Management Review,* summer, 23–34.

Schmuck, R. A. and Miles, M. B. (eds) (1971), *Organizational Development in Schools,* National Press Books, Palo Alto, California

Schmuck, R. A., Runkel, P. J. and Langmeyer, D. (1969), 'Improving Organizational Problem Solving in a School Faculty', *Journal of Applied Behavioral Science,* 5(4), 455–82.

Scott, J. L. (1970), 'Boards' and Superintendents' Perceptions of the Superintendent as an Agent for Innovative Change', University of Northern Colorado, dissertation.

Shepard, H. (1959), 'Organic and Mechanistic Models of Organization', unpublished papers presented at the Esso Laboratories.

Shephard, H. A. (1967), 'Innovation—Resisting, and Innovation—Producing Organizations', *Journal of Business*, 40(4).

Silberman, C. (1970), *Crisis in the Classroom*, Vintage Books, New York.

Smith, L. and Keith, P. (1971), *Anatomy of Educational Innovation: An Organizational Analysis of an Elementary School*, Wiley, New York.

Spencer, E. N. (1967), 'Variables Affecting the Adoption Rates of Educational Innovations in Selected School Districts of Oakland County, Michigan', Wayne State University, dissertation.

Storkel, S. J. (1962), 'The Relationship of Public School Revenue and Adaptability in Selected School Systems of Pennsylvania', University of Pittsburgh, dissertation.

Thelen, H. A. (1964), 'New Practices on the Firing Line', *Administrator's Notebook*, XII(5).

Thomas, A. R. (1973), 'The Innovative School: Some Organizational Characteristics', *Australian Journal of Education*, 17(2), 113–30.

Thomas, A. R. and Bourne, R. G. (1974), 'Aspects of Innovation: The Radford Plan', *The Administrators' Bulletin*, 5(3).

Todd, E. A. (1963), 'The Administration of Change: A Study of Administrative Tenure', University of Houston, dissertation.

Watson, G. (1966), 'Resistance to Change', in Bennis, W. G., Benne, K. D., and Chin, R. (eds) (1969), *The Planning of Change*, Holt, Rinehart and Winston, New York, pp. 488–98.

Willower, D. J. (1963), 'Barriers to Change in Educational Organizations', *Theory into Practice*, 2(5).

Winn, A. (1966), 'Social Change in Industry: From Insight to Implementation', *Journal of Applied Behavioral Science*, 2(2), 170–84.

Wright, D. E. (1970), 'The Impact of Innovative Educational Programs upon the Public Schools of Colorado', University of Denver, dissertation.

Zander, A. (1950), 'Resistance to Change: Its Analysis and Prevention', *Advanced Management*, 15–16, 9–11.

5 Theory about Organization: A New Perspective and its Implications for Schools[1]

T. BARR GREENFIELD

In common parlance we speak of organizations as if they were real. Neither scholar nor layman finds difficulty with talk in which organizations 'serve functions', 'adapt to their environment', 'clarify their goals' or 'act to implement policy'. What it is that serves, adapts, clarifies or acts seldom comes into question. Underlying widely accepted notions about organizations, therefore, stands the apparent assumption that organizations are not only real but also distinct from the actions, feelings and purposes of people. This mode of thought provides the platform for a long-standing debate about organizations and people. Is it organizations which oppress and harass people or is it fallible people who fail to carry out the well-intentioned aims of organizations? The debate continues on issues such as whether it is better to abolish organizations, to reshape them along more humane lines, or to train people to recognize the goals of organizations more clearly and to serve them more faithfully.

In contrast, this paper rejects the dualism which conveniently separates people and organizations; instead it argues that a mistaken belief in the reality of organizations has diverted our attention from human action and intention as the stuff from which organizations are made. As a result, theory and research have frequently set out on a false path in trying to understand organizations and have given us a misplaced confidence in our ability to deal with their problems. If we see organizations and individuals as inextricably intertwined, it may not be so easy to alter organizations, or to lead them, or to administer them without touching something unexpectedly human. More importantly, the view that people and organizations are inseparable requires us to

[1] This is an expanded version of Professor Greenfield's paper, originally entitled 'Theory in the Study of Organizations and Administrative Structures: A New Perspective'.

reassess the commonly accepted claim that there exists a body of theory and principle which provides the touchstone for effective administrative action in organizations. The belief in the reality and independence of organizations permits us to separate the study of organizations from the study of people and their particular values, habits and beliefs. The common view in organization studies holds that people occupy organizations in somewhat the same way as they inhabit houses. The tenants may change but, apart from wear and tear, the basic structure remains and in some way shapes the behaviour of people within. Studies have therefore focussed largely on the variety of organizational structures and their effects upon people. These structures are usually seen as invariate over time and place, as universal forms into which individuals may move from time to time, bringing with them idiosyncrasies which colour their performance of the roles prescribed by the organization (Getzels, 1958, p. 156).

ORGANIZATIONAL SCIENCE AND THE PROFESSION OF ADMINISTRATION

The science of organization has found its way into studies of schools and influenced the training of those who are to administer schools. In this science, schools are a variety of the species organization which can be distinguished chiefly by the nature of their goals and their bureaucratic structure (Bidwell, 1965, pp. 973–4). The science of organization is, therefore, assumed to provide useful knowledge about schools even as it does about other kinds of organizations. Accepting this position, Griffiths (1964, p. 3) rejects 'the opinion that educational administration is a unique activity, differing greatly from business, military, hospital and other varieties of administration' and endorses (p. 118) a 'general theory which enables the researcher to describe, explain, and predict a wide range of human behavior within organizations'.

In a profession of administration based upon organizational science, the task of the administrator is to bring people and organizations together in a fruitful and satisfying union. In so doing, the work of the administrator carries the justification of the larger social order (Getzels, 1958, p. 156), since he works to link day-to-day activity in organizations to that social order. In schools, the administrator may be director or superintendent, principal or headmaster, department head or supervisor. Whatever their titles, their tasks are always the same. They bring people and resources together so that the goals of the organization and presumably of an encompassing social order may be met (Gregg 1957, pp. 269–70). No matter what circumstances he finds himself in, the administrator mediates between the organization and the people within it. The task is difficult; he needs help with it. As the argument runs, such help is fortunately to be found in the emerging science of organizations. Since organizations do have a human component, knowledge abour organizations is usually described as a social science. But social or not, this science like all others is seen as universal, timeless, and imperfect only in its incompleteness.

The claims for a science of organization and for a profession of administration based upon that science have in recent times made a marked impact upon education. For over two decades now, scholars have attempted to improve education by applying organization theory to the conduct of affairs in schools and by training educational administrators in that science (Culbertson and Shibles, 1973). Celebrating its emancipation from the press of immediate practical affairs (Griffiths, 1964), the field turned instead to discovery of the basic relationships and principles which underlie day-to-day concerns. The professor supplanted the practitioner as the source of valid knowledge about administration. If practitioners did not know or accept that they were no longer masters of the basic knowledge which underlay their craft, it did not matter. Even the scholar-practitioner, Chester Barnard, in introducing Simon's classic writings claimed that it was the scholar's knowledge of the 'abstract principles of structure' rather than the practitioner's knowledge of 'concrete behavior' which leads to an understanding of 'organizations of great variety' (Simon, 1957, pp. xlii–xliv). Things are not what they seem, in educational administration as in other realms of reality. We need the scientist and his theory to interpret them to us. His knowledge, though it may be incomplete and is certainly subject to improvement, has the virtue of universal applicability. Acting on this conviction, scholars in educational administration have sought to understand how organizations really work and to use this knowledge towards the improvement of educational practice.

A survey of representative writing in educational administration (see Campbell and Gregg, 1957; Halpin, 1958; Griffiths, 1964; Getzels, Lipham and Campbell, 1968; Milstein and Belasco, 1973) reveals that inquiry in this field has leaned heavily on the belief that a general science of organizations has provided the needed theoretical underpinnings for understanding schools and for the training of the administrators who are to run them. While a general theory of organizations provided the rationale for understanding schools, the sister social sciences provided the research tools and the 'sensitizing concepts' needed to identify and resolve their administrative problems (Downey and Enns, 1963; Tope *et al.*, 1965). Since this happy combination of theory and method yields an understanding of organizations as they really are, it then becomes possible to say how educational administrators may be trained to improve organizations and administrative practice within them (Culbertson *et al.*, 1973). Although the claim is seldom if ever made explicitly, this line of reasoning, linking a general theory of organizations to the training of administrators, implies that we have at hand both the theory and method which permit us to improve schools and the quality of whatever it is that goes on within them. That change in schools proceeds without assistance from an applied organization theory or, indeed, in contravention to it (Fullan, 1972), usually fails to shake our faith in such theory.

It will surely come as no surprise to anyone who examines the references cited to this point that most of them are American in origin, since it was in the United States that the movement to conceive educational administration as a social science arose in the late 1940s. A decade later the movement had taken hold in Canada and some time later in Australia and Britain. As the concept of educational administration as a profession and social science gains ever wider recognition and acceptance, it becomes appropriate to examine the theory and assumptions which underlie the field. In particular we need to ask whether the theory and assumptions still appear to hold in the settings where they were developed before they are recommended and applied to totally new settings. Such an examination is not only appropriate but essential in the face of an alternative view which sees organizations not as structures subject to universal laws but as cultural artefacts dependent upon the specific meaning and intention of people within them. This alternative view, which stems from nineteenth-century German idealism (Deutscher, 1973, p. 326), bears the awkward name phenomenology (Phillipson, 1972), though it might with equal justification be called the method of understanding, as it is in the work of Max Weber (Eldridge, 1971, p. 28). What we call the view is not important. What matters is that there exists a body of theory and assumption which runs squarely at odds with that which has provided the ideological underpinnings of educational administration as it has developed over the past two decades. The ideological conflict between these views rests on two fundamentally different ways of looking at the world. One is the established view both in the study of organizations generally and in the study of educational administration. In this paper, I will outline the alternative view and recommend its application both in organization and administrative theory.

It is surely no accident that the alternative view has its roots in European philosophy and social science. And it is at least noteworthy that this view has a current flowering in Britain, where it is exerting a strong influence in both sociology (Filmer, *et al.*, 1972; Dawe, 1970; Brittan, 1973) and in education (Young, 1971, Cosin, *et al.*, 1971). I do not wish to drive the differences in the views to the point of a spurious contrast between American and European social science. The alternative view which I will outline has its supporters in the United States too (Garfinkel, 1967; Cicourel, 1964; Louch 1966; Wilson, 1970). Two points should be made here. First, and of lesser importance, phenomenology has yet to influence the study of organizations in the United States despite the existence of a long-standing phenomenological tradition in some sociological schools of thought in that country.[2] In Britain, both theory and research on organizations reflect the phenomenological perspective (Tipton, 1973; Silverman, 1970). Second, and more important since it relates to the heart of the issue, the existence of the two competing ideologies illustrates the fundamental contention of phenomenology that there are no fixed ways for construing the social world around us. These ways are products of particular settings and circumstances rather than expressions of universal ideas and values. Our concepts of organizations must therefore rest upon the views of people in particular times and places, and any effort to understand them in terms of a single set of ideas, values and laws must be doomed to failure.

The alternative view rejects the assumption, underlying much of organization theory, that organizations belong to a single species which behaves in predictable ways according to common laws. This view finds forceful expression in the work of Mayntz (1964), a European scholar of organizations:

[2] Deutscher (1973, pp. 324ff) describes these schools of thought and their connections with idealistic philosophy. He also points out (p. 325n) that those he calls the 'Harvard functionalists' make no mention of phenomenology or its proponents in their encyclopaedic history of theories of society. See Parsons *et al.* (1961).

Propositions which hold for such diverse phenomena as an army, a trade union, and a university ... must necessarily be either trivial or so abstract as to tell hardly anything of interest about concrete reality ... After all, the distinct character of an organization is certainly determined, among other things, by the nature, interests, and values of those who are instrumental in maintaining it. (pp. 113–14.)

If people are inherently part of organizations, if organizations themselves are expressions of how people believe they should relate to each other, we then have good grounds to question an organization theory which assumes the universality of organizational forms and effects. This argument suggests that organizations theorists have been so busy defining the forest that they have failed to notice differences among the trees—and worse, have ignored objects in the forest that are not trees at all. It suggests, too, that an academic industry which trains administrators by disclosing to them the social-scientific secrets of how organizations work or how policy should be made indulges at best in a premature hope and at worst in a delusion.

TWO VIEWS OF SOCIAL REALITY

The conflicting views on organizations of which I have been speaking represent vastly different ways of looking at social reality and rest on sharply contrasting processes for interpreting it. These contrasts are summarized in Table 3 in which I have compared the two views and suggested how they differ with respect to a number of critical issues. Each of these issues has implications for the theory of organizations and for research undertaken in line with such theory. Necessarily then, these contrasts also have implications for a number of practical questions in the conduct of affairs in organizations. Some of these will be explored in the concluding section of this paper. Although there are no generally accepted names for identifying the two views contrasted in Table 3, it may suffice to note that the crux of the issue is whether social reality is based upon naturally existing systems or upon human invention of social forms. Social reality is usually construed as a natural and necessary order which, as it unfolds, permits human society to exist and people within it to meet their basic needs. Alternatively, social reality may be construed as images in the mind of man having no necessary or inevitable forms except as man creates them and endows them with reality and authority. In the one perspective, organizations are natural objects —systems of being which man discovers; in the other, organizations

Table 3. Alternative Bases for Interpreting Social Reality

	What is social reality?	
Dimensions of comparison	A natural system	Human invention
Philosophical basis	Realism: the world exists and is knowable as it really is. Organizations are real entities with a life of their own.	Idealism: the world exists but different people construe it in very different ways. Organizations are invented social reality.
The role of social science	Discovering the universal laws of society and human conduct within it.	Discovering how different people interpret the world in which they live.
Basic units of social reality	The collectivity: society or organizations.	Individuals acting singly or together.
Method of understanding	Identifying conditions or relationships which permit the collectivity to exist. Conceiving what these conditions and relationships are.	Interpretation of the subjective meanings which individuals place upon their action. Discovering the subjective rules for such action.
Theory	A rational edifice built by scientists to explain human behaviour.	Sets of meanings which people use to make sense of their world and behaviour within it.
Research	Experimental or quasi-experimental validation of theory.	The search for meaningful relationships and the discovery of their consequences for action.
Methodology	Abstraction of reality, especially through mathematical models and quantitative analysis.	The representation of reality for purposes of comparison. Analysis of language and meaning.
Society	Ordered. Governed by a uniform set of values and made possible only by those values.	Conflicted. Governed by the values of people with access to power.

Table 3 *(cont.)*

Dimensions of comparison	What is social reality?	
	A natural system	*Human invention*
Organizations	Goal oriented. Independent of people. Instruments of order in society serving both society and the individual.	Dependent upon people and their goals. Instruments of power which some people control and can use to attain ends which seem good to them.
Organizational pathologies	Organizations get out of kilter with social values and individual needs.	Given diverse human ends, there is always conflict among people acting to pursue them.
Prescription for curing organizational ills	Change the structure of the organization to meet social values and individual needs.	Find out what values are embodied in organizational action and whose they are. Change the people or change their values if you can.

are cultural artefacts which man shapes within limits given only by his perception and the boundaries of his life as a human animal.

The systems notion posits an organizational force or framework which encompasses and gives order to people and events within it. The system—unseen behind everyday affairs—is real; it *is* the organization. The force of 'natural' in the descriptor is to evoke the view common in systems theory that organizational forms are shaped by powerful forces which in large measure act independently of man. The organizations so formed will be right and good, if the natural forces are allowed free play. Mayntz (1964, pp. 105, 115) has noted that such views in which an unseen organizational hand works for the greater social good are likely to be most congenial to scholars who share a faith in the ideals of the Western liberal democracies. In identifying organizations as social inventions, the alternative view identifies organization with man's image of himself and with the particular and distinctive ways in which people see the world around them and their place in it. This view is the perspective of phenomenology. In it organizations are the perceived social reality within which people make decisions and take actions which seem right and proper to them. (Greenfield, 1973, p. 557). The heart of this view is not a single abstraction called organization, but rather the varied perceptions by individuals of what they can, should, or must do in dealing with others within the circumstances in which they find themselves. It is noteworthy that this tradition—the decision-making tradition (Cyert and March, 1963; Simon, 1964) in organization theory—is frequently cited in scholarly writing, but seldom followed in analyses of organizations. This tradition, culminating currently in the creative insights of James March (1972) into organizational realities, reaches back into the work of Simon (1957; March and Simon, 1958) and thence into the work of Max Weber (trans. Gerth and Mills, 1946) and the German philosophers and sociologists of the phenomenological tradition (Deutscher, 1973, p. 327; Silverman, 1972, pp. 184–5).

What are some of the particular issues involved in the contrast between the systems and phenomenological views? These are suggested in Table 3 where the two views are compared on a number of points. In the discussion which follows, the phenomenological view is emphasized, since it is assumed that the foundations of the system view are the more familiar of the two views.

Philosophical basis

The systems view assumes that the world is knowable as it is. Although the acquisition of such knowledge requires the intervention and help of scientists, theorists and scholars, there exists an ultimate reality which may be discovered by application of the scientific method and similar forms of rational analysis. In systems theory, the prevailing image of the organization is that of an organism. Organizations exist; they are observable entities which have a life of their own. Organizations are like people, although sometimes the image is more that of the recalcitrant child rather than the mature adult. In any case, the theory endows organizations with many human properties. They have goals towards which they direct their activities; they respond and adapt to their environments. Nor can organizations escape the fate of organisms ill-adapted to their environments. Indeed, the fate of organizations depends upon their ability to adapt to an increasingly complex and turbulent environment. Following the Darwinian logic inherent in their image of the organization, systems theorists (Bennis, 1968) see small, quick-witted, democratic organizations replacing the ponderous, bureaucratic forms now expiring around us. The fact that bureaucratic organizations appear as large, robust and formidable as ever does not appear to shake belief in organizations as living entities subject to stringent laws permitting only the fittest to survive. Indeed, our belief in the living organization is likely to be so strong that we fail to notice that the systems theorists have shifted from telling us about the way organizations are to telling us how they ought to be. 'If only organizations were adapted to their environments', the argument runs, 'imagine how quickly these buraucratic forms would disappear'. In thinking about the dazzling prospect of a world in which organizations were creatures closely adapted to a benign, well-intentioned environment, we forget that the role of theory is to tell us the way things are rather than how they ought to be or how we should like them to be. Our image of the organization as an entity, as a living entity, rests upon an analogy. But we fail to draw the conclusion (Willer, 1967, p. 33) that the analogy is useless when discrepancies appear between the image and the phenomena observed.

The phenomenological view of reality contrasts sharply with that of systems theory. This view has its origin in the distinction Kant drew between the noumenal world (the world as it is) and the phenomenal world (the world as we see it). For Kant, a world of reality does indeed exist, but man can never perceive it directly; reality is always glossed over with human interpretations which themselves become the realities to which man responds. And man is always learning, always interpreting, always inventing the 'reality' which he sees about him. In popular form, the Kantian philosophy has been expressed as follows: 'Man does not create his world, but he does make it'. It therefore comes as no surprise to the phenomenologist that people are killed by 'empty' guns. But for the phenomenologist, beliefs are always of greater consequence than facts in shaping behaviour. The bullet may indeed be in the gun, but it is the individual's belief about an empty chamber which causes him idly to pull the trigger. Deutscher (1973) summarizes the phenomenological view as follows:

The phenomenological orientation always sees reality as constructed by men in the process of thinking about it. It is the social version of Descartes' *Cogito, ergo sum*. For the phenomenologist it becomes *Cogitamus, ergo est*—we think, therefore it is! (p. 328)

The role of social science

The implications of the phenomenological view are of critical importance in shaping our views both of the social sciences and of a study of organizations founded on them, as may be seen in the contrasting positions taken by Weber and Durkheim (Bendix and Roth, 1971, pp. 286–97). For Weber, working within his 'method of understanding', 'there is no such thing as a collective personality which "acts" ', only individuals acting on their interpretations of reality. In contrast, Durkheim, convinced of an ultimate, knowable social reality, sought to eliminate the perceptions of individuals and to find 'the explanation of social life in the nature of society itself' (Bendix and Roth, 1971, p. 291). Thus Durkheim spent his life building a sociology around notions of 'elemental' forms which provide the invariable units out of which social life is built. Weber, on the other hand, explored the ideas, doctrines and beliefs with which men endowed their organizations and which provided the motivation for action within them. Durkheim's path leads to generality, abstraction and universality in the study of organizations; Weber's leads to the particularistic, the concrete, and the experience-based study of organizations. Durkheim's path leads to an asceptic study of organizations, Weber's to one which smells of reality.

The phenomenological view leads to the concept of organizations as 'invented social reality' (Greenfield, 1973, p. 556) and to the paradox that, having invented such reality, man is perfectly capable of responding to it as though it were not of his own invention (Silverman, 1970, p. 133). More basically, however, the phenomenological perspective questions the possibility of objectivity in what Weber calls 'the cultural sciences'. While it is possible for such sciences to pursue inquiry within a logically rigorous methodology and for them to take into account certain basic social facts such as where people live and what they do, it is not possible for cultural scientists to give us 'a direct awareness of the structure of human actions in all their reality' (Eldridge, 1971, p. 16). Thus the notion of discovering the ultimate laws which govern social reality becomes an ever receding fantasy which retreats as we attempt to approach it. Such bogus 'laws' as the law of supply and demand were, both for Weber and Durkheim, 'maxims for action', advice to people on how to protect their interests if they wished to be 'fair and logical' (Eldridge, 1971, p. 18). In Weber's view, then, it is impossible for the cultural sciences to penetrate behind social perception to reach objective social reality. Paradoxically, this limitation on the cultural sciences is also their strength, since it permits them to do what is never possible in the physical sciences: the cultural scientist may enter into and take the viewpoint of the actor whose behaviour is to be explained.

We can accomplish something which is never attainable in the natural sciences, namely the subjective understanding of the action of component individuals ... We do not 'understand' the behaviour of cells, but can only observe the relevant functional relationships and generalize on the basis of these observations. (Weber, 1947, pp. 103-4)

While the cultural scientist may not discover ultimate social reality, he can interpret what people see as social reality and, indeed, he must do so according to a consistent, logical, and rigorous methodology (Eldridge, 1971, pp. 9-10). It is such a discipline for interpreting human experience which provides the science in the cultural scientists's work, not his ability to discover ultimate truths about social structure. Thus the purpose of social science is to understand social reality as different people see it and to demonstrate how their views shape the action which they take within that reality. Since the social sciences cannot penetrate to what lies behind social reality, they must work directly with man's definitions of reality and with the rules he devises for coping with it. While the social sciences do not reveal ultimate truth, they do help us to make sense of our world. What the social sciences offer is explanation, clarification and demystification of the social forms which man has created around himself. In the view of some (Dawe, 1970, p. 211), the social sciences may lead us to enlightenment and to liberation from the forces which oppress man. In the phenomenological view, these forces stem from man himself, not from abstractions which lie behind social reality and control man's behaviour within that reality.

Theory about what?

The two views give rise to opposing theories about the world and the way it works, since each sees reality in different kinds of things. Each approaches theory building from a point of view which is normative rather than descriptive. In the natural systems view, the basic reality is the collectivity; reality is in society and its organizations. Assuming the existence of an ultimate social reality, the role of theory is to say how it hangs together or how it might be changed so that it would hang together even more effectively (Merton, 1957; Etzioni, 1960). Thus functional analysis—the theory associated with the systems view—becomes a justification of the way social reality is organized rather than an explanation of it. In this view, the theory becomes more important than the research because it tells us what we can never perceive directly with our senses: it tells us the ultimate reality behind the appearance of things and it establishes a view which is essentially beyond confirmation or disproof by mere research.

The phenomenological view begins with the individual and seeks to understand his interpretations of the world around him. The theory which emerges must be grounded (Glaser and Strauss, 1967) in data from particular organizations. That these data will be glossed with the meanings and purposes of those people and places is the whole point of this philosophical view. Thus the aim of scientific investigation is to understand how that glossing of reality goes on at one time and place and to compare it with what goes on in different times and places. Similarly organizations are to be understood in terms of people's beliefs about their behaviour within them. If we are to understand organizations, we must understand what people within them think of as right and proper to do. Within this framework we would certainly not expect people everywhere to have the same views. In fact, it is the existence of differences in belief structures which provides us with the key to interpreting them. People are not likely to think of their own views as strange. Indeed it is only in contrast to other views that we come to understand our own. Theory thus becomes the sets of meanings which yield insight and understanding of people's behaviour. These theories are likely to be as diverse as the sets of human meanings and understandings which they are to explain. In the phenomenological perspective, the hope for a universal theory of organizations collapses into multifaceted images of organizations as varied as the cultures which support them.

The view of theory as arising from our understanding is expressed by Walsh (1972):

The point about the social world is that it has been preselected and preinterpreted by its members in terms of a series of commonsense assumptions which constitute a taken-for-granted scheme of reference ... In this manner factual reality is conferred upon the social world by the routine interpretive practices of its members. The implication of this is that every man is a practical theorist when it comes to investigating the social world, and not just the sociologist. (p. 26)

Thus, the naturalist tries to devise general theories of social behaviour and to validate them through ever more complex research methodologies which push him further from the experience and understanding of the everyday world. The phenomenologist works directly with such experience and understanding to build his theory upon them. As Kuhn (1970) points out, our theories are not just possible explanations of reality; they are sets of instructions for looking at reality. Thus choice among theories and among approaches to theory building involves normative and—especially in the social sciences—moral questions. Choice among them is in part a matter of preference, but choice may also be made on the basis of which theories direct us to the most useful problems and which provide the most helpful insights into them.

Research and methodology

In the systems view, research is directed at confirming theory. Theory, in this view, is something which scientists build, largely from the arm-chair, by thinking up what must be the ultimate explanation for the phenomena observed. Contrary to accepted opinion, Kuhn (1970, p. 16) has argued that such theory is never open to disproof and serves instead as a 'consensual agreement among scientists about what procedures shall constitute scientific activity and hence which explanations will count as scientific explanations'. (Walsh, 1972, p. 25)

From the phenomenological perspective research, theory and methodology must be closely associated. Theory must arise out of the process of inquiry itself and be intimately connected with the data under investigation. In this view, the aim of theory should be explanation and clarification. Thus research and theory which fulfils this aim must depend not only upon what is being explained but also upon to whom it is explained, and with what. Louch (1966) argues this view as follows:

Explanation, in Wittgenstein's phrase, is a family of cases joined together only by a common aim, to make something plain or clear. This suggests that a coherent account of explanation could not be given without attending to the audience to whom an explanation is offered or the source of puzzlement that requires an explanation to be given. There are many audiences, many puzzles. (p. 233)

Research in the naturalist mode is prone to use experimental methods to establish relationships among variables. The research often substitutes

mathematical models for the substantive theoretical model and is satisfied if statistically significant relationships are found among the variables
of the mathematical model. The aim is to relate variables x and y,
usually with a host of other variables 'held constant'. Little effort is
spent on determining whether x and y exist in any form which is
meaningful to or has consequences for actors within a social situation.
Nor is there much effort to ask whether holding one or more variables
constant yields an interpretable result among those remaining. In physical systems, we can understand what it means to hold volume constant,
for example, while we raise the temperature of a gas and observe the
effect on pressure. But what does it mean when we come to a social
system and speak, as some researchers do, of holding social class
constant while we observe the effect of school resources upon achievement? Whereas the physicist manipulates materials and apparatus in
specific, understandable ways, the social researcher frequently makes
no intervention at all in the social system which he is attempting to
explain. Instead, he does the manipulation of variables in his mind, or
in the workings of his computer. Can we rely on the suggestion that if
we manipulate variables in a social system, we will get the same results
the researcher gets from his intellectual manipulation of them? The
doubt is growing that we will not, as is apparent, for example, from
critiques of school effects research (Spady, 1973, pp. 139–40) demonstrating that schools may account for a great deal or virtually nothing at
all of pupil achievement, depending on which of several alternative but
statistically acceptable procedures the researcher chooses for his analysis.

Phenomenologically based research, on the other hand, aims at dealing with the direct experience of people in specific situations. Therefore
the case study and comparative and historical methods become the preferred means of analysis. These methods are perhaps found in their most
developed form in the work Weber did in building ideal types for
organizational analysis. These types should be seen as 'characteriza-
tions or impressions of ways of thought and styles of living' which
permit comparison and understanding of them (Louch, 1966, p. 172).
What Weber did in building these ideal types was to worm his way
into the heads of bureaucrats, clerics and commercial men in order 'to
discern logical connections among propositions expressing [their]
beliefs about the world' (Louch, 1966, p. 173). The moral consequences
of these beliefs may also be made plain and checked against 'reality'.

The close connection among theory, research and ethics thus becomes obvious.

Thus an organizational theory based upon understanding rejects the emphasis which much of contemporary social science places upon quantification, more complex mathematical models, and bigger number crunchers in the shape of better and faster computers. As Burns (1967, p. 127) has pointed out, better manipulation of numbers cannot substitute for the emptiness of the concepts to which they apply. This fixation on numbers without concern for the concepts they are thought to represent leads to a sickness of social science which Sorokin has called 'quantophrenia' and which Rothkopf (1973, p. 6) likens to the *Leerlauf* reactions described by Lorenz. In these reactions, animals go through elaborate stereotyped performances for hunting or mating when no other living creature is there to see or respond to the performances.

If we move towards improved understanding in our research, we might change our image of what constitutes *the* essential research tool and supplant the computer with Weber's notion of the ideal type. An ideal type provides us with an image of a social situation at a particular time and place. We may then surround this image with others made of different organizations or of the same organization at other times. By looking at these images comparatively, by seeing them almost as the frames of a motion picture, we begin to understand our world better and to comprehend its differences and the processes of change occurring within it. This direction in theory and research leads to an investigation of language and the categories it contains for understanding the world (Bernstein, 1971a; 1971b). It leads also to an investigation of the processes (Scheff, 1973; Garfinkel, 1964) by which we negotiate with each other and so come to define what we will pay attention to in our environment and our organizations.

Society and its organizations

In the systems view, the problem of society is the problem of order. Without society and its organizations, chaos and anarchy would result. The social order is seen as a basically well-working system governed by universal values. In the phenomenological view, the organization as an entity striving to achieve a single goal or set of goals is resolved into the meaningful actions of individuals. Organizations do not think, act, have goals or make decisions. People do (Georgiou, 1973; Greenfield, 1973), but they do not all think, act and decide according to preordained goals. Thus the notion of the organization as a necessary order-maintaining instrument falls and the notion of organization as the expression of particular human ideologies takes its place. In this way, the problem of order becomes the problem of control (Dawe, 1970, p. 212). Or, to put the question otherwise, the problem is not whether order shall be maintained but rather who maintains it, how, and with what consequences. The image which this view calls to mind is the organization as a battlefield rather than the organization as an instrument of order. People strive to impose their interpretations of social reality upon others and to gain command of the organizational resources which will permit them to do so. The warfare in this battlefield usually takes the form of linguistic attack and defence, although the physical forms of warfare fit just as comfortably within the perspective.

Take as an example this exchange between a principal and a new social worker after the social worker had spent considerable time and effort counselling a student who had been persistently truant and tardy.[3]

P: It was really simpler and more effective in the old days when the truant officer just went straight to the student's home and brought him back to school.

SW: Actually, I do the work truant officers did, but I do it a different way.

P: That may be so, but we used to get results more quickly. If the students wouldn't come to school, we expelled them. They had to recognize our authority or quit school. That's what I mean by simple. Now everything is complicated. Why can't we deal with these cases without a lot of red tape?

SW: I prefer to see my work as treatment. The aim is not to wind up a case quickly but to keep the student in school and learning. And in any case, Mr Principal, legally I am the truant officer and you need my backing to expel a student for truancy.

It is surely not hard to see in this exchange a battle going on over what the job of the social worker should be and behind that a struggle over how the school should define its responsibilities to students. The issue is how the job of the social worker shall be defined and who shall control the school's power of expulsion. Each of the protagonists is inviting (and threatening) the other to accept a particular definition of the situation and the way it is proper to act within it.

The conflict view of organizations thus links up neatly with the

---

[3] Personal communication to the author.

decision-making tradition in organizational analysis. In a recent significant contribution Perrow (1972, pp. 145–76) demonstrates how this
tradition, developed brilliantly by March and Simon (1958), complements the insights of Weber. A major concern of Weber was for the
way in which the power of bureaucracies would be used outside the
organization. March and Simon demonstrate how power may be mar-
shalled within the organization. As Perrow points out (p. 196), the
supposed plight of professionals within bureaucracies is a minor com-
plaint compared to what others have suffered from professionals who
have been able to act out their ideological beliefs through their control
of organizations.

We should also be grateful to Perrow (p. 90) for pointing out the
contrasts between Barnard's theory and his practice. For Barnard,
(1938, pp. 46–61) organizations were by their very nature cooperative
enterprises. In this respect, Barnard was a good systems theorist whose
theory dealt with abstractions about organizations and not with the
ideologies of those who ran them. In an astonishing case study, Barnard (1948) spoke to a group of the unemployed who had recently seen
'police clubs flying, women trampled, men knocked down' (p. 64) in
the following terms:

I'll be God damned if I will do anything for you on the basis that you ought to
have it just because you want it, or because you organize mass meetings, or
what you will. I'll do my best to do what ought to be done, but I won't give
you a nickel on any other basis. (pp. 73–4)

In his commentary on this situation, Barnard makes it very clear that he
realized he was in a position of conflict over ideology. But his theoretical concern lies not with the ideologies, but with his proposition that
men under 'states of tension' will do what is 'utterly contrary to that
which is normally observed in them' (p. 62). While he explains in detail
how he won the ideological battle which gave him power to decide
what the men 'ought to have', he makes no mention of his final decision.
The content of decisions is not important in systems theory. However,
Barnard does take pains to denigrate the ideology of the unemployed
workers and their claims for better treatment. He also considers in a
footnote (p. 73–4) whether a person of 'superior position' should swear
in front of those of 'inferior status', and confides that 'the oath was
deliberate and accompanied by hard pounding on the table'.

In this example, Barnard as theorist merely adds the notion of 'states of tension' to his earlier developed principles of cooperative action in organizations. Do these ideas tell us the significant aspects about organizational life with Chester Barnard? The phenomenologist holds that Barnard's ideology is the significant variable shaping the experience of many people in the organizations which he controlled. Without understanding the ideological issues involved in an organization, and in particular without knowing what ideology is in control, the general principles of organization mean relatively little in terms of what people experience in an organization.

Organizational pathologies and cures

The systems theorist looks for pathologies in the body of the organization itself. These stem from ill adaptations of the organization to its environment, to the ultimate goals it should serve, or to the needs of individuals. The solution to these pathologies is obvious: change the structure of the organization to improve the adaptation and thus the performance of the organization. The phenomenologist, on the other hand, sees structure as simply the reflection of human beliefs. If there are problems in organizations—and problems are certainly to be expected—they must therefore rest in conflicting beliefs held by individuals. Solutions to such problems cannot be found simply by changing structures. The root of the problem lies in people's beliefs and the ability to act upon these beliefs.

Thus the argument that we must make organizations more liveable, more congruent with human values and motives, ignores the fact that it is one set of human motives and values which is in conflict with another set of motives and values. There is no abstract entity called organization which can be held accountable—only other people. (Schein, 1973, pp. 780-1)

Our penchant for thinking about organizations as entities, as things with a life of their own, blinds us to their complexity and to the human actions which constitute the façade which we call organization. It leads us to believe that we must change some abstract thing called 'organization' rather than the beliefs of people about what they should do and how they should behave with each other. The more closely we look at organizations, the more likely we are to find expressions of diverse human meanings. The focus of our efforts to improve organizations should not be, 'What can be done to change the structure of this organization?' but, 'Whose intentions define what is right to do among people here involved with one another?' and 'How might these intentions be changed?' The task of changing organizations depends, first, upon the varieties of reality which individuals see in existing organizations, and second, upon their acceptance of new ideas of what can or should be achieved through social action. We know little about either, but it is clear we should understand the first before we attempt to direct the second.

IMPLICATIONS

Where do the ideas based in phenomenology leave the notion of 'organization'? And what of the science that studies organizations? And where does a profession of educational administration which bases its practice on this science now find itself? In conclusion, let me briefly develop some answers to these questions and suggest some directions for future study.

1. Organizations are definitions of social reality. Some people may make these definitions by virtue of their access to power while others must pay attention to them. Organizations are mechanisms for transforming our desires into social realities. But the transforming mechanism lies within individuals. It is found in individuals striving to change their demands or beliefs into definitions of reality that others must regard as valid and accept as limitations on their actions. This notion of organizations as dependent upon the meanings and purposes which individuals bring to them does not require that all individuals share the same meaning and purposes. On the contrary, the views I am outlining here should make us seek to discover the varying meanings and objectives that individuals bring to the organizations of which they are a part. We should look more carefully too for differences in objectives between different kinds of people in organizations and begin to relate these to differences in power or access to resources. Although this concept of organization permits us to speak of the dominating demands and beliefs of some individuals, and allows us to explore how those with dominating views use the advantage of their position, we need not think of these dominating views as 'necessary', 'efficient', 'satisfying' or even 'functional', but merely as an invented social reality, which holds for a time and is then vulnerable to redefinition through changing demands and beliefs among people. Where then may we go from here? Let me suggest some lines of development.

2. We should begin to regard with healthy scepticism the claim that a general science of organization and administration is at hand. Such theories carry with them not only culturally dependent notions of what is important in an organization but also prescriptive ideas of how study and inquiry into organizational problems should go forward. The movement toward international associations for the study of educational administration should be welcomed, but these associations should open windows on our understanding of organizations rather than propagate received notions of organization theory. If the movement can provide a comparative and critical perspective on schools and on our notions of how they should be run, the association will serve a valuable role. Since the dominant theories of organization and administration have their source in the United States, it is these ideas which should receive searching analysis before they are blindly applied in other cultural settings. In Britain, this critical examination of theory and its policy implications has already begun (Baron and Taylor, 1969; Halsey, 1972), though one is hard pressed to find similar critical examinations in other national or cultural settings.

3. Willy nilly, the world does seem to be shrinking towards the global village. Yet there are still strong forces which maintain vivid cultural distinctions within it. Despite these forces, the interests of the mass media, which the academic community seems all too ready to ape (Perrow, 1972, p. 198), directs attention more frequently to the symptoms of social problems rather than to their sources. While the mass media are usually ready with prefabricated solutions to these problems, students of organizations should doubt the utility of solutions which ignore their sources in the truly critical and powerful organizations of our societies. If we are unwilling to understand our own organizations, or if we regard acquiring such understanding as a trivial task, we should be aware that there are often others willing and waiting to apply their own preconceptions and answers to the tasks of defining the organization, identifying its problems, and prescribing solutions to them. Our own experience of our own organizations is a valuable resource. It is with this experience that the organization theorist must begin to understand the nature of organizations. Since an understanding of organizations is closely linked to control of them and to the possibility of change within them, the phenomenological perspective points to issues of crucial importance both to the theorist and to the man of practical affairs.

4. The possibility of training administrators through the study of organization theory has been seriously overestimated. Such theory does not appear to offer ready-made keys to the problems of how to run an organization. Through credentials, such training does appear to offer sound prospects for advancement within administrative systems. While such training may increase social mobility, each society must decide whether it wishes to pursue this goal and, if it does, whether this method is the most appropriate for doing so. If training of administrators is to serve its avowed purposes, then it seems clear that the nature of the training must move in virtually the opposite direction from that advocated in recent years. That is to say, training should move away from attempts to teach a broad social science of organizations-in-general towards a familiarity with specific organizations and their problems. That the training should continue to have critical and reflective dimensions should not conflict with this redirection of training programmes. It appears essential also for training programmes to develop a much stronger clinical base than is now common in most of them. In such training, both the theoretician and the practitioner must be intimately involved.

5. Research into organizational problems should consider and begin to use the phenomenological perspective. This redirection of research should awaken interest in the decision-making tradition of organization theory and in the institutional school of organizational analysis (Perrow, 1972, pp. 177–204) with its emphasis on the *exposé* and ideological analysis of specific organizations (Bendix, 1956). In methodology, research should turn to those methods which attempt to represent perceived reality more faithfully and fully than do the present highly quantified and abstruse techniques. And researchers should avoid prescribing solutions to pressing social problems on the basis of prescriptive theory and research. For example, those who concluded on the basis of the Coleman study that the achievement of black students in American schools might be raised by integrating black and white students were dazzled by the naturalist assumption that a statistical relationship represents social reality. They therefore were led to the error or believing that social relationships may be manipulated in the same way in which variables from the research design can be manipulated. In doing so, they failed to reckon with the reaction of black students to greater integration as a 'solution' to their problems (Carlson, 1972). Indeed researchers and social scientists might consider the cultural

imperialism which is frequently inherent in their recommendations for solving social problems and strive first to understand (Bernstein, 1971b, Sarason, 1971; Holbrook, 1964) the social and organizational world for which they hope to prescribe solutions.

What is needed for better research on schools is better images of what schools are and what goes on in them. 'Better' in this case means creating images of schools which reflect their character and quality and which will tell us something of what the experience of schooling is like. Since schools are made up of different people in different times and places, it is to be expected that images which reflect the experience of schooling must be many and varied. These images would be sets of 'one-sided viewpoints', as Weber called them, each throwing 'shafts of light' (Eldridge, 1971, p. 12) upon social reality in schools.

As the natural systems have provided the dominating model for studies of organizations (Mayntz, 1964, p. 116), the image of the school as a unit of production has dominated investigations of schools (Levine, 1973; Spady, 1973). The production model of the school is a systems variant which sees the school as a set of roles and resources arranged to yield a product which conforms to predetermined goals. We are often so accustomed to this model that we fail to notice the enormous discrepancies between it and what typically goes on in schools. To begin with, most sets of official educational goals would justify schools doing virtually any good thing for the individual or the society in which he lives. Secondly, the products of school are nearly impossible to identify, if by product we mean something which is unmistakably due to the efforts of the school itself. The clearest measure of school product—the results students obtain on standardized and other kinds of tests—correspond poorly to the goals of education and are usually accounted for most readily by influences outside the school. Thus whether schools do anything to achieve a set of vague goals can never be determined within the model of the school as a unit of production.

If we shear from our image of schools the notion of overriding goals and visible products, what are we left with? The image is now that of pure process in which people strive to shape a social environment which is congenial to them and which they believe serves *their* purposes or the purposes which other people ought to have. The image of the school is now not the factory or the system but the public utility (Pincus, 1974) which produces a service which people use for their own ends. It is not surprising in this conception of the school that people involved with it—

teachers, administrators, pupils, parents, etc.—have strong feelings about what services should be provided and how they should be provided. Moreover, it should be apparent that experience with the school's services leads to strong, though not necessarily universally accepted, beliefs about what kinds of service and conditions of service are good and bad and to convictions about which of them are effective and ineffective. However, lacking objective criteria to judge the relevance and validity of their claims, and lacking even a common basis of experience with the school's services, people holding these beliefs and convictions are likely to clash with others having different but equally firmly held convictions. We learn to believe in our own experience of school process and to doubt the validity of others' beliefs. In this way, the proposed model accounts both for the apparent stability of schools—their resistance to change—and for the continuing conflict about what schools are for and how they should be organized and run. It suggests as well that the path to understanding more about schools must lie through interpretations and analysis of the experience of people in schools, not through attempts to decide which structural elements of schools yield outcomes that best approximate their ultimate purposes.

6. The research advocated above and the rationale for it developed earlier in this paper does not imply only the description and analysis of subjective states. Weber is said to have advised researchers first to get the facts about the basic elements of social situations and then to move to a subjective interpretation of them (Eldridge, 1971, p. 19; Bendix and Roth, 1971, pp. 286–91). The 'facts' Weber had in mind were such matters as wages, costs of materials, the people involved, and descriptions of them in demographic terms. These are the typical resource variables which are of frequent concern in analyses of the school from the perspective of the production model. The questions usually investigated are whether the school is making effective and efficient use of its resources in pursuit of predetermined educational goals. Answers to such questions are complex, contradictory and unconvincing, as Spady (1973) has demonstrated. The reasons for such unsatisfactory outcomes are obvious when pointed out, as Gagné (1970) has done. Children do not learn from 'environments', from 'resources' or from the 'characteristics of teachers'. They learn from their specific involvement with people, things and events around them. Thus knowledge of the basic facts about a social situation is only the beginning of an understanding of it. What is needed beyond these basic facts is a

knowledge of how people in a social situation construe it, what they see as its significant features, and how they act within it. Such knowledge can only come from the interpretation of particular experiences in specific situations.

In this respect, it might be useful to think of two kinds of variables in a social situation—outside and inside variables. The outside variables are those which lend themselves readily to quantification and which involve a minimum of interpretation. As has been suggested, these variables provide information about the characteristics of the people and resources found in a social situation. The inside variables are those which may only be expressed through interpretation of experience. Both kinds of variables are important, though in most organizational studies of schools, emphasis has usually fallen exclusively on the former category.

It would be helpful to replace our usual notion of the school as a system with the idea of the school as a set. Where the system idea implies preordained order and functions in the school, the notion of set leaves completely open both the definition of the elements of the school and the description of relationships among them. Defining the school as a set leaves as a problem for investigation what the elements of the situations are and what the meanings of relationships among the elements are. With such a view of the school, we might recognize both external and internal variables; as follows:

External variables. Pupil characteristics: their age, sex, home background, individual abilities and previous learning. School characteristics: building design, facilities and equipment. Classrooms: number of pupils, subject of study, methodology. Teacher characteristics: training and length of service, personality, intelligence, abilities and interests.

Internal variables. What is the quality of relationships among teachers, pupils and others in the school? What experiences do they have in terms of (a) their expectations for the environment, (b) the opportunities and problems they perceive, (c) the efforts they make to learn, help or teach, (d) their feelings of accomplishment or failure? What decisions do different people in the school make and why do they make them? How are people and situations defined and evaluated?

The variables listed above are intended to be suggestive rather than exhaustive. The final point to be made about them is that both of these major dimensions are essential for describing and understanding schools fully. In fact, some of the most revealing analyses will arise from contrasts between the school seen in terms of external variables and the school seen in terms of internal variables. That organizational theory has too frequently directed attention to the external variables and that it has presumed rather than explored their relationships to internal variables are points which have already been made at length.

7. A continued study of organizations from the perspectives of the social sciences is certainly warranted. Schools as one of the most significant of our social institutions deserve particular attention. It seems appropriate, however, for students of schools as organizations to consider the meaning of their studies and to redirect them towards investigations which increase our understanding of organizations as they are before attempts are made to change them. Paradoxically, the efforts which promise to yield the most penetrating insights into organization and the most practical strategies for improving them are those efforts (March, 1972) which deal with the way people construe organizational reality and with the moral and ethical issues involved in these construings.

If, as the phenomenologist holds, our ideas for understanding the world determine our action within it, then our ideas about the world—what really exists in it, how we should behave in it—are of the utmost importance. And if our ideas about the world are shaped by our experience, then the interpretation of experience is also of paramount importance. It is this process, the placing of meaning upon experience, which shapes what we call our organizations and it is this process which should be the focus of the organization theorist's work. And unless we wish to yield to universal forces for determining our experience, we must look to theories of organizations based upon diverse meanings and interpretations of our experience.

BIBLIOGRAPHY

Barnard, C. I. (1938), *The Functions of the Executive*, Harvard University Press, Cambridge, Mass.

Barnard, C. I. (1948), *Organization and Management*, Harvard University Press, Cambridge, Mass.

Baron, G. and Taylor, W. (eds) (1969), *Educational Administration and the Social Sciences*, Athlone Press, London.

Bendix, R. (1956), *Work and Authority in Industry: Ideologies in the Course of Industrialization*, Wiley, New York.

Bendix, R. and Roth, G. (1971), *Scholarship and Partisanship: Essays on Max Weber*, University of California Press, Berkeley.

Bennis, W. G. (1968), 'Beyond Bureaucracy', in Bennis, W. G. and Slater, P. (eds), *The Temporary Society*, Harper and Row, New York, pp. 53–76.

Bernstein, B. (1971a), *Class, Codes and Control: Theoretical Studies towards a Sociology of Language*, Routledge & Kegan Paul, London.

Bernstein, B. (1971b), 'Education Cannot Compensate for Society', in Cosin *et al.* (eds) (1971, pp. 61–6).

Bidwell, C. E. (1965), 'The School as a Formal Organization', in March, J. G. (ed) *Handbook of Organizations*, Rand McNally, Chicago, pp. 972–1022.

Brittan, A. (1973), *Meanings and Situations*, Routledge and Kegan Paul, London.

Burns, T. (1967), 'The Comparative Study of Organizations', in Vroom, V. (ed) *Methods of Organizational Research*, University of Pittsburg Press, Pittsburgh, pp. 118–70.

Campbell, R. F. and Gregg, R. T. (eds) (1957), *Administrative Behavior in Education*, Harper and Row, New York.

Carlson, K. (1972), 'Equalizing Educational Opportunity', *Review of Educational Research*, (42)4, 453–75.

Cicourel, A. (1964), *Method and Measurement in Sociology*, Free Press, New York.

Cosin, B. R., Dale, I. R., Esland, G. M. and Swift, D. F. (eds) (1971), *School and Society: A Sociological Reader*, Routledge and Kegan Paul, London.

Culbertson, J., Farquhar, R., Fogarty, G., and Shibles, M. (eds) (1973), *Social Science Content for Preparing Educational Leaders*, Merrill Publishing Co, Columbus, Ohio.

Culbertson, J. and Shibles, M. (1973), 'The Social Sciences and the Issue of Relevance', in Culbertson, J., Farquhar, R., Fogarty, B. and Shibles, M. (eds), op. cit.

Cyert, R. M. and March, J. G. (1963), *A Behavioral Theory of the Firm*, Prentice-Hall, Englewood Cliffs, N.J.

Dawe, A. (1970), 'The Two Sociologies', *British Journal of Sociology*, 21(2), 207–18.

Deutscher, I. (1973), *What We Say/What We Do: Sentiments and Acts*, Scott, Foresman, Glenview, Illinois.

Downey, L. W. and Enns, F. (eds) (1963), *The Social Sciences and Educational Administration*, University of Alberta, Edmonton.

Eldridge, J. E. T. (ed) (1971), *Max Weber: The Interpretation of Social Reality*, Michael Joseph, London.

Etzioni, A. (1960), 'Two Approaches to Organizational Analysis: A Critique and a Suggestion,' *Administrative Science Quarterly*, 5(2), 257–78.

Filmer, P., Phillipson, M., Silverman, D., and Walsh, D. (1972), *New Directions in Sociological Theory*, Collier-Macmillan, London.

Fullan, M. (1972), 'Overview of the Innovative Process and the User', *Interchange*, 3(2–3), 1–46.

Gagné, R. M. (1970), 'Policy Implications and Future Research: A Response', in Mood, A. (ed) (1970), *Do Teachers Make A Difference?*, US Office of Education, Washington.

Garfinkel, H. (1964), 'The Relevance of Common Understandings to the Fact That

Models of Man in Society Portray Him as a Judgmental Dope', in Deutscher (ed) (1973, pp. 330–8), op. cit.

Garfinkel, H. (1967), *Studies in Ethnomethodology*, Prentice-Hall, Englewood Cliffs, N.J.

Georgiou, P. (1973), 'The Goal Paradigm and Notes towards a Counter Paradigm', *Administrative Science Quarterly*, 18(3), 291–310.

Getzels, J. W. (1953), 'Administration as a Social Process', in Halpin (ed) (1958, pp. 150–65), op. cit.

Getzels, J. W., Lipham, J. M. and Campbell, R. F. (1968), *Educational Administration as a Social Process: Theory, Research, Practice,* Harper and Row, New York.

Glaser, B. G. and Strauss, A. L. (1967), *The Discovery of Grounded Theory*, Aldine, Chicago.

Greenfield, T. B. (1973), 'Organizations as Social Inventions: Rethinking Assumptions About Change', *Journal of Applied Behavioral Science*, 9(5), 551–74.

Gregg, R. T. (1957), 'The Administrative Process', in Campbell and Gregg (eds) (1958, pp. 269–317), op. cit.

Griffiths, D. E. (ed) (1964), *Behavioral Science and Educational Administration*, The Sixty-third Yearbook of the National Society for the Study of Education, University of Chicago Press, Chicago.

Halpin, A. W. (ed) (1958), *Administrative Theory in Education*, Macmillan, New York.

Halsey, A. H. (ed) (1972), *Educational Priority: E.P.A. Problems and Policies,* Vol. 1, HMSO, London.

Holbrook, D. (1964), *English for the Rejected*, Cambridge University Press, Cambridge.

Kuhn, T. (1970), *The Structure of Scientific Revolution*, University of Chicago Press, Chicago.

Levine, D. M. (1973), 'Educational Policy After Inequality', *Teachers College Record*, 75(2), 149–79.

Louch, A. R. (1966), *Explanation and Human Action*, University of California Press, Berkeley.

March, J. G. (1972), 'Model Bias in Social Action', *Review of Educational Research*, 42(4), 413–29.

March, J. G. and Simon, H. A. (1958), *Organizations,* Wiley, New York.

Mayntz, Renate (1964), 'The Study of Organizations', *Current Sociology*, 13(3), 95–155.

Merton, R. K. (1957), *Social Theory and Social Structure*, Free Press, New York.

Milstein, M. M. and Belasco, J. A. (eds) (1973), *Educational Administration and the Social Sciences: A Systems Perspective*, Allyn and Bacon, Boston.

Parsons, T. *et al.* (1961), *Theories of Society: Foundations of Modern Sociological Theory*, Free Press, New York.

Perrow, C. (1972), *Complex Organizations: A Critical Essay,* Scott, Foresman, Glenview, Illinois.

Phillipson, M. (1972), 'Phenomenological Philisophy and Sociology', in Filmer, *et al.* (1972, pp. 119–63), op. cit.

Pincus, J. (1974), 'Incentives for Innovation in the Public Schools', *Review of Educational Research*, 44(1), 113–43.

Rothkopf, E. Z. (1973), 'What Are We Trying to Understand and Improve? Educational Research as *Leerlaufreaktion*'. Invited address to the meeting of the American Educational Research Association, New Orleans.

Sarason, S. B. (1971), *The Culture of the School and the Problem of Change*, Allyn and Bacon, Boston.

Scheff, T. J. (1973), 'Negotiating Reality: Notes on Power in the Assessment of Responsibility', in Deutscher (ed) (1973, pp. 338–58), op. cit.

Schein, E. H. (1973), 'Can One Change Organizations, or Only People in Organizations?' *Journal of Applied Behavioral Science*, 9(6), pp. 780–5.

Silverman, D. (1972), 'Methodology and Meaning', in Filmer *et al.* (1972, pp. 183–200), op. cit.

Silverman, D. (1970), *The Theory of Organisations*, Heinemann, London.

Simon, H. A. (1957), *Administrative Behavior: A Study of Decision-Making Process in Administrative Organization*, 2nd edn, Free Press, New York.

Simon, H. A. (1964), 'On the Concept of Organizational Goal', *Administrative Science Quarterly*, 9, 1–22.

Spady, W. G. (1973), 'The Impact of School Resources on Students', in Kerlinger, F. N. (ed) *Review of Research in Education*, No. 1, Peacock, Itasca, Illinois, 7 pp. 135–77.

Tipton, Beryl F. A. (1973), *Conflict and Change in a Technical College*, Hutchinson Educational, London.

Tope, D. E. *et al.* (1965), *The Social Sciences View School Administration*, Prentice-Hall, Englewood Cliffs, N.J.

Walsh, D. (1972), 'Sociology and the Social World', in Filmer *et al.* (1972, pp. 15–35), op. cit.

Weber, M., trans. Gerth, H. H. and Mills, C. W. (1946), *From Max Weber: Essays in Sociology*, Oxford University Press.

Weber, M. (1947), *The Theory of Social and Economic Organizations* (Parsons, T., ed), William Hodge, London.

Willer, D. (1967), *Scientific Sociology: Theory and Method*, Prentice-Hall, Englewood Cliffs, N.J.

Wilson, T. P. (1970), 'Conceptions of Interaction and Forms of Sociological Explanation', *American Sociological Review*, 35(4), 697–710.

Young, M. F. D. (ed) (1971), *Knowledge and Control: New Directions for the Sociology of Education*, Collier-Macmillan, London.

PART TWO

Issues in Context

6 Structure and Educational Decision-Making: The Roles of Central, Regional and Local Authorities

B. O. UKEJE

In this paper I shall, firstly, discuss the general problems of structure in educational administration, and then proceed, on the basis of the issues raised, to consider the roles of central, regional and local authorities in decision-making. I shall use my country Nigeria as the background but will also illustrate, where possible, with examples elsewhere.

PROBLEMS OF STRUCTURE ✓

The problems of structure in educational administration naturally involve the administrative process of organizing which, according to Newman (1963, p. 143), consists of two aspects, namely:

1. dividing and grouping the work that should be done into individual jobs, and
2. defining and establishing relationships between individuals doing these jobs.

In the educational enterprise and in terms of the job to be done—provision of relevant, efficient and effective education—there are two kinds of structure:

1. the organizational structure of the school system; and
2. the management structure of the controlling organs.

The principal issues in trying to handle these two problems, also as identified by Newman (1963, pp. 144-5) include the following: (i) how to divide the activities into groups; (ii) the relationships between individuals; and (iii) the over-all organizational structure.

Most organizations are composite, that is to say they do not use one method of grouping. In education we normally organize in terms of location—local school boards for example, in terms of clientele—primary, secondary, teacher training, etc., and in terms of functions—finance division, etc. Any particular arrangement will be determined by the purpose of the enterprise, its size, the people involved in it, stability and maturity levels, the technology employed and the major obstacles to be faced. These factors are then the major constraints to organizational patterns.

Often it is desirable to distinguish between those units or sections that are responsible for the performance of major operations and those units (auxiliary units) that are established to facilitate the work of the main units. The size and nature of the enterprise normally determine the extent of its needs for separate auxiliary units.

In most developing countries, however, problems are created by the rapid multiplication of new administrative units which have to be co-ordinated with each other and with the existing departments. New functions tend to be given separate organizational expression. But as Swerdlow (1963, p. 9) has pointed out 'Carried to the extreme, the proliferation of new organizations produces such diffusion of power that the task of central direction and coordination becomes extremely difficult'. This has been the experience in Nigeria between the newly created State School Boards on the one hand and the Local or Divisional School Boards and the School Committees and Board of Governors on the other hand.

The second basic issue of organizing is the kind of relationship between individuals which should be formally established. How should authority and duties be delegated? How much decentralization is necessary and desirable? Experience suggests that some of the basic objectives of good organization are:

1. to provide a clear cut definition of responsibilities and relationships—who is responsible for what and to whom is he responsible?
2. to avoid conflicts of authority and overlapping of jurisdiction—one man cannot serve two masters;
3. to provide a framework for adequate coordination of functions—all the elements and units must work harmoniously together and all parts should fit well together;
4. to facilitate executive control; and
5. to create an environment in which voluntary cooperation can be engendered.

It is also necessary to observe that the assignment of responsibility must be accompanied with the requisite authority for its execution. Here authority, as defined by Simon (1957, p. 125), means 'the power to make decisions which guide the actions of others'.

The delegation of authority is normally tied up with duties and obligations. The act of delegation of authority is simply giving someone permission to do certain things. It is an assignment of duties to subordinates with the granting of the necessary permission to make commitments (use authority) in order to perform the duties. Each subordinate is then responsible to the executive for the satisfactory performance of the duties. Ultimate responsibility, however, rests with the executive, hence it is often said that responsibility cannot be delegated.

The third basic problem of organization is that of the organizational arrangements. The structure of any organization is a reflection of its purpose. To organize is to set the stage for the achievement of some purpose. Just as the primary function of the architect is to consider the purposes of the building, the primary function of the organizational structure is to consider the purposes of the enterprise. But the goals or purposes are affected by time and social factors. As Simon (1960, p. 44) has stated: 'Organizational forms must be a joint function of the characteristics of humans and their tools and the nature of the task environment'. Thus when one or the other of these change significantly, we would expect corresponding modification in the organizational structure. In the developing countries these factors are changing very rapidly, hence there is a state of 'structural fluidity' in most of those countries.

Goals are a critical determinant of organizational structure. Thus the starting point for the design of an organizational structure is the determination of the objectives and activities of the enterprise. Once this is done structure can be developed by considering the following steps outlined by Newman (1963, p. 274):

1. The determination of the primary departments, that is the major operating divisions into which the work of the enterprise may best be divided. The primary departments should, of course, be examined periodically in the light of changes in policies and functions.
2. The next problem is the determination of the level at which operating decisions are to be made. In determining a structure of organization it is necessary to know where the centres of operating power lie. This leads to the issue of centralization versus decentralization. The level of decentralization of operating decisions determine the major blocks in the structure.
3. The next issue is the determination of the ancillary or facilitating units.

4. A vital problem is that of the top management organization. There is, for instance, a serious problem in all the Ministries of Education in Nigeria because of the duality of Permanent Secretaries as Head of Administration and Chief Inspectors of Education as head of the professional functions of the Ministries.

5. The final issue is the determination of the structural arrangements. This is the actual arrangement of the operating departments and the facilitating units.

A basic problem is how to devise an organizational structure through which education can be made more relevant, efficient and effective within the context of a particular culture. In Nigeria where, in most instances, the language of the home is different from the language of education, there are doubts as to whether the six year period for primary education in some states is long enough for the development of functional basic skills of reading, writing and computation. This has to be weighed against the political and financial problems of providing free basic education for all; the longer the duration the higher the cost of this political obligation.

THE ROLE OF CENTRAL AUTHORITY IN DECISION-MAKING

Wide variations exist as to the role which central authorities have played in the general problem of educational provision, development and control—that is, the general problem of educational decision-making. In general, educational systems are a reflection of social and political forces and consequent changes. Some are a result of certain evolutionary processes while others are a result of sudden revolutions. However, there is not always a perfect correlation between types of educational control and types of political systems. For example, France which is a democracy maintains a highly centralized and authoritarian system of education.

Cramer and Browne (1956, p. 4) have outlined four types of educational control all the world over and therefore a corresponding number of types of decision-making roles played by various controlling authorities. They are: (i) strong local responsibility and a decentralized system epitomized by the United States of America, Canada, Switzerland and Japan; (ii) strong National or State responsibility with centralized control as in France, the Philippines, the Irish Republic,

Australia and West Germany; (iii) responsibility divided between national and local units such as in England and Wales, Sweden, New Zealand, Denmark, India and to some extent Nigeria; and (iv) national control of policy but decentralization of administrative details, which is found in the U.S.S.R., East Germany, Argentina, Bulgaria and China.

In states with predominantly local responsibility, central authorities play an important role in the formulation of broad policies but a peripheral and complementary role in the provision and control of educational activities.

In states with divided responsibility, the control of education and processes of decision-making are shared between the central authorities and the state bodies. In such nations, there is a mixture of centralized direction in matters of broad policy with local autonomy in matters of details. Ultimate authority on national policy rests with the Minister for Education or central authorities but local autonomy is often carefully respected. Communications from central authorities, apart from matters of broad national policy, come as suggestions. Thus in Nigeria the decisions of the Joint Consultative Committee on Education, the National Educational Research Council and similar bodies go to the States only as suggestions. However, decisions involving a change of the school year, the salary scale of teachers and national examinations have been binding on the States. Voluntary agencies play a prominent part in the provision of education in such nations. The central authorities normally do not operate or own schools but this is changing in the developing countries where the central authorities are taking a more and more active part in educational provision.

In nations with strong national or centralized control, decisions on educational policy and even practices are handed down to the local bodies from the central authorities. In nations like the U.S.S.R., Germany, Argentina, Bulgaria and China, the central authorities control the policy making organs but decentralize the machinery for implementation to the local units.

In federations like the United States, Canada and Nigeria, the greater part of educational activities as a rule take place in the States; the management and controlling functions are shared between the federal and the State authorities. In general the central authorities formulate educational policies through consultative committees and develop plans for the coordinated and rational development of the entire system.

In most countries, the direct participation of the central government in the provision of education came very late and often as an attempt to correct deficiencies in the existing school programmes and to equalize educational opportunities. The type of role which the central authority has played in educational decision-making has largely been determined by factors such as (i) the degree of importance it attaches to education; (ii) the acceptable purpose of education; (iii) the historical past; and (iv) the political theory of the nation.

In most of the developing countries where education is increasingly being regarded as an investment and as an instrument not only for national development but also for national survival, the central authorities are demanding increasing involvement in the business of education. Again, because of their colonial past most of the developing nations have had the tradition of either total missionary control of education or a system of partnership between the State and the Church. These systems in development administration are, however, changing rapidly as a result of political changes in those States. Nigeria is a typical example of such changes.

Another important factor for national variations is the fact that the purpose of education tends to vary from one nation to the other. In the Soviet Union, for instance, where education is predominantly used as an instrument for the attainment of Communist ends, the entire educational system is government-owned, financed and controlled. In New Zealand, the concept of equality of educational opportunities led to centralized financing and centralized administrative structure which has left the local education boards with fewer powers in major policy matters. In Nigeria, education is being used as an instrument for national unity hence the Federal Military Government is building Unity Schools, two in every State of the Federation, and it has decided to provide universal, free and compulsory primary education from around 1976. In France, the concern over efficiency and intellectual development has led to extreme centralization of structure, decision-making process, and control.

The Example of Nigeria

Now let us consider the case of Nigeria as an example of a federal structure, shared responsibility, and development administration. Since independence in 1960, the awareness of the power of education in national development and the hope to employ it as an instrument for the advancement of national objectives has necessitated more and more

Table 4. Organizational Structure for Federal Educational Administration in Nigeria

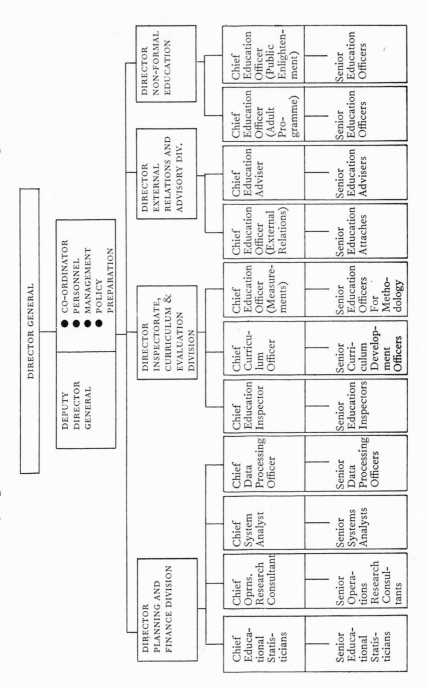

direct involvement of the Federal government in the educational enterprise at all levels and in all dimensions. The structure of the Federal Ministry of Education itself has changed remarkably and is still changing. Table 4 shows a new structure soon to be introduced, in which the four major divisions are (1) Planning and Finance, (2) Inspectorate, Curriculum and Evaluation, (3) External Relations and Advisory, (4) Non-formal Education.

In its process of decision-making, the Federal Ministry of Education (i) works with advisory bodies and commissions to draft educational policies just as in India and in the United Kingdom; (ii) renders financial assistance in the form of Grants, Bursaries and Scholarships—this directly or through bodies like the Universities Commission, again as in India and in the United Kingdom; (iii) maintains and operates federal institutions—three federal universities, a Federal School of Science, Federal Advanced Training Colleges and Federal Unity Schools; and (iv) organizes, mostly through the National Education Research Council, educational conferences, seminars and workshops. It has also established a National Universities Commission similar to the Grants Commissions in the United Kingdom and India.

The present trend of more and more direct involvement of the Federal Government or authorities in education is justified on the grounds that education is an instrument for national unity and provides a means of rectifying the imbalance in educational opportunities among the States. Thus the Federal authorities share with the State authorities in educational decision-making at all levels and in particular in regulating, leadership, coordinating, controlling, research, planning and operational functions.

THE ROLE OF REGIONAL AUTHORITIES IN DECISION-MAKING

In federations it is normal to find intermediate governmental agency between the national authority and the local school unit. This is the state or regional authority in education; and this is the situation in the United States of America, Canada, Australia, Nigeria and India.

As with the central authorities, the role played by the regional authorities has varied from nation to nation and tends to be determined basically by such factors as (i) the historical development of the educational system; and (ii) the political theory of the nation. In general,

Table 5. Suggested Structure for Nigeria State Ministries of Education

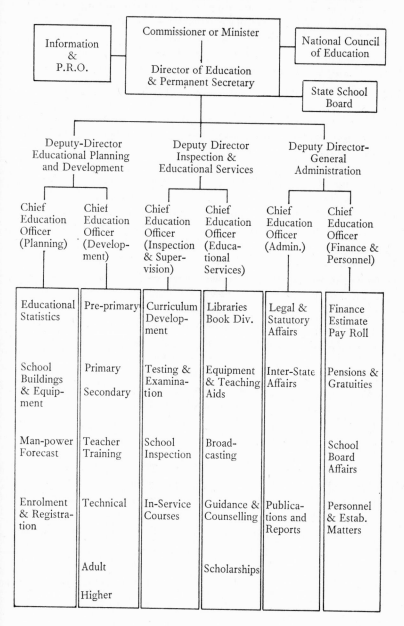

however, in most of the federations the greater part of the provision of educational activities takes place in the states while the management and control functions are shared between the federal and the state authorities.

In each of the twelve States in Nigeria there is a Ministry of Education headed by a Commissioner, who is responsible to the State Executive Council or Legislature. Structural divisions within the Ministries are not uniform and are subject to change, but there is in each State a State School Board or Board of Education. A new structure which has been proposed for all the States is given in Table 5.

In Nigeria, as in Canada, the State authorities exercise control over courses of study, examinations, textbooks, teacher training, minimum requirements for school buildings. They also control teachers' salaries and school fees, where applicable. They are largely responsible for the provision of funds and facilities for the operation and management of primary and post-primary schools. In fact, some of the States spend upwards of 40 per cent of their annual budget on education. The State School Boards are particularly involved in the provision of scholarships, running of workshops, conferences, in-service courses and the establishment of such educational services as libraries, curriculum development centres, school broadcasting, and special education for the handicapped. In addition, they help to set up local organs of management and control such as Divisional School Boards or Local Education Authorities, Boards of Governors and School Committees.

Thus the regional or State authorities share decision-making processes with central authorities in educational leadership, regulatory functions, coordination, research, planning and management.

THE ROLE OF LOCAL AUTHORITIES IN DECISION-MAKING

The trend particularly with the developing nations, is that with increased expansion in education more and more decision-making powers are delegated to the Regional bodies and thence to the local bodies. In most cases, however, such as in India and in most of the Nigerian States, the local or divisional bodies have little real responsibility and have consequently proved neither effective nor enthusiastic. In addition, most of them have little funds for any initiative.

The United States is, however, a typical example of almost full local autonomy in educational decision-making in regard to primary and secondary schools. There, local vigour, local initiative and local support are at their highest level. For instance, in the financing of primary and secondary schools, local communities contribute, in general, some 52 per cent while about 40 per cent come from the State and only some 7 per cent from the Federal sources. By law, education is a state function but this function is largely performed by the local communities. This is in keeping with the principle of democratic participation. Each State is organized into school districts which differ according to local conditions and cultural and historical backgrounds.

The power of the local school districts in the United States include the power to hire and fire school employees, purchase school sites, build and equip buildings, purchase supplies and services, determine the curriculum, levy taxes to pay for the school operations, and exercise control over students and pupils. Each district has an elected board of education that determines the educational policies of the district within the framework of the laws and policies of the State. Each board has a chief executive officer, the superintendent, who advises the board and is the executive head of the district's school system. A major responsibility of the school board is the preparation and adoption of the school budget. The actual preparation of the budget is carried out by the superintendent and his staff and submitted to the board for approval. The board has almost complete autonomy in spending the school funds as provided in the budget.

In Nigeria the Local Education Authorities or Divisional School Boards are a recent creation. In the Northern States, they are called Local Education Authorities while in the Southern States they are called Divisional School Boards. By law, members of the Divisional or Local Boards are appointed by the Governor of the State on the recommendation of the Commissioner for Education. By law, while the State Boards are responsible for the provision of post-primary institutions, the Local School Boards are responsible for the provision of primary schools. For example, the Public Education Edict, 1970 of the East Central State assigned to the Divisional School Boards in the State the following functions in regard to primary schools in the State:

(a) to appoint, promote, transfer, discipline and dismiss teachers and other staff required to be employed at or for the purpose of a State primary school;

(b) to maintain any premises forming part of or used in connection with any such school;

(c) to acquire on behalf of the Administrator and to obtain equipment, furniture and other movable property required for the purposes of any such school;

(d) to provide recreational facilities and provide school meals;

(e) to collect school fees and other revenue.

The Divisional School Board, the Edict further stipulates, may appoint a School Committee for any school in its area which, 'subject to, and in accordance with regulations and such directions as may be given by the Commissioner, shall generally see to the welfare of the school'.

These Divisional School Boards generally have little funds and are mostly inexperienced; thus in practice the State School Board still performs most of the functions assigned to them by the law. The regional or State authorities are still the main organs for decision-making even for the primary schools.

In spite of this, a good deal of local support and local participation in educational decision-making has come through Parent-Teachers Associations and Boards of Governors, where these exist. Boards of Governors have often succeeded in eliciting community support in the form of provision of funds and facilities for the schools. They have also taken decisions with regard to school rules and regulations. The P.T.A's, that are just emerging in parts of the South, have been involved in vital local school decisions. Some have voluntarily levied themselves for the provision of facilities for the schools and have contributed immensely in maintaining sound school discipline. In many areas the African concept of self-help is still found.

In this paper I have tried to sketch the inherent relationship between the problems of structure, the issues of organizational decision-making and the special circumstances of a nation. If this has raised many questions, then I will have achieved my purpose.

BIBLIOGRAPHY

Banghart, F. W. (1969), *Educational Systems Analysis*, Macmillan, London.

Barnard, C. I. (1938), *The Functions of the Executive*, Harvard University Press, Cambridge, Mass.

Campbell, R. F. and Gregg, R. T. (1957), *Administrative Behavior in Education*, Harper and Row, New York.

Cramer, J. F. and Browne, G. S. (1965), *Contemporary Education: A Comparative Study of National Systems*, Harcourt, Brace and World, New York.

Diesing, Paul (1962), *Reason in Society: Five Types of Decisions and Their Social Conditions*, University of Illinois Press, Urbana.

East Central State of Nigeria, *Public Education Edict, 1970*, Government Printer, Enugu.

Federal Ministry of Education, *Statistics of Education in Nigeria (1970)*, Federal Ministry of Information, Lagos.

Halpin, A. W. (ed) (1970), *Administrative Theory in Education*, Macmillan, New York.

Lewis, L. J. and Loveridge, A. J. (1965), *The Management of Education*, Pall Mall Press, London.

Lyden, F. J., Shipman, G. A. and Kroll, M. (eds) (1969), *Policies, Decisions and Organization*, Appleton-Century-Crofts, New York.

Moonman, Eric (1961), *The Manager and the Organization*, Pan Books, London.

Newman, W. H. (1963), *Administrative Action: The Techniques of Organization and Management*, Prentice-Hall, Englewood Cliffs, N.J.

Nigeria Educational Research Council (1970), *Report of the National Curriculum Conference, 8th–12th September, 1969*, Federal Ministry of Information, Lagos.

Reller, T. L. and Morphet, E. L. (eds) (1962), *Comparative Educational Administration*, Prentice-Hall, Englewood Cliffs, N.J.

Simon, Herbert A. (1957), *Administrative Behavior: A Study of Decision-Making Processes in Administrative Organization*, Macmillan, New York.

Simon, Herbert A. (1960), *The New Science of Management Decision*, Harper and Row, New York.

Swerdlow, Irving (ed) (1963), *Development Administration: Concepts and Problems*, Syracuse University Press.

Tead, Ordway (1951), *The Art of Administration*, McGraw-Hill, New York.

7 Creativity of the School: Some European Approaches

RIEN VAN GENDT

There seems to be a common assumption in most Western societies that the educational system must move deliberately away from being a custodian of stability towards the promotion of social change, cultural development and economic progress—or at least that it should be an important component in such a process. In this context, the culture-transcending role of the school has begun to displace its culture-transmitting function. Partly as a consequence of this, the last decade has been a period of ubiquitous innovative activity in the educational system. In short, innovation was (and still is) *en vogue*.

However, looking at actual developments in different countries one observes that, despite much talk about innovation, schools are somehow incapable of reacting effectively to the challenge it offers. Sometimes an initial movement in a desired direction has been cut down to a trivial exercise by constraining factors. Sometimes new practices have been adopted without adequate diagnosis of their effectiveness in the functions to be performed. Sometimes change is generated by an individual teacher but never takes root in the school as a whole and so perishes with the originator.

Hence this axiom should be kept to the forefront in any consideration of the problem: innovation has a reality only in the context of the goals or aspirations of those involved in the system. It should be purposeful and not a discontinuous event. Nothing is inherently good or valuable in innovation *per se*. Change is not good in itself and one should not jump on the bandwagon of innovation without first approving of the direction in which it is going. The topic to be considered is the ability of the school to adopt, adapt, generate or reject new practices whether they are initiated from outside or engendered internally. The major purpose of any related activity will be to improve this ability and so to strengthen the problem-solving capacity of the school.

An important underlying assumption of our analysis is that schools could be more actively involved in the process of innovation. If they are viewed merely as passive elements in a national 'innovation policy', then the effectiveness of such a policy will be doubtful. Imposition of innovation from without often creates strains and confusion inside and may well bring the school to respond in a way that is inimical to the institutionalization of the change proposed. Thus, the formal adoption of new practices at some higher administrative level does not necessarily imply their actual use in the schools. This is not to say, however, that there is no potential problem-solving capacity among the professional staff in a good many schools in most countries. There certainly is, and if this were taken into account when schemes for improvement were being planned (both by bringing such staff into consultation and allowing them some discretion as to the means of implementation in their own schools) there would be much greater likelihood of innovation successfully permeating the whole system.

But there we must make an important reservation. The true test of successful innovation is the extent to which it takes root in, and pervades, the school as a whole—not the performance of individual teachers in the relative isolation of their own classes. Hitherto the teacher has been regarded as the most important factor in the innovation process and much attention has been paid to his individual development, first to modify his own behaviour and then to trigger off a multiplier process among his colleagues. This has fostered a myopic concentration on single roles in teaching and screened out other factors of equal importance such as internal relationships, authority structures and the extent of the school's own discretion in dealing with such matters as finance and material resources. Our contention here is that in the present analysis of problem-solving capacity, the smallest organic unit that should be considered is the school—not the individual teacher or his class.

In focussing thus on the school, however, we must not in our turn be myopic. External relationships are just as important as internal and our approach must take proper account of the administrative system at local, regional and national level, professional support, and other relevant influences in the school's environment. In the present context, improving the school's problem-solving capacity to deal with change is synonymous with strengthening the creativity of the school—'creativity' referring to its own ability to deal with new practices. This does not necessarily mean that the school is the creator of innovation but that it has the potential to adopt, adapt, generate or reject it.

Analysing the concept of creativity calls for a multiple-factor approach, for there are many factors that may inhibit or encourage the problem-solving capacity of a school, the principal being:

1. The financial resources allocated to it;
2. Pre-service training of teachers, headmasters and administrators;
3. In-service training of teachers, headmasters and administrators;
4. The employment conditions of school staff (e.g. possibilities of promotion or transfer);
5. Adequacy of staff skills;
6. Efficacy in the appointment and evaluation of staff;
7. Provision of capital equipment;
8. Provision of professional support to the school;
9. Provision of learning materials, the relation with producers and the selection and purchase of teaching aids;
10. Relations between the school and its administering authorities;
11. Relations between the school and other influential outside bodies or individuals;
12. Attitudes of staff towards innovation and their capability of putting it into practice;
13. Social organisation within the school;
14. Authority relationships and decision-making processes within the school;
15. The expectations of individual parents, employers and other citizens with a concern for education.

To propose a single model for structuring these various factors and their relationships—a mega-solution for all countries—is impossible on account of the multiplicity of variation in local characteristics. All that can be done is to create something appropriate to a specific national context at a known point in time. The factors mentioned above are interrelated. This does not prevent separate analysis of a single factor or a single cluster of factors; but it should be appreciated that, while this might point to the desirability of restructuring one or more of the constituent factors, such action would not be justified as a means for strengthening the problem-solving capacity of the school until its influence upon all other factors or clusters had been confirmed as beneficial or, at least, innocuous.

In the following paragraphs we will describe a number of research and development projects in West European countries that are relevant for the strengthening of the decision-making capacity of the school as

that capacity relates to innovation. In this context we will not deal with developments on the local, regional or national level that are not connected to corresponding research activities, nor with research projects that are not meant to result in practical applications. Therefore we will select those examples that are on the borderline of research and practice. Three preliminary remarks have to be made:
— the selection of projects is more or less arbitrary, illustrative rather than exhaustive;
— the presentation of a particular project is based more on our own perception of the nature and scope of this project than on the official view of the person(s) responsible for the project;
— the presentation is not in all cases based on the most up-to-date information.

NORWAY

The Planning Department of the Royal Ministry of Church and Education is in the process of designing and elaborating a system of allocating financial resources to local schools, which aims at finding a balance between local freedom on the one hand and pursuit of the central objective of equality of educational opportunity on the other.

The existing system in Norway could be described as one of central government subsidies to local communities for school expenditures. The rationale behind a system of central subsidies is to provide the same quality of educational supply to all schools in the country; moreover the subsidy is combined with a strict legal regulation concerning input-factors which leaves little scope for local freedom. Subsidies are given to local authorities according to their fiscal capacity. At present the proportion of teacher salaries covered by subsidies varies from 25 to 85 per cent. The legal regulations that limit the use of teacher resources relate to the number of hours taught in the class, extra hours that are taught, class size, teaching obligations, teacher qualifications, teacher salaries, etc. Although there is some scope for local freedom, the limits on the use of teacher resources in fact centralises decision-making.

Strengthening the creativity or problem-solving capacity of the school implies a careful analysis of what decisions would be taken at the various administrative levels and especially at the school level.

The Norwegian experiment[1] attempts to increase the possibilities for more local freedom without affecting the realization of the central equality objective. The experiment, restricted to the allocation of financial resources, introduces standard costs per pupil as a basis for subsidy. A thorough investigation of the cost structure of the primary schools has been made in which all running costs were included. Differentiation was made according to two factors. In the first place, the standard costs per pupil has to vary. Costs per pupil in small schools tend to be higher than in big schools, which means that different cost-standards exist for non-graded schools, two-graded, three-graded, etc. Secondly, the subsidy percentage for each municipality varies according to its fiscal capacity. When all the relevant data are gathered, it is possible to arrive at the subsidy to be paid to each local community. This system may be investigated at certain intervals, e.g. every third year.

The main benefit of the system is that it combines equality with freedom. More specifically the advantages are:

1. standard costs are calculated on the basis of chosen standard inputs of all major cost factors. Thus twisting the demand in favour of using teacher resources is avoided;
2. expansion of the subsidy base to 100 per cent of the running costs makes it possible to compensate more than before for differences in financial capacity;
3. standard costs per pupil will make it possible to remove regulations of teacher input, even though they may be wanted for other reasons.

The local freedom thus achieved implies among others the possibility to transfer hours between categories, classes and schools according to local needs, the possibility to organize pupils in groups of various sizes on pedagogical grounds, the possibility to organize the school day in lessons and intervals of various length, the possibility to make the curriculum more flexible than before. This freedom may be achieved within the limits of certain central regulations, such as the fact that no single class is allowed to have more than thirty pupils, and that examinations are still centrally organized.

---

[1] For further information, see Bakke, E., 'Financial Instruments and the Decentralization of Decision-Making', in: OECD (CERI)—*Creativity of the School* (Technical Report No. 1), forthcoming.

SWEDEN

The nine-year compulsory school was introduced in Sweden in 1962 and the first curriculum recommended democratic forms of work in rather vague terms. However in the autumn of 1970 a new, or revised, curriculum came into force in which the democratic aspects are more clearly presented and explained. The curriculum states explicitly, 'The school is to lay the foundation of and further develop those qualities of the pupils that can maintain and reinforce the democratic principles of tolerance, cooperation and equality of rights among people'. As early as 1968 the positive attitude to increased school democracy resulted in the appointment of a fact-finding group within the National Board of Education with the task of 'elucidating needs, possibilities and forms of cooperation in schools'. In the same year the School of Education of the University of Malmö started a project 'Student democracy and co-planning at different educational levels', on which work continues, following the presentation of interim results in 1972.[2]

The work of the Malmö project was divided up into three main sections:

Part I dealt with school democracy in grades 1–6 of the comprehensive school.

Part II took up corresponding questions in grades 7–9 and in upper secondary schools and

Part III studied problems concerning student democracy in higher education.

We will focus on Parts I and II. Data have mainly been gathered by means of questionnaires, although attitude schedules, interviews, sociometric tests, personality tests and minutes of meetings also have been used. The statistical treatment consisted of descriptive measurement, non-parametric methods, analysis of variance and factor analysis.

With respect to Part I, it appears that pupils have to exert their influence on the teachers' decision-making in a direct way. One of the findings of the project is that pupils have about 40 per cent against teachers' 60 per cent chance of influencing the decisions within the class on questions concerning amenities, about 30 per cent chance with regard to disciplinary questions, 10 per cent chance in questions concerning the teaching and 45 per cent with regard to recreational activities.

[2] For further information, see Wetterström, M., *Some Results from Research in School Democracy in Swedish Schools,* OECD, DAS/EID/73.2.

The pupils' influence is thus greatest in questions concerning recreational activities, followed by questions concerning amenities, discipline and teaching. As to changes desired in the distribution of influence, the teachers stated that the principal should have less say in all aspects of school life and that they themselves should have less influence in teaching and recreational activities, areas where they at present have the greatest influence. They wanted more influence in questions concerning working hours and conditions, and at the same time wanted to see the pupils increasing their influence in all aspects. In fact there was surprising agreement among the various groups (teachers, pupils, headmasters) about how influence should be divided within the school.

The groups differed however in their perceptions of the present distribution of influence. For instance, comparison of answers received from headmasters and teachers indicated that teachers consistently give headmasters a greater degree of influence than the headmasters themselves have done. The reverse is also true; in fact each group underestimates its own influence and overestimates the influence of the other. Another consistent difference is that the teachers stated that the pupils' influence is less in all aspects than the headmasters did

With respect to Part II (grades 7–9) pupil influence is organized in an indirect way such as through representation in the student council, which is one form of pupil participation. Pupils in each class choose two representatives for the council. The attitude of the pupils in grades 7–9 and their interest in the student council proved to be positive. As a follow-up an attempt was made to extend the experience with student councils to grades 1–6 but evaluation indicated that the effects were very small. It was concluded that more radical measures are necessary if any meaningful effects on participation are to be achieved at this level.

Summarizing, it can be said that Swedish schools are in general positive towards democratic forms of work, both because of the expectation that they will contribute to interpersonal relationships within the school and because they are expected to have an influence on the social education of pupils. Although so far the participation bodies have had a very limited decision-making power, the pupils in schools nevertheless have a certain amount of influence, largely dependent however on the head of the school.

NETHERLANDS

The potential capacity of the school to deal with innovation is to a large extent dependent upon the structure of external professional support to the schools and to the educational system as a whole. This support comes mainly from the three national pedagogical centres and the thirty or so regional centres for educational innovation and guidance.

The work of the regional centres lays particular emphasis on a direct working relationship with the schools in a region. For the moment these schools are nursery schools, primary schools and schools for special education, although the services of regional centres are being increasingly extended to various types of secondary education. Most of the centres were established on the initiative of the schools themselves in cooperation with local authorities, school boards and parents' representatives.

The tasks of the centres are as follows:

1. counselling of teachers, parents and educational authorities. This comprises the provision of information, the organisation of workshops, conferences and expositions, the assessment of teaching materials, audio-visual aids, etc.
2. guidance to individual pupils. This is a central task and presupposes a good relation with the schools. The centres are involved in the identification of problems via the measurement of performance and intelligence, the diagnosis of the problems of individual pupils, the provision of support (psychological, authodidactic, remedial teaching) and evaluation.
3. research on innovation with respect to educational problems. This comprises research with respect to strategies for innovation, the effects of specific innovations and the progress of individual pupils.
4. cooperation with other institutions providing professional support to schools, among others the three national pedagogical centres.

In contrast to the regional centres, the national centres are subdivided according to denomination. Their activities embrace all branches of education with the exception of the universities and some branches of non-university higher education. The main objective of national centres is not the guidance of individual pupils but the innovation of education in general. An important problem is created, however, by the fact that effective relationships between the network of regional centres on the one hand and national centres on the other, are absent.

The present situation appears to be a transitional stage between a period with an uncoordinated disjointed system of professional support and a new era with an integrated approach towards innovation and guidance.

WEST GERMANY

Responsibility for the school system in West Germany lies with the eleven individual states (Länder), each of which regulates standards, organization, curricula, etc. In the field of educational research and development the Länder may call for cooperation and support from the Federal Government (Bund). In addition to the Länder administration and the various planning agencies set up to further the purpose of any individual Land there are various bodies for planning and coordination on the national level, namely:

1. the 'Deutscher Bildungsrat' (Educational Council), an independent national advisory body for Bund and Länder;
2. the 'Ständige Konferenz der Kultusminister der Länder' (Permanent Conference of the Land Ministers of Education and Cultural Affairs), the main instrument for bringing coherence to inter-Länder coordination;
3. the 'Bund-Länder-Kommission für Bildungsplanung' (Bund-Länder Commission for Educational Planning), a body combining the ministers responsible for matters of education at both levels.

The Education Council said in the 1970 report concerning the future structure of the educational sector, that many planned pedagogical innovations cannot be achieved without a corresponding reform of educational administration and more specifically a reform of school management. A reform of the administration is required in order to decrease the present degree of centralization, which is limiting the scope for local initiative. Increasingly the necessity is felt to bring the educational administration in line with the growing complexity of the teaching-learning process, and this has resulted in a number of changes in the administrative infrastructure.

Initially the emphasis has been on changes in the higher levels of the hierarchy. For instance the ministries of education in the various Länder have been strengthened by the establishment of planning bureaux, commissions have been established for specific problem areas, research projects have been commissioned to research and development institutions and cooperation between Bund and Länder has been improved. More recently a shift of attention in the direction of school management can be observed. One important project in this context is being carried out by the *Deutsche Institut für Pädagogische Forschung* in Frankfurt. The project is called 'Organisation of school management' and aims at the development of alternative models for school management. It deals with the issue of decentralization and proposes the introduction of school regions that should have wide discretion, and be served, in groups, by a regional educational support centre. The philosophy behind the project is related to strengthening the creativity of the school.

FRANCE

The French educational system may be said to be characterized by a highly centralized organization, i.e. it is the Ministry of Education that takes virtually all the decisions with respect of schoolmapping, curricula, examinations, distribution of budgetary funds, etc. Nonetheless in both administration and teaching, the various parties involved can exercise a certain discretion within predetermined boundaries. Thus it is possible for the rectors, regional inspectors of schools[3] and headmasters to adapt the national regulations to conditions at their respective levels, while every teacher is free to organize his way of teaching and to choose his methods within the framework of centrally decided curricula and official directives concerning the timetable. Although the many constraints are not negligible, they are far from being decisive and personal initiative and patient persuasive action can help to reduce some of the administrative obstacles. In fact there is an advantage of being far from the centre of control.

In relation to educational innovation three situations may occur:

1. decentralized initiative may receive a more or less favourable response which according to the case enables it to flourish or dooms it to failure;
2. a central decision may reach more or less effectively the levels where it is to be applied;
3. the central decision and decentralized initiative may converge and,

---

[3] France consists of twenty-five Académies which are territorial divisions placed under the authority of a rector. According to population density each Académie includes between two and seven departments. The educational administration in each department comes under the authority of a regional inspector.

according to each case, may be successful or relatively unsuccessful. We can illustrate each of these by a specific case.

As an example of the *first* situation, the 'new classes' experiment in pilot lycées can be mentioned. This example relates to the introduction in a few pilot schools of new teaching methods such as pupils making visits, preparing surveys outside the classroom, finding documents, using various methods of expression, teamwork, etc. The central authority accepted and, to a certain extent, protected and encouraged this venture. Flexible adaptation of certain regulations was sanctioned especially as regards daily routine, special care being taken in the choice of staff, particularly of headmasters, in the event of their transfer. Nonetheless, the flow of innovation introduced by this experiment is still confined for the most part to a small minority of teachers and schools. At the level of the central administration it is not unanimously felt that the methods tried should be generally adopted in view of the existing institutional structure, the existing staff and budgetary repercussions.

An example of the *second* situation is the reorganization of the first cycle of secondary education. In pursuit of the extension of compulsory schooling to the age of sixteen, decided upon in 1959, the Ministry of Education has put a remarkable effort into the design, organization and building of a new type of school, the Collège d'Enseignement Secondaire (CES) for pupils between 11/12 and 15/16 years of age. The objective was to create single establishments that would replace the variety of educational courses hitherto offered to this age group. Despite the considerable effort made to introduce the new system it can be observed after ten years that this innovation has not been realized on a large scale. The reason for this situation lies in the inflexibility of the existing institutional structure and the lack of imagination of some of the implementers. Furthermore the fact that communication lines are very long in a centralized system causes distortions and delays. Various institutional factors and factors of resistance were thus unfavourable to the efficient introduction of the innovation.

The introduction of 'modern mathematics' provides an example of the *third* situation. Revision of the content and methods of mathematics teaching was first recommended by a few teachers who had been experimenting privately with the subject and was then taken up by several groups who coordinated their experiments with the strong support of the Association of Mathematics Teachers. Subsequently the Ministry authorised a programmed teaching research project and appointed a committee to look after it. A few years ago reform in mathematics teaching was officially instituted.

A national body, the *Institut National de Recherche et de Documentation Pédagogiques*, is examining the problem of providing professional support for schools. In particular, the *Institut* has been analysing the conditions or factors influencing the success or failure of educational innovations. It appears that three groups of factors have to be considered:

1. those operating within the institutional system, e.g. the communication between different levels of a structure, the possibility of starting experiments.
2. those relating to staff; e.g. the inclination of staff to take the initiative for innovation, the way the decisions of the central administration are received, the effect of continuous, recurrent education that gives attention to the introduction of innovation. It is recommended that teacher guidance systems should be established, part of their job being to train staff, offer opportunities for teachers to meet and pool experience, etc.
3. those relating to the social environment. The public does not always understand the rationale of innovations.

The development of mutual understanding between national and institutional levels requires a careful analysis of the roles the *Centres Régionaux de Recherche et de Documentation Pédagogiques* and the *Centres Départementaux de Documentation Pédagogique* might play as decentralized services of the *Institut National*.

CONCLUSIONS

Measures for improving a school's capacity for problem-solving must be conceived, in so far as possible, with knowledge of all factors influencing its organization and its conduct. In other words the problem of creativity should be approached in a comprehensive way.

As an illustration let us consider the relation between the school and outside administrative and non-administrative institutions. The two following situations should be regarded as extremes of a continuum. In the first, a school has considerable discretion, for instance, to transfer items from one account to another (i.e. virement) or to allow its teachers freedom to plan their own activities. This, however, does not necessarily render the school eagerly receptive to new ideas or practices, even when some staff members consider them to be useful. Various internal factors may stand in the way, for example, a negative attitude on the part of staff reluctant to change established patterns, the sheer weight of the extra work load, lack of time, inability to take proper advantage of the freedom provided or the absence of outside professional support.

In the second situation, a school may be intrinsically very receptive to innovation so far as its internal structure and the attitudes and capabilities of staff are concerned, but is subject to outside influences (local authorities, school boards, examiners or parents) which put a damper on creative experimentation. In both these cases it will be difficult to ensure that an innovative spirit becomes absorbed into the school's ethos without danger of 'tissue rejection' at some later date.

The comprehensive approach that should be adopted to the strengthening of the problem-solving capacity of the school makes demands on the administration of education. The administration needs to be able to cope with all the dimensions of the creativity problem, and this is facilitated if:

— there is teamwork among the educational administrators assigned to deal with various issues;

— the individual educational administrator broadens his view and becomes more of a generalist.

It is desirable that the preparation of educational administrators should have regard to these requirements, providing experience in teamwork, encouraging a multidisciplinary approach, and drawing on specific case studies such as those described in this paper.

8 Curriculum Change in Developing Countries

JINAPALA ALLES

The developing nations are heterogeneous and this has relevance to the study. Several factors—the achievement of political independence, the efforts to attain enhanced rates of growth, the population explosion, etc.—provoked an unprecedented demand for school education, at first, characterized by quantitative expansion, but later by a concern for quality. Curriculum change has, therefore, taken a diversity of forms. It is difficult to generalize, and this is evident when one recognizes the nature of the process of change in education (Huberman, 1973). However, an attempt will be made to present some trends in curriculum change in developing countries.

It is useful to recognize certain broad 'time periods' for developments in curriculum change; 1960–1970 will be considered of significance; the pre-1960 period represents an earlier phase of activity; the 1970's is the beginning of another phase. In several countries, exploratory work had occurred prior to 1960, and in others the 1970's are characterized by features attributable to the pre-1960 period. The selection of the decade can be further justified. The output of literature in this field in the mid-sixties has increased over *ten-fold*, when compared with selected suitable indicators of relevant literature output in the mid-fifties (Havelock, 1971). In the wider perspective of educational planning, the 'sixties' are marked by transitions leading to a 'turning point' in educational planning in the 'seventies': the stress of the '60's on reaching 'quantitative targets has evolved to include intensive concerns for the purposes and processes of learning leading to an enhancement of the quality of life of learners' (Platt, 1973).

The principal initiatives for change were taken in science and mathematics curricula, at the secondary level. The trends which emerge from a consideration of the principal efforts in curriculum change in science and mathematics reflect the broad strategies of initiation, development and consolidation of curriculum change as it has taken place in the developing world in the 'sixties'.[1] Efforts at curriculum change have been made in other study areas. The introduction of the indigeneous languages as media of instruction has entailed programmes in language curriculum development, linked with significant socio-political aspects with high emotional involvement from groups and individuals. The diversification of school programmes has entailed pre-vocational programmes at the second level.

This last activity has emerged from a postulated 'dys-function' between traditional school learning programmes and the 'world of work' (World Bank, 1971). Efforts have been made to adapt the curriculum to those proceeding, in some cases, to the end of the primary level, and, in other cases, to that of the secondary level. In almost all countries, Social Studies also have been an area of concern. The achievement of useful insights into the process of curriculum change, the dynamics of curriculum change, and the emergence of efforts at institutionalizing curriculum change is realizable by an intensive consideration of the science-mathematics study area. The paper will focus on the process of curriculum change and refer to products of curriculum change only incidentally.

The term *Curriculum* will be used within the connotations indicated below:
— *Curriculum* is a structured series of *intended* learning outcomes;
— *Instruction* entails inter-action between learners and those who faci-litate and support learning—teaching agents;
— Selection is an essential characteristic of curriculum specifications and the source from which curriculum is selected is the available cultural content—disciplinary and non-disciplinary;
— Evaluation of curriculum and instruction involves validity of both selection and structure; and the effectiveness of instruction is re-flected by the extent to which the final outcomes correspond with intended outcomes.

However, the term *Curriculum* will be used to refer to the combined set of specifications, namely, the curriculum specification and the in-structional specification. Where a distinction is to be made, the separate terms will be used.

---

[1] In fact, in this context one would indeed need to analyse problems of curricu-lum change in out-of-school contexts, and in the evolution of informal learning sub-systems (Unesco, 1972c, *Learning to Be*). These aspects will be kept in view, but no analysis and specific comment will be attempted.

The activities in curriculum change in developing countries have been limited to the learning situations in the conventional schools. In a few instances, curriculum change efforts have been made in other contexts; but these instances are isolated and few. On account of this, this paper is limited to a consideration of the sub-set of learning activities taking place in the school. It leaves out of consideration many significant learning situations, especially those taking place informally in the home, in the community; semi-informally, in the church, the mosque, the shrine and the temple; formally, in other learning contexts outside school, sometimes with the intervention of mass media. These latter activities, especially the importance of the informal learning which take place in the home and other out-of-school locations, mediated by others besides conventional teachers, are being increasingly recognized as important. This will be the case in the more developed countries. The concern for these other informal learning situations as resources for providing 'basic education' relevant to development, especially in rural contexts, will become critically significant to some of the 'least advanced developing countries' which operate under very severe resource constraints.[2]

THE INITIATION OF CURRICULUM CHANGE

The Situation Prior to the 'Sixties'

Prior to the Sixties, a massive effort in educational development was progressively mounted in the developing world in diverse ways with different emphases. The general character of the scene is reflected in the extract below:

The African nations are in the midst of an enormous transformation. As they emerge to political independence, they are also moving swiftly from the traditional ways of living toward 20th Century industrialism. Spurred onward by the worldwide revolution of rising aspirations, they yearn to throw off external direction, economic backwardness, illiteracy and disease ... And to this end they are launched on a long course of modernization which is certain to change their existence into new and as yet not fully known communities ... (Unesco, 1961)

---

[2] These and cognate issues were developed schematically by Dr Alles in a scholarly appendix to his paper which, because of limitations of space, regrettably could not be included in the present volume. (*Editor*)

One of the essential tasks facing these states was that of building systems of education geared to changing needs.

Education is the very core of development in Africa. It is one of the main levers for speeding up its progress in all spheres ... Education thus has a strategic position in the great battle for progress. The type of man who will govern Africa tomorrow is potentially contained in the curriculum of education today'. (Unesco, 1961)

From the point of view of improving the quality of education, the above analysis reveals the approach prevalent in this phase:

It has been thought advisable to dwell mainly on the subjects of study in which the most far-reaching changes will be needed. But, needless to say, all subjects will be affected. In the natural sciences, for instance, substantial adjustments will have to be made with respect to the study of soils, plants and animals—for example, the groundnut rather than the sweet pea should be taken to illustrate papilionaceous plants. Even in mathematics, especially at the primary level, the material used in setting problems should be familiar to the pupils in their daily lives ...

The recasting of the curriculum must not be merely a patching up, consisting in the withdrawal of some chapters, the expansion of others and the discarding of certain topics in favour of others ... Finally, the question of textbooks must be considered with due appreciation of its urgency, for without suitable textbooks there can be no real curriculum reform. (Unesco, 1961)

Prior to the 'sixties', curriculum renewal, implied the issuing of circular instructions by administrating agencies, making amendments and modifications to 'skeletal' syllabuses and examination specifications. This resulted in amendments in pupil texts. Except for such alterations, the pattern of work in the classroom had, for better, or for worse, a certain degree of comparative stability. Quality improvement was not wholly forgotten.

Another very encouraging feature of the programme of educational development in most countries of this Region is the concern that is being evinced about the maintenance of the quality of education which is inclined to deteriorate when programmes of rapid quantitative expansion are embarked upon. (Unesco, 1962)

It will be clear that 'curriculum change', with the connotation that it has today, had not yet emerged clearly in the early 'sixties'. However, during this period in the 'pre-sixties', notwithstanding the limitations in insights relating to curriculum change, inspired teachers have taught imaginatively; and resilient young learners have survived the stereo-typed patterns of experiences to which they were exposed in class-rooms.

The emergent countries accepted that the school was a critical in-stitution that had a bearing on the future—the future being envisaged in varying ways in the many different contexts. With the expansion in enrolment, the decision makers recognized that a large percentage of the primary school populations would not be proceeding to the secon-dary level, and a very large proportion would terminate their formal schooling at the end of the secondary grades. This was in marked con-trast to the earlier attitude, especially towards second level education, that it was a preparation for the next higher level in the school system. Having regard to the earlier commitment to higher education and the fact that the curriculum and instructional specifications had been taken over with little adaptation from foreign contexts, these specifications and the manner of implementing them were particularly well adapted to the limited group proceeding to further education. The higher edu-cation system dominated the school learning context as seen in the secondary school leaving certificate examinations. The schools served a socio-economic elite, the characteristics of this elite varying but little from one developing country to another. The expectation of the secondary school pupil was entry to higher education. With political independence, there was an increasing emphasis placed on access to education. Enrolments increased more and more as schools came to be located in rural contexts. Access to these schools for the deprived populations became a partial reality; the percentage proceeding beyond the second level was small indeed. Questions were raised as to how relevant the secondary school curriculum and the secondary school examinations were for the 'terminal group'. Attempts were made to 'identify' early the terminal and non-terminal learning populations. This exercise in the developing countries was less successful than it was in some developed countries. As an awareness of equity and social justice emerged, a significant pressure group sought the reorientation of curricula in schools, to make them more appropriate to the large majority who were not proceeding beyond second level education.

In the emergent nations a literate population in conventional terms was needed, but it was even more necessary to prepare a *scientifically* literate population able to participate in development involving the application of science and technology. The question was asked: What complex of science learnings and mathematical skills is relevant to the 'terminal group'? The earlier tradition especially in science learning and mathematics learning was to teach these subjects to the secondary school pupil on the unexplored assumption that most of these pupils would, in the future, function as scientific workers at one level or another. The examinations were designed to test knowledge of facts and principles relevant to such later formal pursuit of science. Science as it was happening in the home, in the market-place, in the farm and elsewhere, was noteworthy by its absence in the school curriculum. The problem of presenting science knowledge, skills and attitudes, and assessing whether the young learn these in a way relevant to their own life-tasks was subjected to partial analyses, and partially resolved in the developed world in the 'fifties–sixties'. This activity had repercussions in the developing world, especially at the secondary level. A similar comment would apply to the learning of mathematics. Questions analogous to these were raised for the first and second level in social studies, languages, and other areas of the school curriculum.

The 'Sixties'

The developing countries entered the 'sixties' against this background of increasing enrolments, the opening up of the school to more than an elitist group of learners, the recognition of the role of the school for terminal studies, the acceptance of the worthwhileness of such terminal programmes of study, and the recognition of the possibility of undertaking such study in rewarding ways. The perspective of curriculum development in the 'sixties' is reflected in the extract given below:

... Curriculum-making in Asia follows the traditional pattern. Ad hoc committees of teachers and other specialists are formed which decide what subjects are to be taught in a grade and the allocation of instructional time. Syllabi and courses of study are then developed which set forth itemized lists of the topics and sub-topics in each subject. Thereafter textbooks are prepared—by a State agency or private publishers—to conform to the syllabi and courses of study. In recent years, new developments, notably in science curriculum, are taking place in many countries of Asia. These represent an innovative approach to curriculum development ...

The selection of a subject to be taught involves among other things analysis of the nature of that subject, definition of the objectives for which it is taught, understanding of the capacity and 'readiness' of the pupil, the methods of teaching appropriate to the nature of the subject and the capacity of the learner, the learning aids and materials relevant to these methods, and assessment of what the teaching and learning may have accomplished. Curriculum-making therefore has a much wider and dynamic function.

There are three principal foci of the curriculum; knowledge, the learner, and the society. The rapid increase in the amount and complexity of knowledge is the outstanding feature of modern times. New disciplines of study have emerged and the boundaries of established disciplines can no longer be sharply defined. These developments have profound implications for the curriculum as the principal medium for translating knowledge into learning ... Learning can no longer be equated with learning of facts, for facts are becoming too numerous. The curriculum must reflect the most up-to-date knowledge and present it in a valid form, selecting from a vast and growing stock that which is essential ...

... One of the important tasks in curriculum-making in Asia is to adjust the content and methods of education to this widening range and variety of ability and aptitude (of learners).

Another set of changes is induced by steady advances in the psychological understanding of the nature of learning, of the conditions in which learning takes place, and of the individual differences among the learners. While a definitive body of knowledge still lies in the future, the insights that have so far been gained add new perspectives to curriculum-making.

... Both economic and social needs are mediated through the curriculum and curriculum-making has to be sensitive to the responsibility of the schools to educate the individual in understanding social change ... It goes beyond the question of educating for social adjustment and is concerned more with presenting social *issues* and *problems* to the learner and to help him in bringing to bear on these issues the attitudes of an inquiring mind which it is the purpose of education to cultivate. Issues of race relationship, poverty, deprivation, international cooperation, etc. create a climate of demand for more attention to be given to the kind of social problems with which the pupils have to live when they step out of the four walls of the classroom.

Curriculum development and examinations ... should be closely linked as interdependent functions but they seldom are so linked. In all countries examinations are, in one form or another, an important factor in education; in the countries of the region, they dominate the educational process. It is widely believed that measures for curriculum reform and general qualitative improvement may fail to yield anything more than marginal benefits so long as corresponding reforms are not mde in the examination systems. (Unesco, 1971)

After the initial efforts at giving more of the same traditional type of schooling, there is now a growing concern for more meaningful development than in the earlier period. It was recognized in the 1960s that curriculum change was more than a passive addition to syllabuses and examination specifications. Major reconstruction and regeneration were seen to be not only desirable, but urgently necessary. This was inescapable in the experimental sciences. Science education at the secondary level became a political commitment of many ministries. Even in poor countries large resources were allocated for the construction of laboratories, purchase of equipment, teacher education in science, and concurrently for curriculum change in science teaching at the second level. An interesting example of such an effort is that of Sri Lanka.

In several contexts, significant and major efforts were mounted also in the field of examination reform linked to curriculum change. The initiation and implementation of significant reform was facilitated by such insights as the taxonomic analysis of educational goals (Bloom *et al.*, 1956). These constructs found application in India (Bloom, 1971). A similar activity in a smaller national population, but on a nation-wide scale, was attempted in Sri Lanka (I U P A C, Unesco, 1968). This document for Sri Lanka illustrates the effort in the field of chemistry learning at the second level. But related exercises in examination reform linked to curriculum renewal were carried out for other study areas in the curriculum. The study of the curriculum change efforts in other countries—in several selected states of India, in West Africa, more particularly Ghana, S.E. Asia, Nigeria, Latin America, Kenya, etc., are illustrative of similar efforts in curriculum change.[3]

Isolated Efforts Cohere—Nationally, Regionally and Internationally

National governments recognized the significance of curriculum change and provision appeared in budgets; directoral staff were identified and coordinating machinery evolved. In some, the initiatives were taken within Ministries of Education, in others University-Study Groups pioneered such work, in still others professional associations sponsored these efforts. The isolated efforts cohered diversely depending on authority structures, vested interests, and other situational contexts.

The concern of the International Union of Pure and Applied Chemistry and of Unesco in chemical education in Sri Lanka (I U P A C-Unesco, 1968) is evidence of a widespread concern. This is also seen in

[3] See, for instance, Haggis (1969), Gilbert and Lovegrove (1972), Bergvall (1969), Howson (1970), Raju (1973), N E R C (1970), U N D P (1973), Kothari (1972), N C E R T (1970–1, 1970–2), S E A M E O (1972).

School Science Teaching the report of a Commonwealth Conference on Science Teaching (Commonwealth Education Liaison Committee, 1964). Science curriculum change exercises provided the leading edge of curriculum change. This is reflected in Unesco's own efforts in this field: Pilot Project for Chemistry Teaching in Asia (Unesco, 1972a); Pilot Project for Physics Teaching in Latin America (Unesco, 1969); the corresponding Biology Project in Africa. These project activities provided a much needed exchange of experiences among the national and international professionals concerned in this area of activity. It led to such meetings as that on Curriculum of General Education in 1968 (Unesco, 1968), and to Mathematics in Commonwealth Schools (Commonwealth Secretariat, 1969). Under the leadership of the National Institute of Educational Research, Tokyo, a major survey was undertaken (NIER, 1970).

There emerged also a recognition of the importance of high-level education for 'curriculum change agents'. Concurrently came the recognition of the critical importance of in-service teacher education linked to curriculum regeneration. This was recognized in 1968 in Moscow, and subsequently a concrete follow-up was made at Granna in Sweden in 1971 (IEA, 1971). The importance of continuing leadership development and the interchange of experiences has also led to the emergence of an International Curriculum Organization.

The institutionalization of curriculum change and the form of the institution in a given country has a character specific to it and often has been conditioned by the immediate preceding patterns of curriculum change that took place in the country concerned. It is a function of the authority structure, and pressure groups interested in education. Education is the concern of all: and a wide variety of pressure groups function, one set in one country, and another in another. The particular functional components within the institutions evolved for curriculum change in a given country reflect certain traditions in the society in which it is, and some aspects, such as the procedures for preparing learning materials, including pupil-texts, may be a reflection of the vested interests within the country. An interesting survey of the institutional provision for curriculum change is provided in a recent report (IEA, 1971).

Curriculum change, related to education research and development, is no longer an activity that can be left to the isolated enthusiasms and the commitments of individuals or small groups of professionals, university educators, subject specialists or professional associations. There is a growing commitment of institutional frameworks located within national education systems. The information which is available concerning the various types of institutions is as yet inadequate to make any assertions regarding their styles of functioning. Undoubtedly this would vary widely from one institute to another as the wide variety of socio-political-economic environments modifies their styles of operation.

Diffusion, Implementation and Evaluation

When one examines the documentation on curriculum change (e.g. SEAMEO, 1972; Unesco, Latin America, 1973a; Liberia, Ministry of, 1972; Kenya, 1972; Educational Development International, 1974; Commonwealth Secretariat, 1969; Unesco, 1968; Alles, 1967a and 1967b) one observes a clear recognition in all instances that curriculum design and development must be followed by a coherent programme of diffusion, implementation and evaluation with relevant feedback. In-service teacher training has been a major concern in all curriculum change exercises; those who mediate in learning can do so effectively only when the relevant resources are allocated for the implementation of the design and other guidelines. Most curriculum change programmes have taken note of the importance of follow-up with the production of teacher guidelines, pupil texts, equipment and materials relevant to implementation, evaluation instrument and the means for accumulating significant feedback.

Curriculum change involving innovation is difficult to initiate and maintain, even at the design level; but this is not an insoluble problem, because, at this level, the number of individuals involved is limited, and usually they are committed people with self-confidence, willingness to take risks and other leadership potentials. On the other hand, curriculum implementation on a nationwide basis, entails carefully designed programmes of in-service teacher education, production and distribution of teacher guidelines, pupils' texts and production of equipment and materials. Even when these problems can be resolved the organization and implementation of in-service teacher education at levels of high commitment and effectiveness is a major problem. The actual additional recurrent financial commitments for carrying out such a change is, in absolute terms, large, but in relative terms, 'small', that is, percentage-wise it may amount in each year to an additional cost of the order of 1 to 5 per cent of the total recurrent expenditures of the school system. In practice, however, the diffusion and implementation sequences have presented exceedingly intractable problems. Hence, while relatively successful programmes of diffusion and implementation on a *pilot* basis are seen in many contexts, nation-wide implementations which are even partially satisfying are rare.

The critical factor in achieving a durable change is the rationality and acceptability of the design itself. But internalization and large-scale implementation demand more than these criteria for successful realization at the field level of the change. Authorities use different techniques for implementing change. The strategy generally used is rarely purely a 'line' one; it is usually a 'mixed' strategy of winning involvement at the school level and using strong persuasion, psychological and economic 'sanctions', legislative and administrative direction, of one type or another. If one limits oneself to winning participation, then the changes are more durable, but take a long time to be realized. Time is a resource for developing countries. When authority structures and pressures are used for implementation, the changes are seldom internalized by the adopters, unless they are practised long enough to change habits and patterns of behaviour. Curriculum change, in short, is not a matter of changing things, but of changing persons; when it involves large numbers of persons, this entails severe difficulties and long-time intervals (Huberman, 1973). It follows that experience of comprehensive carefully designed evaluation, even at the pilot-stage level, is limited in the developing countries, while nation-wide efforts of curriculum changes are only in their preliminary stages of design and field application.

CURRICULUM CHANGE—A WIDER PERSPECTIVE

Research and Development in Education

Curriculum change is seen now in a wider research-development perspective (Berlin, 1972; Unesco-UNICEF CEDO, 1972; Unesco, Hamburg, 1972). But translation of this insight into a reality is a difficult task. Many participants in developing countries recognize this clearly because they have sensed the excitement, the satisfactions—and the risks—of this activity, an awareness achieved by participation in curriculum change in the harsh environments of developing countries. It is often easy to advise—to be a consultant in this field. But the tasks of nurturing change attempts on a national scale, supporting and guiding them through difficult phases of work, keeping enthusiasms of individuals and groups alive through long sessions of work—these are activities and experiences which can only be acquired by leadership at the front-lines in the face of fire from many national pressure groups, not the least of which are entrenched bureaucracies. These problems are accentuated by the absence of a coherent policy on education at the national level.

Curriculum change, as a research and development function can survive only in organizational ecologies supportive of such exploration. Our experience in the field of experimental science research is extensive and need not be reiterated here. It is relevant, nevertheless, to raise a question such as:

— Do the institutions have an ecology appropriate to their function and nature as research and development units in education?

This is an important issue because once the activity has proceeded in an inappropriate setting, the vested interests will harden; and the result will be that only 'motions' of curriculum change will survive.

It is necessary to recognize also the communication flows, the internal dynamics, and the energetics of curriculum change agencies. Systematic analyses may yield insights, if not a scientific awareness, about the curriculum change processes. But much of the practice of curriculum change will have the features of a fine art for some time longer.

One must reflect also on the structure and functions of curriculum change units in the next decade. The information available is too meagre to reach any valid conclusions, but one may raise a critical question:

What type of leadership does one find at the helm of these units?

In the sixties, these relatively small units were headed by young leaders with strong commitments. It was then still not prestigious to direct such units. Today it is tending to be the contrary. What are the dangers? What precautions can be taken to ensure vital leadership? Will the hand of bureaucracy spell, if not death, inaction? These are but a few of the concerns in curriculum change.

Achievement of Continuity of Developmental Work

The initiation of curriculum change has been difficult, but a larger issue remains: curriculum change to be valid, must be a continuing effort through time. If continuity of change is not achieved, then the situation will emerge where the revised curricula become thémselves 'the new dogma', and stagnation ensues. This demands that continuous evaluation—in both formative and summative modes (Bloom *et al.*, 1971)—however difficult, need to be pursued, and imaginatively institutionalized. This is much easier said than done.

Pragmatic operational factors demand the institutionalization of continuous curriculum change. But ...

The aims of institutions get lost as they mature. The enterprise goes on because it started and runs for the sake of running.

Hence, instead of a growth of meaningful work sequences and interaction patterns, a relatively tragic identification of curriculum change with designations, impressive name boards and formidable edifices may follow. The substance and the dynamics of curriculum change may then disappear, the external forms being left to survive!

The Future

It is good to remind ourselves of 'how sudden and enormous the transformation has been between the old world of tribes and kingdoms and nations states, and the new global society that may lie ahead, and of what immense and novel efforts we will have to make to survive in this strange new world that we have already entered' (Webster, 1971). It will be vital to review learning systems at a time when the purposes of education is a prime area of debate. There is the need for a wider learning programme for those concerned in these change efforts. Identifying alternative purposes, seeing through their full implications, making choices, and doing this with an awareness of the complex interdependence of today's societal frameworks may require the development of subtle capabilities in the management of learning systems.

Because all of this work takes place in situations of change, and in the face of uncertainty, it follows that the analysis must be dynamic and not static, the policy planning continuous and not sporadic, and the process as it applies to educational policy integrated with similar processes operating in other sectors of activity. (Webster, 1971)

Curriculum change agencies by their very nature need to consider the future. A critical competence is that of living with uncertainty and ambiguity. A massive volume of future-oriented literature is emerging and systematic techniques of conjecturing about 'alternative possible futures' has rapidly become a professional area of activity (Webster, 1969).

Curriculum change agencies will need to strengthen their own 'futures-casting' capacities for, with their very limited resources, the developing nations could ill afford to make many more errors than have already been committed. Change offers the possibilities of choice and yet, at the same time, the rapidity of change makes the choice more difficult. Curriculum change agencies will need to avoid the most immediate disease of tomorrow, namely disorientation by the unforeseen arrival of the future.

BIBLIOGRAPHY

A A AS (1970), Science Education News, Washington, D.C.

Alles, J. (1967a), *Notes on Structural and Functional Aspects of an Educational System Relevant to Educational Administration*, Ministry of Education, Colombo, Sri Lanka.

Alles, J. (1967b), *Theoretical and Conceptual Frameworks Relevant in Curriculum Development*, Ministry of Education, Colombo, Sri Lanka.

Alles, J. *et al.* (1972), *Costing First and Second Level General Education*, Chapter 3, 'Educational Cost Analysis in Action: Case Studies for Planners', Vol. 1, International Institute for Educational Planning, U N E S C O, Paris.

Bergvall, P. and Joel, N. (1969), *Pilot Project on the Teaching of Physics*, U N E S C O, Paris.

Berlin, G. (1972), *Aspects of Curriculum Development*, Unesco Regional Office for Education in Africa, Dakar.

Bloom, B. *et al.* (1956), *Taxonomy of Educational Objectives: The Classification of Educational Goals, Handbook 1, Cognitive Domain*, McKay, New York.

Bloom, B. *et al.* (1971), *Handbook on Formative and Summative Evaluation of Student Learning*, McGraw-Hill, New York.

Commonwealth Education Liaison Committee (1964), *School Science Teaching*, Report of an Expert Conference held at the University of Ceylon, Peyadeniya, Ceylon, 1963, H M S O, London, 1964.

Commonwealth Secretariat (1969), *Mathematics in Commonwealth Schools*, Report of a Specialists Conference, 1968, Commonwealth Secretariat, London.

Coombs, P. H. *et al.* (1973), *New Paths to Learning for Rural Children and Youth*, U N I C E F, New York.

Educational Development International 1974, A Journal of the Centre for Educational Development Overseas, 2 (1), January 1974, London.

Gilbert, P. G. and Lovegrove, M. N. (ed) (1972), *Science Education in Africa*, Heinemann, London.

Haggis, S. (1965), *Ten Years of the Ghana Association of Science Teachers—Retrospect and Prospects*, Addresses given at the Tenth Annual Conference (1955–65), Ghana Association of Science Teachers, Kwame Nkrumah University Press, Kumasi.

Haggis, S. (1969), *Ghana—Establishment of a National Science Teaching Improvement Centre*, UNESCO, Paris.

Havelock, R. (1971), *Planning for Innovation through Dissemination and Utilization of Knowledge*, University of Michigan, Michigan.

Howson, A. G. (Ed) (1970), *Developing a New Curriculum*, Centre for Curriculum Renewal and Educational Development Overseas, Heinemann, London.

Hubermann, A. M. (1973), *Understanding Change in Education: An Introduction*, UNESCO, I.B.E., Geneva.

IEA (1971), The International Seminar for Advanced Teaching in Curriculum Development and Innovation, Granna, Sweden.

IIEP (1973), *IIEP Occasional Papers*, UNESCO International Institute for Educational Planning, Paris.

IUPAC-UNESCO (1968), *Evaluation in Chemistry*, Report of International Workshop, Ceylon, Bangkok.

Japanese National Commission for UNESCO (1971), *Meeting of Experts on Educational Planning in Asia*, Final Report, Japanese National Commission for UNESCO, Tokyo.

Joel, N., *Improving the Initial and In-service Education of Science Teachers by Involving Them in the Process of Designing New Science Courses*, UNESCO, Paris.

Johnson, M. (1967), 'Definitions and Models in Curriculum Theory', *Educational Theory*, 17(2), Chicago.

Kothari, D. S. (1972), *Education for Developing Countries in a World in Transition*, University Grants Commission, New Delhi.

Ministry of Education—Colombo (1969), *Education in Ceylon (1969)—A Centenary Volume*, Vols. I, II, III, Colombo.

Ministry of Education, Liberia (1972), *The Liberian Curriculum Revision Programme*, Monrovia.

National Council for Educational Research snd Training (1970a), *Work Experience as an Integral Part of Primary Education*, NCERT, New Delhi.

National Council for Educational Research and Training (1970b), *Objectives of Primary Education*, NCERT, New Delhi.

National Institute for Educational Research (1970), *Asian Study on Curriculum*, Vols. I, II, III, Tokyo.

Nigeria Education Research Council (1970), *Report of the Educational Curriculum Conference*, 1969, Lagos.

Platt, W. J. (1973), *The Fauré Report—a Turning Point in Educational Planning* (Mimeographed), UNESCO, Paris.

Postlethwaite, N. (1974), A personal communication.

Raju, B. (1973), *Dynamics of Curriculum Change in Developing Countries*, Faculty of Education, University of Nairobi, Nairobi.

Ratnaike, J. (1974), *Staff Mission Report—Malaysia*, UNESCO, Bangkok.

Science Education in Latin America (1972): Report of the Regional Seminar on the Improvement of Science Education in Latin America, (Montevideo, 5–15 December 1972).

SEPA, *Science Education Programme for Africa (1972–73)*, *SEPA Annual Report*, 1972–73.

South-East Asian Ministers of Education Organization (1972), *Seminar on Strategies for Curriculum Development in South-East Asia*, S E A M E O - R E C S A M, Penang.

UNDP (1973), *The UNDP Programme in Nigeria—Report of the Evaluation Mission*, 1973, U N D P, New York.

UNESCO (1961), *Final Report—Conference of African States on the Development of Education in Africa*, Addis Ababa, U N E S C O, Paris.

UNESCO (1962), *Report of Meeting of Ministers of Education of Asian Member States Participating in the Karachi Plan, Tokyo, 1962*, U N E S C O, Bangkok.

UNESCO (1968), *Meeting of Experts on the Curriculum of General Education, Moscow*, U N E S C O, Paris.

UNESCO (1971), *Third Regional Conference of Ministers of Education, and those Responsible for Economic Planning in Asia, 1971, Singapore*, U N E S C O, Paris.

UNESCO (1972a), *Final Report and Evaluation of the U N E S C O Pilot Project for Chemistry Teaching in Asia (1964–1970)*, U N E S C O, Paris.

UNESCO (1972b), *Growth and Change: Perspectives of Education in Asia, Educational Studies and Documents, No. 7*, 1972, U N E S C O, Paris.

UNESCO (1972c), *Learning To Be: The World of Education Today and Tomorrow*, U N E S C O, Paris.

UNESCO (1973a), La Oficina de Ciencias de la U N E S C O para America Latina, (Montevideo), 1973, *Le Ensenanza de las Ciencias en America Latina*, U N E S C O, Paris.

UNESCO (1973b), 'Prospects: Education for Rural Development', *Quarterly Review of Education*, 3(2), Summer 1973, U N E S C O, Paris.

UNESCO (1973c), 'Prospects: Learning to Be: A Renovation of Education, Curriculum Innovation in the South Pacific', (Bishop, G. D.), *Quarterly Review of Education*.

UNESCO (1974), 'Curriculum Planning and Some Current Health Problems, *Educational Studies and Documents, No. 13*, U N E S C O, Paris.

UNESCO Regional Office for Education in Asia (1972), *Education in Asia*, Bulletin VI, No. 2, March 1972, U N E S C O, Bangkok.

UNESCO Regional Office for Education in Asia (1973), *First Level of Education in the Asian Region*, Bulletin No. 14, June 1973, U N E S C O, Bangkok.

UNESCO-UNICEF (1971), *Planning for Integrated Science Education in Africa*, Report of a Regional Workshop, U N E S C O - U N I C E F Co-operation in Integrated Science Education, 1971, Associated Press of Nigeria, Nigeria.

UNESCO-UNICEF-CEDO (1972), *The Development of Science and Mathematics Concepts in Children*, Report of a Regional Seminar, U N E S C O Regional Office for Education in Asia, Bangkok.

United Nations (1968), *Education, Human Resources and Development in Latin America*, United Nations, New York.

Webster, M. M. (1969), *Educational Planning and Policy—An International Bibliography*, Syracuse University Research Co-operation, Syracuse.

Webster, M. M. (1971), *Educational Planning in Transition, Emerging Concerns and the Alternative Futures Perspective*, Syracuse University Research Co-operation, Syracuse.

World Bank (1971), *Education Sector Working Paper*, World Bank, Washington.

9 Educational Administration in England and Wales: The Major Issues

J. G. OWEN

I

The major issues of administration are concerned with the way in which the tasks of government are changing. In England and Wales, as in every country with a developed system of education, demands become more complex, more insistent and larger. Education comes in new forms as it tries to meet a continually widening range of needs. It steadily affects more lay people, costs more, involves a larger number of official agencies and is subject to increasingly complicated regulations, formalities of guidance and informal pressures.

In response, administration is expected to become something different from what it was even five years ago. But administration, as a mixture of shared rules, policies and judgments, is an abstraction. Behind the abstraction sits the administrator who, in turn, has to be more accountable, more aware of change, undogmatic and fast moving in his responses to new demand. Yet he is expected also to ensure the stability of a major piece of traditional cultural machinery.

Changes in the conventions of control and administration are not very publicly known. Nevertheless observers and participants see three things clearly: central and local government are not in step, administrators and politicians now have more to do with each other and there is inconsistency within the unavoidable relationships on which administration depends.

Central government leaves a great deal of decision about policy, about the direction of a movement, about standards and purposes to local choice. This means that education in England and Wales is by far the largest public service which involves direct contact with the majority of families in the land. Local connection, local involvement and local purpose has justified local control of a national statutory service. But at the same time, local control of governmental services in 1974 is diminishing in its independence. Crises of economy and crises about the distribution of resources have led—and this has been clear enough in recent months not to need underlining—to louder appeals to consider the national interest. There have been urgings to contribute to a national rescue bid. This has been made necessary by economic, social, political and international events. Crises and conflicts become matters of daily dealing. Behind them lie fundamental questions of what we can afford, how long we can afford it and—if we have to choose between things which we cannot equally afford—the justification of our choices of priority.

Parliament and lay committees make the decisions: but they do so when the implication of each choice and the narrowing of each pair of alternatives has been worked out by the administrator. In England and Wales he is regarded as, on the whole, enjoying a unique freedom from direct political pressure. But his independence may be an illusion in two ways: first, if things go wrong he can never win (nor is he meant to). Second, he cannot by now be an effective administrator if he assumes that he can maintain his independence come what may. The classical bureaucrat is on the way out: the political bureaucrat has arrived.

II

To some minds it is change in the nature and structure of government which leads to shifts in outlook on the part of the administrator. The more active the role of government and the role of administration in both guiding and responding to social change, the more involved the administrator becomes. He is inside, he is part of the thing that he administers.

This involvement is not only a matter of politics: in education there are moral involvements—not new but, year by year, different in their seriousness. An example arises in the quandary of an experienced Head of a comprehensive school who suspended a fifteen year old boy from his school when the police had charged him with the possession of cannabis. Later the boy admitted to the police that he had not only possessed cannabis but had also sold it in school. Further, he had possessed and sold LSD in school. He was placed on probation; in time he was ready to return to school. The Head wanted an assurance that the boy would not revert to his earlier ways: the boy's father protested that the Head was making too much of it all. His son, he said, knew of members of staff who did precisely the same thing. Why was the Head not concerned with them?

In his spirited way the Head (and his own deputy had heard the allegation, too, and this made a difference) demanded that the father and the boy should substantiate the allegation about staff involvement in drugs or withdraw it. Otherwise, the boy would have to remain out of school. Under the regulations, precedents and convention of English law about education the Head knew that he did not have much to stand on and that the problem had to be passed to the out-of-school administrator. He, for his part, could not decently overrule the Head, but nor could he deprive a child of education. One punishment had been enough: further exclusion from school would be unjust.

Is this the type of incident about which a straightforward administrative decision can be made? Or does it involve a wider range of issues about the misuse of drugs, about mental health, about the *mores* of present day teachers and about the rights of pupils and students? And is it new? No, but it does exemplify what teachers everywhere, the administrator within school and the administrator outside, may accept as a normal demand.

Comparable in its own way—for the diversity rather than the newness of demand—is the fairly recent English experience of having to treat the disputes and grievances of teachers on an industrial basis. The administrator cannot remain detached and certainly cannot be unchallengeable when a local education authority has to accept that a decision can be made which goes against established policy. The type of challenge to an authority's decisions which previously was encountered only in comparatively rare pieces of litigation will now be met more often. New for England—and nothing wrong with it—except that we have had to be later in learning how to cope.

It is in these other ways that administration becomes more visible. It becomes involved in the area of moral conduct and social behaviour and it becomes inseparable from the relationship where a considerable privacy of contact has previously existed between a teacher and his employer. It becomes political, too, more open to argument, demand, pressure and challenge. As its visibility grows, the rules of administration become known to a larger number of people. It becomes something which it is easier to understand, to circumvent and sometimes to subvert.

III

Other changes of a general kind are worth noting: as recently as 1969 it was still possible (Baron and Taylor) to treat the administration of education as something which happened outside rather than within schools and colleges. It seemed straightforward to assume that to have a proper administrator inside an institution was less important than the idea that a Head or a Principal should above all be a teacher. This meant that it was difficult to see a parallel between a Principal and a Chief Education Officer. By now, it is admittedly more clear that the main difference lies in its being easier to define the administrative power of the Head or Principal; it is becoming more clear, too, that much that can be said in description of the work, influence, frustration and changing role of the out-of-school administrator could, with equal validity, be claimed for the Principal. Nevertheless, the administration of education (as opposed, perhaps, to the management of an educational institution) is still regarded as having more to do with external administration. And this assumption underlies what is said in the greater part of this paper.

Things have, of course, changed. This can be attributed to there having been alterations, by national regulation, about the way in which colleges of education and colleges of further education should be administered. This has been linked with a movement towards the greater autonomy of the governing bodies. At school level a somewhat comparable change in the importance of institutional administration has been noticeable, but here it is less any set of regulations or any national re-definition of a school's relationship to a local education authority which has mattered than the fact that many secondary schools have been reorganized, have become larger and have had more demands made on them. Primary schools, too, have changed under the influence of the Plowden and Gittins Reports.

Gradually, the extra-institutional administration of education has become less specialized and more central. It remains an area in which the government administrator admittedly does not meet his school or college colleague on equal terms but there is now at least a forum in which the language begins to become a common one. Because of this, a summary (such as that of Glatter, 1972) of recent movements in theory and practice of administration in education has been timely in reducing isolation and separateness. And the increase of a sense of sharing in administration has also brought more education into administration.

The connection of administration with education *per se* has been compelled by a number of governmental decisions. The aim of those decisions has often been plainly political. Nevertheless both the main results and the side-effects should be beneficial.

As a first example, the newly imposed task of putting teacher education, higher education overall and further education into new relationships with each other in England and Wales has, for the visitor from another country, a certain obscurity about it. It has to be explained that teacher education forms part of the entity known as Higher Education. It also has to be explained that three other constituents of Higher Education are the universities, the polytechnics and those colleges of technology or of the arts which offer first degree courses. These may, but do not always, contain some component of teacher education. In itself the education of teachers has, since 1947, been conducted largely on a separate basis.

To put a number of parts of post-school education together by governmental decree, to ask that a new pattern should be created, to ask for an alteration in the size of each contributor's offering both to the total of educated manpower and to the pool of trained teachers (as well as that this re-jigging should be the responsibility of local education authorities) amounts to a large demand on administration.

How well the demand can be met requires sympathetic understanding of what it is that each group of institutions as well as each college for itself should have expected. Educational expectations, academic aims, views about a contribution to the overall purposes of teacher education in higher education—all these have been well documented and well argued. The ground is well mapped and guidance in producing a plan for this kind of reform has been provided by a White Paper and by one or two subsequent regulatory government circulars.

A comparable pattern has been followed for another exercise, which again required administrators to display both sympathy and understanding for a non-administrative issue; in this instance it was concerned with nursery education.

Nursery education had lain in a neglected field in England and Wales since the early 1950s. The surge of wartime (and postwar) enthusiasm for day-nurseries, nursery schools and nursery classes had faded away. Mothers had gone back home to look after their children and their employment chances, too, had dwindled sharply. Patterns of an emergency life had gradually shaded into a civilian ordinariness. Against this background schooling had once again become something which started in year 5—and not before.

The English and Welsh administrator had, admittedly, been peppered throughout the late 1950s with ambitions and urgings from special groups—from the Nursery Schools Association, from the Pre-School Playgroup Association and from those who before the Plowden Report was published, saw how important it was for the efforts of family (particularly those of the mother) and of school to be linked in some preparatory way before full schooling began.

The degree to which an administrator was moved by these special pleadings on the part of avowedly minority groups depended on his mobility of mind, his age, his sympathies and his openness to suggestion.

But how was the administrator expected to respond to an official directive to re-start the process of providing nursery education? It was intended to be done on a basis of giving complete coverage in less than a decade and of making this provision, too, in a way which allowed some differentiation to be exercised between children and families in greater and lesser need.

The administrative response could be in one of two styles: it could be that of someone who treated it as an exercise in logistics—buildings, staff, equipment, the money side of things—or as a chance to provide a lead into school education in a way which would enlarge the overall benefit of early teaching. But within this latter view, too, there is more than one way of looking at things: nursery education can be thought of as accelerating the acquisition of things to be learned in such a way as to compound the benefit of schooling at the age of, say, nine or ten. This is the spirit of pre-preparatory schools in the private sector. Alternatively, nursery education can both enrich what the child gets from his parents and family and, if this can be claimed not too crudely, it can partly separate him from those dull influences of an uncaring home which stultify his learning.

Provided that administrators did not take the purely logistic approach there were, thus, subtleties of thought and planning which had to take into account matters which were almost purely pedagogic. Many administrators and committees had therefore to learn things afresh, to know where (if they were fortunate) to turn for good advice—and they also had to digest ideas and plan schemes quickly. The spur of a national programme was an excellent incentive for concentration and speed of effort. And the only cloud of irony which passes over this picture of stimulus and enthusiasm is the possibility that the economies of crisis and the search for sacrifice can nibble away at a field of activity which combines what is educationally essential with what is politically attractive—and not too expensive.

Thus, even when educational changes have had to be made from a tradition which lies outside the school and college, the administrator has had to develop or acquire a grasp of educational detail which is unusual. In the same way, the principals of colleges and the heads of schools who are by now so firmly involved in a variety of levels of consultation that differences between them and external administrators become steadily less easy to see—these have found it essential to understand the so-called pure administrative background. Budgets, government controls and the interrelation of agencies have had to become part of the daily thinking of people who until now had thought that the daily complications of staff, students, timetables and accommodation were enough.

IV

In the opening up of administration to pressures which were more plainly educational, the interconnection of what happens in public services has come to matter a great deal. This goes beyond the need that decisions should be taken corporately for the sake of some abstract ideal of corporateness. New responsibilities have made it necessary for education to be firmly dovetailed in part of its work with other personal social services, particularly where the responsibilities of care, guidance, support and education for socially frail families come together. Those who are severely subnormal in their mental capacities, too, move from the age of education to the age of adult work—or of some degree of protectedness from the rest of the adult world. At this point the services of education, of health authorities, of social services and of a number of voluntary organizations need to come together.

In a comparable way the administration of education within a local education authority and the administration of community and personal health services in an area health authority have to mesh with each other in order to ensure that not only the health of the school child and student but also the preventative and environmental aspects of a total health service are beneficially organized.

The way in which education services have to look beyond their traditional limits in order to allow interrelated policies to be created and acted upon is not strange. All that needs to be said is that the connections created by statute in the past five years sometimes seem to have been rather late. At the same time they have in several instances been matched by good local initiatives which go beyond the requirement of central government. And if, indeed, we had to summarize new issues in educational administration within the area of new development and new responsibility, we would be bound to notice that education has become part of a larger environment; it has moved nearer to the ideal of contributing to an educative community. Within this movement, the administration of education is credible only if it can meet educational challenge on the ground of education itself and if it can translate the twin ideals of enlarging and renewing educational opportunity into arrangements which can be believed and afforded.

V

Part of the job of being believed depends on knowing what it is that is being dealt with. The administrator has to know the language, ideas, practices and frustrations of the school and college educator. Often, however, he can only reveal that he knows enough to be trusted if he actually speaks with the educator. He must speak to some purpose. That purpose is now almost invariably bound up with consultation.

To analyse the reasons which account for the growth in both the fashion and the necessity for consultation would no doubt be complicated. It probably has much to do with the development of ideas and practices about the democratization of public life, about the increase in people's participation in activities which earlier had been arcane, obscure and fit only for the understanding of mandarins. Consultation, too, often amounts to an administrator explaining in a credible way why the answer has to be no; expansion, renewal or development cannot go forward—because there is little money or because building programmes are restricted or because of tight teacher quotas.

Within schools and colleges the Principal or Head has found a comparable increase in the amount of explanation which is expected of him. Assistant teachers become sceptical about headmasterly infallibility. Parents, too, want to know not only why school rules should apply to their children but to find out why obstacles and permissions stand in the way of their children at the time of examinations. The Headmaster realises that one of his most frequent exercises in explanation, consultation and pacification has to be carried out in face of the cry, 'You cannot deny my child the right to fail'. But beyond individual families lie parent associations and local pressure groups. And these can be the focus of virtually continuous consultation and explanation. It is not the governors and managers of schools who need consultation to anything like the same degree. They are seen as part of authority and work in support of the Head—not least at those times when that most articulate and well-informed body of a Head's questioners, the assistant teaching staff, are in full cry (King, 1973). No doubt the improvement of education itself contributes indirectly to the process. But, whatever the ultimate justification may be, consultation and explanation has become a fixed part of public life.

To the administration of education at a local level these demands present no particularly new problem. Education committees, their members and their officers as well as Heads and Governors have certainly for the past two decades been involved in a massive programme of public explanation and debate about schemes of school reorganization.

At national level, however, the debate has not been so obvious. Admittedly, Secretaries of State have differed in the way in which they have responded to advice. They have not all confined themselves to knowing what their official advisers, or their political intimates or even their statutory consultative bodies have wished them to hear. When, for instance, the Schools Council produced its second set of proposals for major change in examinations at 18 plus, a very broad presentation of consultation was balanced by the opinion which a Secretary of State formed after what seem to have been completely informal and rapid soundings—and soundings which were not intended, of course, to secure a representative balance of opinion.

Any country with a fairly old system of public education is unlikely to have a natural capacity for providing national policy makers with a freshly sensitive picture of what people want, need or expect. On the other hand it should not be the prerogative of younger countries to promote both nationally and regionally those programmes of conference, public view-seeking and large seminars which mark the history of educational development in New Zealand and Australia, in some Canadian provinces and American states. By contrast, the English now reveal themselves as having a distaste for discussion unless it leads to a desired political or administrative end. Or, more refinedly, they value large debate when they are politically on the minority side or when they are still in an administrative quandary about which horse to back.

Despite history, consultation now forms a distinctive part of administrative life. It creates the constant need to balance views in order to give due weight both to traditional consultees (with somewhat predictable views on most issues) and to newer pressure groups. Thus, for example, education authorities must by tradition (and because it is a good practice) consult teacher unions. A well-known pattern exists for doing this and in some ways it produces the nearest thing there is to a national consultation. Unions usually take their overall standpoint— even if not the particular local view which is expressed—from their headquarters and from their national executives.

By contrast, pressure groups such as those of A C E, C A S E, N A G A M,[1] the Comprehensive Schools Committee, the Child Poverty Action Group, can easily fall outside the administrator's list of favourite callers. Not all local education authorities will include them in a formal process of consultation: the pressure groups will have to ask (sometimes insistently) for their views to be considered.

Administration is faced with no insuperable problem in the job of balancing opinions before conclusions are shared. It does, however, seem likely that within the next decade the administration of education (and the administration of other personal social services, too) will have to decide whether it is only the expression of political pressure—and here is meant the pressure of the majority political party at any one time—which can be given full weight If, in the expanding pressures of consultation, more heed is to be paid to the views of lesser-known and shorter-lived minority groups, then much will depend on the skill and credibility of those groups. A great deal, too, will depend on the size of the backing which they can secure from a less directly interested majority of parents and voters.

[1] A C E, Advisory Centre for Education; C A S E, Confederation for the Advancement of State Education; N A G A M, National Association of Governors and Managers.

VI

Behind any view about the developing need which the administrator experiences for open, frequent and unforced consultation lies the question of what consultation is for. It serves the purpose of finding out what is needed. What that amounts to can, in turn, include questions of large policy (teacher supply, the rate of expansion in higher education, the vocational purposes of continuous education). It can thus supplement the process of long term planning and it may even serve—not too justifiably—as a substitute for planning.

But whatever the purpose, the administrator in seeking expressions of view from the public or from professionals has to learn how to use, how to control and how to trust consultation. Experience is building up.

In a smaller and less visible context consultation matters in another (and very crucial) way to the administrator. At the level of central government the senior secretaries of government departments have no doubt always been aware that their ministers must put up a convincing show with or against other members of the government if the Cabinet and the Treasury are to allow more money to be spent and services to be expanded. The Cabinet no doubt acts highly corporately. At the least it acts with unanimity. This is the nature of high-level political agreement.

At the level of senior *officers* within government departments degrees of cooperation and fusion of aims are less obvious. Even at times of considerable crisis there is an air of roads, the Channel tunnel, hospitals, the care of old people, schools and Concorde all vying with each other. The advice given to ministers seems to be exclusive and single-minded —and to be shaped by a senior civil servant's view about the preservation of cherished programmes and the retention of a departmental identity.

The openness of mind on the part of senior civil servants within central government has been scrutinized in a number of comparative studies. In one survey (Robert Putnam, 1974) the bureaucrat who excluded politics as a matter of any seriousness and who would prefer that policies, countries and people were run only by pure-minded and well informed administrators was thought to be on the decline. Bright young senior men in Britain's civil service, for instance, were now thought to be characterized as more politically conscious, more 'programme-committed', more egalitarian and more tolerant towards politicians and pluralism. This may be happening because the traditional European civil servant represented until recently one of the last bastions of an older social order. The bastions are crumbling, but not without conflicts of principle and loyalty.

At the level of local government things may be different. They were changing in the late sixties when the management of local government came under review in the Maud and Mallaby Reports (1967). They changed further after the later publication of the findings of the Redcliffe-Maud Commission (1969), after the decision to re-shape local government and while the 1972 Local Government Act was being passed. At that time, too, another management report was prepared by the Bains Committee (1972). The Committee was made up mainly of representatives of the legal and financial officers of local authorities. Their report urged the need to create structures of management in local government which would compel officers to share their planning and to avoid the waste and inefficiency to which unrelated efforts might sometimes allegedly lead.

There are ten principal administrative services in first-tier local government: the work of the Chief Executive and his small secretariat is to ensure that a County Council is efficiently served. He coordinates nine others. Of these, six are largely support services: the County Secretary provides legal and general administrative services, common to all other departments; the Personnel Officer does the same thing for staff; the Treasurer manages money for the spending departments; the County Architect designs and builds buildings for other departments; the Estates Surveyor buys and sells sites for those buildings—and for developers who can commercially add to the financial strength of the county. The County Planning Officer ensures that the efforts of other departments do not ruin the visible environment. He also ensures that the controllable parts of the environment are, if possible, improved. In addition to these six there are three substantive departments: the County Engineer designs and builds roads, bridges and sewerage works, the Director Social Services provides for the personal social services and the Chief Education Officer manages the department which provides all education outside the universities, the private sector of schooling and the individual training schemes of separate specialist professions.

Within this pattern most departments contribute something distinctive to the totality within which, for instance, an education service is ad-

ministered. Others, too, give invaluable help—as National Parks Officers, Chief Librarians, Museum Curators or as Amenities, Tourist and
Industrial Officers. But by and large those departments which do not
directly provide public services support those departments which do.
How support is given is decided partly by regulations of government but
largely by local conventions and agreements. How substantive services
are provided is a matter, again, which is largely guided by central
government but which is mainly decided at local level.

Consultation and coordination between a Chief Executive and nine
principal officers is of inarguable benefit. But it has to be noticed that
the majority of the total team are neither constantly nor directly in
contact with a public; they do not offer a direct service. The three
departments which give the largest direct services have thus an added
dimension of accountability and a second responsibility of consultation.
Within education—the biggest spender and the service which is in
touch with virtually every family for quite a long period during each
person's life—we attempt to manage things in such a way that the
public can know what we do, that teachers understand our schemes and
that other committees and administrators are informed about our aims.

To try in this way to be satisfyingly sensible all round means that
special weight has to be given to the statutory differences created by
making a Local Education Authority something which is not quite the
same as a local authority *per se*. It is different, mainly in its singleness of
purpose and in the need to have corresponding differences in procedure
to match that purpose.

It is not difficult for administrators and committees responsible for
other services either to sustain or to erode the efficiency of education.
The habits by which a good education authority is to be supported can
be forgotten, ignored or continually refined. Part of the function of new
local authorities is to review and monitor the work and programmes of
their own committees and departments. This should give adequate
assurance that what is good will be fostered and what is bad will be
thinned out. And this should be the limit of outside involvement with a
department's work. But are there potential weaknesses inside the administration of education itself? Yes: there are now bound to be, as a
result of local government reorganization, more men in senior positions
who have a background of local government bureaucracy, not a background of education. Unless these people, generally men of long
experience and good sense, can re-learn the importance of putting

education before other loyalties—such as the loyalty to bureaucracy as a thing in itself—a great deal could be lost.

What all this amounts to is that corporate relationships should not impinge on what the administration of a single department does about its main task. Hence it should be a needless fear that consultation and cooperation within local government should create any more difficulty than normal patterns of cooperation with interests which lie outside.[2] Nevertheless the corporate approach can carry dangers for an education authority. Within a small corporate team an imbalance of personality, a limitation of intellectual breadth, an over-soft leadership or any crude searchings for power can lead to interference in areas of work where valuable traditions can be destroyed.

VII

One of the main reasons which make it essential to have good understanding and cooperation lies in the need for the resources of local and central government to be distributed in the best way. Education is different in not being, as some have mistakenly called it, simply another service of local government. It is, instead, a separate function with its own administration, accountable both to a large local council and to a national department of government. This dual accountability places emphasis on the administration of resources. In a time of acute competition for expenditure this is an issue of importance.

It need hardly be said that the days of straight accretion—of both services and cost—seem to be long gone. Administrators are already in the habit of reviewing expenditure more deeply year by year. Fringe developments have always been vulnerable; recently, basic matters of the service's fabric have also been under the sharpest scrutiny.

If priorities have to be decided fairly, heavy demands are made on the energy and intelligence of staff in reviewing (and advising on) choices. They must see through the complexity of diverse claims and must be in a position to explain and to make credible guesses at the reasons which make nursery expenditure likely to pay off more than expenditure on Further Education, or the reasons which explain why the development of special education must be held back if the protein content of school dinners is not to be diminished.

[2] Universities may be the clearest example of cooperation on a third front, with other professionals within education but outside local government.

Both the analysis and the forecasting of demand and cost is the source of weakness in educational administration. Admittedly, refinements of method are well-developed in a few local education authorities and in general administrators are aware that they must understand the degree of accountability that is expected of them. But who will tell the administrator what to prove? Increasingly this compulsion lies with central government. And there then arises the danger that decision, accountability and final responsibility will not rest with the same people. There will, for instance, be contradictory plans for a nationally expanded service and, within twelve months, regulations which reduce these to unrecognizable form. There will be frustration, too, as the irritation of earmarked expenditure (as has always been the case with the allocation of local funds by central government for major capital projects) gives way to a seemingly more liberal idea of decisions being made at local level within block allocations. But the block fund will, one knows, always be too small. Liberality will be an illusion. And with so many shadows and false claims about them, how will administrators and committees work constructively under new pressures and fresh frustrations?

VIII

The relationship between the officers of an administration and its elected members will clearly have much to do with the degree of tolerance and constructivity which can emerge. Not all those issues which, for instance, are mentioned in this paper will be matters of frustration. There will certainly arise demands for inventiveness and energy. There will also be demands for a level of understanding between the lay and professional halves of administration without which the system was in the past able to run quite satisfactorily. It was possible a decade ago for the officer to advise—always, as it would be said, objectively and fearlessly. Committees and the members of councils could act on or reject this advice. If, of course, either happened too frequently, one side or the other became cynical—but this was known and expected (Kogan and Van der Eyken, 1973).

Regrettably, demands become larger and action moves faster. There is less leisure for two stabs at a single policy. Advice still has to be objective (in the sense of apolitical and unprejudiced) but there is no room for what is simply a gesture of sincerity. Authentic differences of opinion are unavoidable and mere posturings are unhelpful. Pain and frustration, too, follow insidiously, in the way which, before his early death, Derek Morrell described:

... I find it yearly more difficult to reconcile personal integrity with a role which requires the deliberate suppression of part of what I am. It is this tension, and not overwork, which brings me regularly to the point where I am ready to contemplate leaving a service about which I care very deeply.

Injudicious cooperation will lead to accusations of officers and chairmen living in one another's pockets: advice will be said to be trimmed. Issues will be raised about expediency and compromise—and all this will be distasteful. But it is just as necessary to point to the virtues of cooperation—and to the cost of cooperation—as it is to remember that laymen and professionals will and never can be of entirely the same view. Each side must be well-informed about the conditions and difficulties through which the other is working: each side must decide where not to disagree and, in the same terms, where disagreements may be inevitable. What the education service cannot afford is purposeless wrangling, indecisive gestures and waverings after decisions are made. But does the risk of these abortive activities amount to a major administrative issue? Will the search for middle ground between the administrator and the politician lead to the kind of nerveless and finally boring caution which brings downfall to the moderates within politics? Or will tenacity to a hard line of difference lead to some kind of extreme confidence which again, in political terms, can bring its own disaster?

If administrative skill is needed to foster successful relationships, to quell suspicion and to promote the enactment of productive ideas, then administration has to concern itself very seriously with the new relationship of politics, resources and educational policy. And in many ways this is probably the key issue. Education is firmly in the centre of public debate. Wars have become fewer, defence matters (or at least costs) less, gross social inequalities survive but are being battled against. What are those parts of public service which can, against a background like this, make life better? Subsidized housing, health services, personal family services, education—this quartet calls for common ideals and different practices; it also calls for shared rationalizations and diverse outcomes. The social underpinnings are familiar and have points of similarity. If administrative issues differ in their importance, it is because in each of the four the resources, the clients and the climate of sympathy and tradition is different. But despite differences of a practical kind, there may be similarities of goal which can both embrace and transcend distinctions of theory.

CONCLUSION

As the process of organizing a public activity grows larger, the risk increases that organization may become an end in itself. When administrators begin to serve what appear to be only those ends which they themselves recognize, the dangers of complacency and introspection become obvious.

The current issues in educational administration in England and Wales seem likely, at the least, to guide us away from excessive introspection. If issues are new, this is largely because the scheme of things to be administered has changed a great deal from the pattern of concerns which beset English contributors to the first conference in 1966. In particular, five new trends are discernible.

First, the normal development of the education service has brought new statutory responsibilities. This has made it essential that administration should understand and encompass new areas of educational thinking. It ranges from higher education to nursery education and from a new connection with health services to a development of connections with a still young system of jointly administered personal welfare services.

The development of education also brings in train other demands— not the demands of regulation or of new statute but those which accompany the need to support movements of renewal and reform. The reappraisal of curriculum and examinations, of systems of educating those who would not otherwise be included in compulsory education and of voluntary education in terms of community learning and adult education—each of these demands that administration should be able to be close alongside the job of education. There is less and less justification for remote control.

A second group of stimuli to which administration is at present adapting itself in England and Wales is concerned with consultation, response and cooperation. New demands are being made which result from surveys and reports when, for instance, the emergence of parental interest in education has to be taken into account. They stem from new relationships between teacher and students, from new ways in which lay people are involved in the government and management of schools and colleges and from the work of organized pressure groups. Most of all, new demands emerge from that rapid extension of ideas about cooperative organization which is labelled corporate planning.

Traditional issues in new settings form a third category of concern. Principally, these are matters of resource. In the distribution of resources the pattern of national control is changing; the scale of local responsibility is also changing. It leads to new problems of demarcation; new rules are having to be made—and not simply about money. How does the parish pump relate to Whitehall? How can the demand be met for a more broadly informed public approach to education?

The fourth range of problems emerges from changing styles of behaviour on the part of central government. This is not simply a matter of economics and politics. It revolves around questions of consistency, about the degree of tenacity which is revealed towards declared policies, about steady development or stop-go emergencies. What is new here is not the existence of these problems but the frequency with which administration has to alter its stance in order to make sense of changes elsewhere—and which it might not fully understand. And as the complexities grow, the administration of education ironically finds itself with a weaker national voice. It faces the risk of being lumped in with locally administered services of lesser significance.

The last handful of new issues stems from a more or less comparable change in relationships. At local level there is now a universal preoccupation with party politics. This in turn brings to prominence new hierarchs in a context in which administrators themselves can be cardinals or acolytes. But it matters less whether they have a visibly high or low position in the overall control of education than that they and their lay counterparts should serve the same cause.

By good fortune and, no doubt, because this is one of the things at which local government reorganization aims, the gap between layman and professional is narrowing. We are living through a stage at which policies are being reviewed, made or done away with and at which both committees and officers know in detail what they are handling. Things have had to be revised or learned anew; the grasp of those who run the show is therefore a firm one. In time this grip will slacken somewhat— no doubt in a manner which will be beneficial as well as unavoidable. But until changes are complete, differences cannot be expected to disappear very rapidly. The need for cohesion between administrators and politicians is clear; it can do a great deal to avoid the wastefulness of historical differences. In a most important way, too, it can enlarge the concept of administration in education—and this is very necessary at a time when things might otherwise become altogether too big for a traditionally single-handed administration to manage.

BIBLIOGRAPHY

Baron, G. & Taylor, W. (eds) (1969), *Educational Administration and the Social Sciences*, Athlone Press, London.

Department of Education and Science (1967), *Children and their Primary Schools* and *Primary Education in Wales* (Plowden and Gittins Reports), HMSO, London.

Department for the Environment (1972), *The New Local Authorities: management and structure* (Bains Report), HMSO, London.

Glatter, R. (1972), *Management Development for the Education Profession*, Harrap, London.

King, R. (1973), 'The Head Teacher and his Authority' in Fowler, Morris and Ozga (eds), *Decision-making in British Education*, Heinemann, London.

Kogan, M. and Van der Eyken, W. (1973), *County Hall: the role of the Chief Education Officer*, Penguin, London.

Ministry of Housing and Local Government (1967), *Report of the Committee on the Management of Local Government* and *Report of the Committee on the Staffing of Local Government* (Maud and Mallaby Reports), HMSO, London.

Putnam, Robert (1973), 'Bureaucrats and politics', in *New Society*, London, 27(588).

Royal Commission on Local Government in England 1966–69 (1969), *Report* (Redcliffe-Maud Report), HMSO, London.

10 Educational Administration in Scotland: The Major Issues

T. R. BONE

DIFFERENCES BETWEEN SCOTLAND AND ENGLAND IN EDUCATION

The Scottish system of education is not merely separate from that existing in England and Wales; it is distinctly different, being the product of a quite different process of evolution; and the administration of the Scottish system does not provide an example of convenient devolution of control from London, with the features of the southern part of the United Kingdom reproduced in the north; but instead presents in its form and structure a Scottish response to Scottish problems, individual and distinctive at least quite as often as it happens to coincide with the English arrangements to deal with similar situations.

There was a time, as everyone knows, and a long time at that, when the Scots could claim to have a much better system of public education than the English. By act of Parliament of 1696, there was to be a school in every parish in the land, and if it was not until about 1800 that this legal requirement had been fulfilled, there was not even a similar enactment in England till 1870. Scotland had a national system of examinations for secondary schools by 1888, while England did not have any such system until well into this century, and even now it is not a national one. Until about 1960 access to genuine secondary education was much easier in Scotland than in the south. The Scots forced university graduates who wished to be teachers to train as early as 1906; the English made it compulsory in 1969 for primary schools, and only in 1973 for secondary schools.

I could give other examples, but unfortunately the advantages of the past can become the encumbrances of the present, and the boasts of yesterday become the foolishness of today. There is much to be proud of in the traditions of Scottish education (Scotland, 1969), but the Scots as a nation cannot afford to look backwards or inwards too often; too much is happening in the rest of the world, and we are in danger of being left behind, with institutions inappropriate to the needs of the years immediately ahead.

Partly because of the size of the country and its long held sense of national identity, and partly because of the authoritarian cast of the church which dominated the Scottish way of life in general, and education in particular, for over three hundred years, Scotland has had a strong tradition of central control in education. In 1872, when the state took over from the church, the newly appointed Scotch Education Department ('Scottish' since 1918) had no difficulty in imposing a highly-centralized system of administration, with a large number of small local school boards to provide the schools and see that the children attended them, while the central authority set the standards for the country, and through its inspectors ensured that those standards were met (Bone, 1968). The emergence of county authorities did not affect this principle, though naturally stronger local authorities needed less supervision in matters of detail.

By the time the mood of the country, and the growing professionalism of teachers, demanded a relaxation of the Department's paternalistic approach, the centralized system was firmly established, and though it came to be felt that power should be shared more widely, and that some of the share should go to those who actually taught the children, it was taken almost for granted that this should be achieved by the establishment of new central controlling mechanisms, all responsible for the whole country, rather than that the different areas of Scotland should go their own ways, and though the regional education authorities now coming into existence may in time create new patterns, at present the most distinctive features of Scottish education all involve central control.

One of the best examples of this concerns the arrangements for the award of the certificates which set the standards for secondary education, and which do much to determine the entrance requirements for higher education, whether at university or college. From 1888 until 1964 the certificate examinations were effectively controlled by the Scottish Education Department, mainly through its own inspectors. In 1964, however, an independent Scottish Certificate of Education Examination Board was established, partly to meet teacher demands for participation in the shaping of the examinations which exert so much influence on the curriculum, and partly to free the inspectors for more constructive work. The Board contains representatives from the universities, colleges, central institutions and local authorities, with the largest single group upon it being the teachers, but the inspectors have not quite disappeared from the scene, since the examination syllabuses are in the hands of separate subject panels, working under the Board, and on each of these panels HM Inspectorate is represented, and plays there a not unimportant role.

Mention of the colleges of education and the central institutions (colleges of technology, music, art, domestic science etc.) raises another point of difference from England. Almost all of these had their origins in local effort of some kind, often supported by the churches, but in the closing years of the nineteenth century and early years of the twentieth they all moved into a position of complete financial dependence on the Scottish Education Department. They each have their own boards of governors (teachers being strongly represented where the colleges of education are concerned) (Cruickshank, 1970) and are not subject to the local education authorities in any way, but the Department exerts considerable influence through its control of their funds, and so for instance in 1972 was easily able to impose restrictions on the intake of students wishing to become primary teachers. Probably it was because of the early establishment of central control that these institutions tend to be larger than their English counterparts, the Department preferring the economies of large scale enterprises to the less predictable development of rival local establishments.

The influence of the centre is also evident in curriculum change, though less effectively so. Until 1955, suggestions for change in this sphere appeared usually in official reports or memoranda written by the Department's inspectors; now these documents are normally produced under the aegis of the Consultative Committee on the Curriculum, a more broadly based body, with representatives from schools, colleges, universities and local authorities. (SED, January 1974). Unlike the English Schools Council, however, the members of this body do not represent their fellows but are selected by the Secretary of State—i.e. the Department—for their personal knowledge and expertise. This body's suggestions for change are supported by HM Inspectors, who try to see that particular innovations are adopted over the whole country. But this is a much more difficult matter for central control, and naturally the response of the schools varies in different parts of the country, the attitude of the local directors of education being an important factor, as is the extent of the backing given by the local authorities' advisers.

On the recommendation of the Consultative Committee, four national Curriculum Development Centres have been set up, all directly financed by the Scottish Education Department but located in the major colleges of education. Jordanhill,[1] for instance, houses the national Centre for Social Subjects, which produces and evaluates resource materials in History, Geography, Economics, and Modern Studies, and these materials naturally exert wide influence on teaching in the subjects concerned, though there is no compulsion on schools to make use of them.

A further example of central control which is described in greater detail in the following chapter, is the General Teaching Council. This is an institution unique to Scotland, established in the late 1960s against determined and virulent opposition, which controls admission to teaching in this country, ensuring that no one can teach who does not hold the approved qualifications or their equivalent (Bone, 1974). With a majority of teachers among its members, it has eliminated unqualified teachers from service in this country and has made a valuable contribution to discussion about the most appropriate forms of teaching (GTC, 1972). This body has given Scottish teachers an unequalled measure of control over entry to their profession, though it has done so at the expense of one or two of the hardest pressed of the local authorities, which formerly in times of shortage might have employed persons not quite qualified, but now cannot do so.

SOME GENERAL SCOTTISH PROBLEMS IN EDUCATION

Many of Scotland's problems are related to the geography of the country, and to the uneven distribution of the population. Such natural resources as coal and iron ore are concentrated in the Central Lowlands stretching roughly from Ayrshire over to Fife, and industry inevitably has brought the vast bulk of the population to that area, especially to the western side of the belt, leaving the rest of the country sparsely habited. Ninety-eight per cent of the land surface of Scotland is still classified as 'countryside', but over eighty per cent of the people live in the towns, and about half of them, two and a half millions, live in the Clydeside conurbation alone.

[1] The Glasgow phase of IIP 1974 was held at Jordanhill College of Education.

One consequence of this is the problem of providing education in the rural areas. When a handful of young children live in a few crofts at the end of a lonely Highland glen, their schooling can become a highly expensive matter, if a teacher can be found willing to work there at all, and if half of a school's roll can suddenly disappear when one family moves to another location, planning for that school becomes highly uncertain.

More serious, in that it affects far more people, is the problem of industrial depression in the west central region, where traditional industries like shipbuilding and heavy engineering are in serious decline, and where a radical restructuring is required. Too much capital and labour has been concentrated in industries which have either been subject to major changes in the technology of production, or for whose products there is no longer demand: it is a classic disease, and the classic symptom of high unemployment has been evident for many years. For school administrators the result has been the problem of adequate provision in huge areas of social, economic and educational disadvantage.

The most obvious need is to obtain sufficient teachers willing to teach in these areas—in some of the huge housing estates on the fringes of Glasgow, in the northern part of Lanarkshire, and in parts of Renfrew-shire, Dunbartonshire and Stirlingshire. Financial inducements have been tried, by a system of extra payments to teachers in 'designated schools', and have had some success, but the problem will persist at least until there are virtually no other jobs for teachers to find. Already some of those who train to be primary teachers in Aberdeen and Edinburgh choose not to teach rather than come to the areas of need, and it is often argued that the distribution of Scotland's colleges of education is inappropriate, since three of the five which train graduates are located in the east.

But even when adequate numbers of teachers are available, as the Scottish Education Department is confident there will be in a few years' time (S E D, 1973), the educational administrator's difficulties will not be overcome, since he hopes to achieve more than the placing of a qualified body in front of a class. The teaching of reluctant learners presents problems which go near to defying solution, at least in state systems where large numbers of pupils are involved, and where every class cannot have a teacher of exceptional ability, charm, enthusiasm, persistence, and dedication.

A new factor has appeared in the Scottish equation, however, which may well in time affect the distribution of population and the economic ills which lie at the root of so many educational difficulties. This is the oil and natural gas which have been discovered off the coast of Scotland and which will be coming ashore in large quantities by the end of this decade. The Scottish Council for Development and Industry (SCDI, 1973) has estimated that between 25,000 and 35,000 new jobs for Scots should be created as a result of oil and gas developments, but, even more important, the opportunities associated with the existence of these industries should attract a flow of investment to the relevant parts of the country which could transform the whole economic outlook for Scotland. If proper advantage is taken of the situation, both by Government and industry, there could be a restructuring which resulted in a shift of workers to new types of employment in new areas of the country. The population map could look quite different in about fifteen years' time.

Whether that happens or not, it is essential that co-ordinated planning takes place, and it was for that reason, before the oil was discovered at all, that the need for regional authorities was recognized, with stronger powers and greater co-ordination among the various agencies that shape the development of communities. Hence the appearance, in May 1975, of a totally new structure for the local government of Scotland, with considerable effects for education—to be discussed later in this paper.

But local government is in turn affected by national government, and the newest of the important factors affecting Scottish education, even more recent than the oil, has been the emergence of the Scottish Nationalist Party as a political force to be reckoned with. In the General Election of February 1974 they won seven parliamentary seats, and took an important share of the votes in many other constituencies, with a programme which laid great emphasis on nationalizing 'Scotland's oil', and which invited voters to decide whether they wished to be 'rich Scots or poor British'.[2] At the time of writing it is not clear whether this Party's success will be more than a temporary phenomenon, but the pressure generated by it is leading to devolution of certain decision-making powers from Westminster to a Scottish Assembly.[3] Education

[2] In the General Election of October 1974 the Scottish Nationalist Party held those seven parliamentary seats and won another four.

[3] Promised by the Labour Government in the Queen's Speech in October 1974.

is among the services which will be devolved in this way, and the consequences of the change cannot be predicted at this stage. There may be little difference in practice, but it is possible, and indeed likely, that the Scottish Assembly will attempt to resist other pressures which are continually tending to lessen the differences between education in Scotland and in other parts of the United Kingdom.

SOME PARTICULAR PROBLEMS FOR ADMINISTRATORS

A. *Consequences of the Re-organization of Local Government*

Following the Report of a Royal Commission on Local Government in Scotland (1969), a Local Government (Scotland) Act (1973) is giving Scotland a two-tier structure of regional and district authorities similar to that now existing in England. The new Councils were elected in May 1974 and take over in May 1975 after running for a year in harness with their predecessors. The process of appointing the senior officials began shortly after the Council had been elected.

It is dangerous to generalize about the regions, since they vary from some which are reasonably compact and homogeneous to others which are vast and exceedingly diverse in nature. One (the Highlands) covers 9,813 of the total 29,596 square miles of land mass in Scotland, while another (Fife) contains 505 of those square miles. One (Strathclyde) has a population of 2,578,000 persons, out of a total for the country of 5,228,000, while another region (Borders) has 99,000 of those persons. But in spite of the differences, and the apparent anomalies, they are probably all (with the exception of Fife—which retained its old identity through Government weakness at a moment of pressure) right in the way that matters most—right in terms of planning for economic development.

The most immediate consequence of re-organization is the loss of independent power of action by the local units. Each of the regions embrace what have previously been a number of separate counties or cities, each with its own county or city council, and each with its own officials in the various spheres of administration. Thus there have been thirty-five local education authorities, with thirty-five directors of education, and thirty-five teams of officials under those directors, with small variations in practice in every area. From May 1975 there will be only nine regional and three island authorities, and it is obvious that there will be many difficulties in reconciling all the different interests which will be found within them. Not unnaturally, this is a time of great uncertainty for the local officials in education, and many are wondering not only what kind of new structure they will find themselves in, but also what place they themselves will have in that structure.

The typical pattern of local government in Scotland has been that of a general council with a number of independent committees, each serviced by an independent administrative department. The formulation of policy in any particular sphere and the process of devising plans to implement that policy are the responsibility of the committee and its officials, and there is very little attempt at co-ordination across the whole range of the authority's activities. This excessive departmentalism has been one of the features most attacked in the preparations for the new regional authorities, and the Paterson Report (Scottish Development Department, 1963), the Scottish equivalent of the English Bains Report (Department for the Environment, 1972), has argued for a unified approach to the formulation and implementation of plans to meet the needs of the communities. It seems likely that Paterson's ideas will be a major influence on the new structures which will shortly emerge.

What we are likely to have is a corporate approach to planning, with a central policy committee in each region, supported by service committees of the familiar kind (though each with greatly enlarged geographical spheres of influence), and by a management team of officials, led by a chief executive of some kind who will have no direct responsibility for any individual department. The other members of that management team will be the heads of the service departments—e.g. Development, Housing, Amenity Services (parks, libraries, etc.), Public Services (transport, refuse collection etc.), Education, Health, Social Work and Police. The Director of Education will have to see himself in that team as being concerned not solely with his own department, but with the wider objectives of the whole authority, and will have to accept limitations on his own departmental plans in the interests of co-ordination.

The result will be the ending of the quasi-autonomous position of the education authority, for now a function like personnel management is likely to be conducted over all the services of the region, with agreed policies for allocation of resources, recruitment, training, welfare, and promotion. The region will have to work out not merely how many teachers it will need, but also how many librarians, technicians, social workers, youth leaders and policemen, and recruitment in one field will have to be related to that in another.

All this will be difficult enough in each of the nine regional and three island authorities throughout Scotland, but it will be immensely so in the west, where the new Strathclyde Region is responsible for almost half of the country's population. In planning terms, Strathclyde is the right unit, but in educational terms it is far too big. None of the new regional authorities in England and Wales approaches it in the number of people it has to cater for. Almost certainly it will have to be divided into sub-regions, and the problem will then arise of deciding which functions must be the concern of the centre and which can be left to the sub-regional organization. At the time of writing it is very far from clear what will happen.

The move to the regions will also pose difficulties for the Scottish Education Department, partly because the corporate management style of the regional authorities may not well accord with the traditionally independent departmental style of the civil service in Scotland, and partly because the power of the regions may make them less dependent on the advice and expertise of the centre, and less willing to accept restrictions. The regional authorities' team of local advisers, for instance, may feel much less need of the help of the Scottish Education Department's inspectors, and may not ask for it. Indeed, it is not only the local officials who feel personal concern at the changes.

Again, the size of the Strathclyde region raises special difficulties. When the Convener of its regional authority can say that he has been elected to speak for half the population of Scotland, the question arises as to who the Secretary of State is speaking for if they differ—the other half? The balance of control is certainly in some danger, and the central authority can only defend its position by falling back on Parliament, which could lead to a diminution of the power of St Andrew's House (the home of the Scottish civil service), as it became more and more an intermediary between the Government in London and the Scottish regions. But that situation could so easily be upset by the many unpredictable variables, including the Scottish Nationalist Party, that it would be foolish to attempt to forecast its development.

B. *Getting the Schools Right*

(i) *Problems of Staffing.* Since the early 1950s Scotland, in common with many other countries, has had a severe shortage of teachers, and much planning, energy and expenditure has been devoted to efforts to overcome that shortage. Three new colleges of education were built in the 1960s to produce more primary teachers; a Special Recruitment Scheme was introduced to bring into teaching people who had to be financially assisted to obtain the necessary qualifications for training; and a high proportion of the output of university graduates were attracted into secondary teaching. Gradually the situation improved, partly because of the greatly increased supply, and partly because of Scotland's birth rate (which has declined each year for the past eight years).

In 1972 the Scottish Education Department's forecasts began to suggest that unless some brake were put on the growth of teacher numbers, there would be an oversupply for the primary schools by about 1976, and a similar situation in the secondary schools a few years later. Policy changed. The Department felt able to announce target staffing standards for the primary schools (SED, 1973), with a maximum of thirty in each primary class, and to assert that these could be achieved while at the same time the entrance requirements to training for primary teaching could be raised, the Special Recruitment Scheme could be modified so that it produced only secondary teachers, and the intake to primary training in the colleges could be restricted (SED, 1973).

The Department then turned its attention to the secondary schools, and published a report on Secondary School Staffing (SED, 1973) which broke new ground in many ways, being based on a comprehensive survey of the organization and staffing of the schools, linked to mathematical modelling techniques, and putting forward not a simple concept of teacher-pupil ratios, but suggestions of school complements arrived at by the application of agreed ratios to pupil numbers at different stages and in different subjects. This allowed for a much more flexible use of staffing resources, and marked a considerable advance over previous thinking. To achieve the standards and improvements set forth in this document, a national pupil-teacher ratio of about 15:1 was needed, and the forecasts indicated that this might be achieved by 1976–77. Knowing that these teachers would not be evenly distributed over the country, however, and that authorities in the west would have difficulty in obtaining their share, the document said that it would be more realistic to set 1977–78 as the target year in which these standards would be reached in all areas (SED, 1973).

Unfortunately for the Department, these forecasts now seem at least a little premature. In a few years' time it may well be that supply will be greatly improved, and the shortages over, but at present, largely because of the raising of the school leaving age (which was calculated for) and apparently much higher wastage rates among young teachers (which were probably underestimated), the situation is bad, especially of course in the west of Scotland. The teachers in many secondary schools in the past session have found themselves with very large classes, very few correction periods, and numbers of fifteen-year-old pupils who were very reluctant to be in schools. Naturally it did not help much for the Department to keep saying that it would be all right in a year or two, and there have been working-to-rule situations in some schools, threats of strikes in others, and a demand for an inquiry into teachers' conditions (rejected by the SED). Indeed it would be fair to say that discontent among Scottish teachers has been as high in 1973–74 as at any time in the past ten years.

Probably the situation will be a little better in 1974–75 (though there are directors of education in the Glasgow area who are very pessimistic about that), and by about 1976–77 the staffing standards will have been achieved in most parts of the country. But if they are to be reached in the west there will have to be a determined effort of some kind to move the surplus teachers from the east and north-east over to the western central region. A start has been made by asking the authorities in the east to restrict their intake this summer (SED, 1974), but sterner measures may be needed. And when that happens, the old fear of direction of labour will concern the teachers' unions.

There will also have to be direction of another kind by authorities themselves, or at least by one new authority, Strathclyde. In 1974, for the last time, new teachers are seeking employment with Glasgow, Renfrewshire, Lanarkshire and Dunbartonshire, and they can (and do) attempt to play off one of these against the others when it comes to offers of posts. In the summer of 1975 everyone in the west of Scotland will be applying to Strathclyde, and presumably the new regional authority will take advantage of this to force them to take posts in the schools where the need is greatest.

There is a problem in the primary school too. At present primary staff are scarce in the west, but, though that may pass, it is very possible that the standard of 30:1 which the Department has set as an acceptable ratio may not satisfy the teachers' unions. At a time when they see little hope of major salary improvements (because of Britain's economic position), they must fight for better conditions of service, and 30:1 seems a lot less generous to the teacher in the classroom than it does to the administrator. The latter tends to have a long memory, and can remember when the position was a lot worse; the new teacher is not interested in that, and 30:1 does not seem very good to her.

One special difficulty is that the primary calculations do not allow for preparation periods for teachers. These are at present only possible when a visiting teacher of Music or Physical Education is taking the class (when of course the class teacher should ideally be present to integrate the activity into the rest of the work), but now some of the younger politicians among the Glasgow teachers are beginning to agitate for staffing ratios which would genuinely allow all primary teachers one preparation or correction period per day. The educational arguments for this are completely sound, but the effect on the Department's calculations if this were granted would be extremely serious.

(ii) *Problems of Curriculum and Methods.* Like most other educational systems, the Scottish has been engaged in a continuing programme of curricular and methodological change over the past ten or so years. The targets have been set, normally nationally, in two ways—by the publication of documents arguing for new approaches in the schools, and by changes in the examination syllabuses—and the attainment of these goals has been vigorously pursued by H M Inspectors and (with more or less vigour according to the persuasion of the directors of education) by the local authority advisers.

Where examination changes are involved, curricular and methodological changes follow almost inevitably, and it is noticeable that the new approaches have been adopted on a much larger scale (indeed almost universally) in the certificate classes of the secondary schools than they have in primary classes, non-certificate classes, and non-examinable subjects. Physics changed very quickly in the 60s, even Latin changed very considerably in the 1970s, but Physical Education in the schools has not really changed very much, though one would think from reading the relevant publication of the Consultative Committee on the Curriculum (1972) that it should be very different from what it was.

The other main agencies in the promotion of change are those responsible for the training of teachers, both at the initial and the in-service stages. The Colleges of Education tend to use the national documents—

like the memorandum on Primary Education in Scotland (1965) or the curriculum paper on Technical Education in Secondary Schools (1972) —as basic study material for students in the relevant areas, and so those entering the schools are usually familiar with current thinking about their subjects, but whether they keep up with that thinking or not depends on themselves, and on the arrangements for in-service courses available in the district where they go to work. Fortunately there has been a marked increase in in-service provision in the past two or three years, partly in the colleges of education, and partly in the new teachers' centres built by the authorities.

One should not give the impression that the only impetus for curriculum development comes from the centre; there has been some exceedingly good work done by groups of teachers in some of the local authority areas, especially in some of the areas of greatest staffing difficulty, notably Glasgow and Renfrewshire. Yet it is national support, and especially national examinations, which are the surest means of securing change.

The greatest problems are still in the field of teaching pupils who, at the age of thirteen, fourteen or fifteen, are clearly unable to benefit from an examination-based course, and though a great deal of work has been done in this area, universal solutions have not been found. Inspiring teachers, with considerable preparation, or with some dependence on good resource materials, can motivate them towards fruitful learning experiences, but it is hard work, and not all teachers succeed. Discipline problems are occasionally severe, and indeed there was so much concern about this in the first part of session 1973–74 that the Secretary of State agreed in January 1974 to set up a Committee of Inquiry into Discipline and Truancy.

It is not a problem which will easily be solved, but obviously an improved staffing position would help.

(iii) *Problems of Structure.* As secondary schools underwent a process of comprehensive reorganization in the second half of the 1960s and early 70s (now very near to being complete), they became inevitably larger and more complex, and their traditional management structure became less suited to the changing educational, social and organizational needs of the time. Consequently, various experiments were tried in the late 1960s in some schools with the appointment of housemasters, and tutor group leaders to supplement the normal pattern of Headmaster, Deputy, Woman Adviser, and Principal Teachers of the various subjects. But these moves did not go far enough, and in 1971 the Department published a memorandum on *The Structure of Promoted Posts in Secondary Schools in Scotland* (1971) which advocated the introduction of (a) many more promoted posts, with, in particular, two or three Assistant Headteachers, each with specialized co-ordinating functions, between the Deputy Head and the Principal Teachers, and (b) a separate system of promoted posts for the guidance of pupils—personal, curricular, and vocational.

This system has now been introduced in most places, and should make for considerable improvements. The problems have been greatest in the area of guidance, where no qualifications or suitable training courses existed before the appointments were made, and sometimes those given responsibility for guidance had little suitability for that role. Courses now exist, provided by the colleges of education, and the situation will gradually improve.

More important in the long run is the problem of definition of the role of the Assistant Headteachers. In some schools one is responsible for the first two year groups, another for the third and fourth, and another for the fifth and sixth. A different pattern is to have one Assistant Headteacher in charge of guidance (often the former Lady Adviser—suitable or not), a second in charge of 'administration' (which may mean dealing with the timetable, pupils' absences, college students on practice, etc.), and a third in charge of curricular matters. And a third pattern, not frequently used, is to have the subjects grouped in three faculties, each with an Assistant Headteacher for co-ordination. In all of these patterns at least one of the Assistant Heads, and sometimes more than one, is supposed to co-ordinate the activities of a number of subject departments, and difficulty arises when the Principal Teachers resist the attempts of a non-specialist to interfere with their subjects. If the inspectors and advisers tend to pay a courtesy call on the Headteacher, and then go direct to the Principal Teachers, missing out the Assistant Heads, it does not help.

The new structure has helped, however, in making for a more participative style of management in Scottish schools. Traditionally they were authoritarian in organization, like the system they were part of, and decisions were taken by the Headteacher alone. Now it is usual for there to be some kind of Board of Studies (often just the Head, Deputy, and Assistant Heads together, but sometimes with elected representatives of the Principal Teachers), and for this to be supported by committees of various kinds, often convened by Assistant Heads. The process has some way to go yet (few schools have ordinary teachers on the Board of Studies, and none I know of has pupils), but the situation is much healthier than it was. It should also make for more effective schools.

RELATIONSHIPS WITH ENGLAND AND WALES

Though the Scottish system of education is separate from that in the rest of the United Kingdom, and is subject to separate laws, a separate Minister of the Government, and a separate branch of the Civil Service, it is of course in many ways similar to that in England and Wales (Osborne, 1968), and is becoming increasingly more so. No British Government could allow serious differences in the level of provision, for instance, to exist in different parts of the kingdom, and when the school leaving age was recently being raised from fifteen to sixteen this obviously had to be done simultaneously on both sides of the border, though the Scots were markedly less enthusiastic about the change than their English counterparts. The ending of selection for secondary education, and the move to comprehensive schools, came at the same time in both systems, though it was more easily achieved in the north.

The extent to which developments in Scottish education today are influenced by those in England is sometimes disputed (Kellas, 1973; Millan, 1974), but by and large it is not so much Cabinet Ministers, or even the Treasury, which is bringing Scotland gradually nearer to the English position; the forces at work are much more subtle, and in the end much more powerful. First, there is the impact of educational research and writing, for though Scotland has a laudable tradition of research, more is inevitably done in England, and far more books on education appear in the south and then come to be studied by teachers in training in Scotland. This is especially true of sociological research and writing, which has had so much influence in recent years. Secondly, there are national United Kingdom institutions which affect education all over Britain, and which inevitably are dominated by English ideas, the most recent of these being the Open University and the Council for National Academic Awards, which both exert a profound influence on the nature of the work being done.

Thirdly, and most important of all, is the changing nature of British society. When the Scottish system was evolving in its own distinctive way (from 1560 to about 1914), Scottish society was very different from its English counterpart, notably in matters of economics and religion. But today there is little difference between Scottish and English society, and such differences as do exist are tending to be reduced, thanks largely to the influence of the communications media. Indeed if one accepts that educational change tends to be a reflection of social change, then the ways in which our society is changing—with smaller families, shorter working hours, less need for unskilled labour, greater availability of leisure, a general rise in material and cultural expectations, a loss of confidence in the values inherited from the past, and a weakening of traditional assumptions about authority—are all ways in which English society, and that of all industrialized nations, is changing too. It would be very surprising if the schools of Scotland, and the arrangements for education, did not gradually come to be more like those of our nearest neighbours.

BIBLIOGRAPHY

Bone, T. R. (1968), *School Inspection in Scotland, 1840–1966*, University of London Press for Scottish Council for Research in Education, London.

Bone, T. R. (1974), 'The General Teaching Council for Scotland, an Assessment of its Achievements', *London Educational Review*, 3(2).

Consultative Committee on the Curriculum (1972), Curriculum Paper 10, *Technical Education in Secondary Schools*, HMSO, Edinburgh.

Consultative Committee on the Curriculum (1972), Curriculum Paper 12, *Physical Education in Secondary Schools*, HMSO, Edinburgh.

Cruikshank, M. (1970), *History of the Training of Teachers in Scotland*, University of London Press for the Scottish Council for Research in Education, London.

Department for the Environment (1972), *The New Local Authorities, Management and Structure* (Bains Report), HMSO, London.

General Teaching Council for Scotland (1972), *The Training of Graduates for Secondary Education*, HMSO, Edinburgh.

Kellas, J. G. (1973), *The Scottish Political System*, Cambridge University Press, London.

Local Government (Scotland) Act (1973).

Millan, B. (1974), 'No Danger from England', *Times Educational Supplement (Scotland)*, 8 February 1974.

Osborne, G. S. (1966), *Scottish and English Schools, A Comparative Survey*, Longmans, London.

Royal Commission on Local Government in Scotland (1969).

Scotland, J. (1969), *The History of Scottish Education*, University of London Press, London.

Scottish Council for Development and Industry (1973), *A Future for Scotland*, HMSO, Edinburgh.

Scottish Development Department (1973), *The New Scottish Local Authorities, Organisation and Management Structures* (Paterson Report), HMSO, Edinburgh.

Scottish Education Department (1965), *Primary Education in Scotland*, HMSO, Edinburgh.

Scottish Education Department (1971), *The Structure of Promoted Posts in Secondary Schools in Scotland*, HMSO, Edinburgh.

Scottish Education Department (1972), Circular 819, 14 March 1972.

Scottish Education Department (1973), *Education in Scotland in 1972*, HMSO, Edinburgh.

Scottish Education Department (1973), *Secondary School Staffing*, HMSO, Edinburgh.

Scottish Education Department (1974), 'The Central Organisation of Curriculum Development', Circular letter of 7 January 1974.

Scottish Education Department (1974), 'Recruitment of Teachers for Secondary Schools—Session 1974–75', Circular 892, 4 February 1974.

11 The British Educational Scene: Selected Aspects

Through lectures, group discussions and visits, supplemented by detailed documentation, IIP participants were able to examine many facets of educational administration in the United Kingdom. Due to limitations of space, it is only possible in this chapter to present extracts from three relevant papers; these highlight some issues of special interest to the overseas participants.

1 Control and Guidance: The Role of the Inspector

W. A. GATHERER

The history of the two British educational systems over the last century reveals a persistent, if erratic, movement towards the lessening of central control over curricular policies and teaching methods.

In an important sense, of course, no teacher can ever be wholly controlled with regard to what he teaches and how he chooses to teach. Control of the transmission of knowledge must always be crude, directing only the outward labels and the general content of what goes on in the classroom. In discussing educational control, therefore, we are compelled first to define what is meant by 'control' and 'authority'. A useful starting-point is Dennis Smith's summary of the various forms of controlling power vested in the directing agencies:

1 *Power derived from Authority:*
   (i) legal authority, based upon statutory or similar provisions;
   (ii) professional authority, deriving from special knowledge and competence;
   (iii) diffuse authority, associated with position in a status hierarchy.
2. *Power derived from control of resources:*
   (i) financial;
   (ii) certification: control over the nature and distribution of qualifications.
   (Smith, 1971)

As most educational systems in the modern world have discovered, a well staffed inspectorate constitutes a versatile combination of various forms of authority. Inspectors have *legal* authority vested in them by statute. This is buttressed by *professional* authority deriving from their educational knowledge and expertise. They possess *diffuse* authority which is inherent in their academic and social status. And they have, in varying quantities, much practical power because of their personal supervision of curricula and teaching methods. In many countries, at different times, they have administered certification schemes. Occasionally, as was the case in the last century in Britain, they have controlled the allocation of finance to educational institutions.

It had been Kay-Shuttleworth's intention when the inspectorate was established that Her Majesty's Inspectors should derive their authority principally from their professional prestige, and for most of our recent history this has also been the motivation of the government inspectors in Britain. Teachers, however, have not always viewed the inspectors' powers with equanimity. The odium engendered by the 'payments-by-results' aspect of the Revised Code system of inspection in the latter half of last century lingered on into the twentieth century. Inspectors were seen as a race apart—strangers whose visits to schools caused much uneasiness and disruption of routine. They represented the remote authority of government and carried the stigma of unpopular policies. They were sometimes seen, as by the Scottish educationist William Boyd, as a threat to the professional dignity of the teacher and as agents of a system which was 'educationally sterile' because they visited schools as outsiders with 'powers that paralyse originality'. (Bone, 1968; Cruickshank, 1970).

There seems to have been a significant difference between the educational philosophies which actuated the English and Scottish inspectorates during the first half of this century. The educational objectives of the Scottish inspectors were traditional and conservative: they inspected schools formally, reporting on teachers in accordance with a prescriptive, conventionalized procedure. Though many were men of acknowledged charm and ability, they appear to have cultivated a rigidly uniform style of address and conduct.

In England, the inspectors were at the forefront of change. It was they who wrote the *Handbook of Suggestions* issued in 1905 and re-issued in 1909, 1918, 1926 and 1937 which strongly emphasised the freedom and responsibility of the individual teacher, and which, in succeeding editions, became 'steadily more sympathetic to progressive theory' in primary education (Selleck, 1972). While their Scottish colleagues were stolidly preserving the traditions of the established school curricula, they were contributing to the liberalizing work of the Hadow Committee,[1] organizing conferences which stimulated fresh thinking on educational approaches, and collaborating with university education departments in research and development work.

One reason for this difference in approach and style may have been the existence in England of a dual inspection system. The presence of local inspectors and advisers undoubtedly relieved the government inspectors of some responsibility for formal school inspection, and may have encouraged them to look more comprehensively at the educational development of the system. Their closer involvement with the teachers locally must certainly have influenced the government inspectors' deployment of their own energies, for the local advisers and organisers did much of the work that elsewhere was performed by Her Majesty's Inspectorate, such as advising the local authority on the progress of schools, organizing in-service courses for local teachers, and giving person-to-person advice in the classrooms. Owen (1973), estimates that there are, currently, about 2,500 advisers in England and Wales.

In Scotland there were no local inspectorates or advisorates. The government inspectors in Scotland thus maintained closer links with the local authorities than was necessary for their English colleagues: even today in the majority of districts the only comprehensive range of curricular advice available to Scottish schools is offered by Her Majesty's Inspectors. Advisers, of whom there are about 150, are located mainly in the cities.

After the second world war a reorganized English inspectorate cultivated a new 'civilized, professional relationship' with teachers (Blackie, 1970). Recognizing that they were now meeting teachers with equal, and sometimes superior, academic and professional qualities, they promulgated the notion that the management of curricular development was best achieved by partnership between the local advisorates, the teachers and themselves (Lester Smith, 1969). They concentrated on the long-term needs of the system: research, in-service training,

---

[1] The Consultative Committee chaired by Sir Henry Hadow produced some influential reports including *The Education of the Adolescent* (HMSO, 1926) and *The Primary School* (HMSO, 1931).

and the production of useful surveys, reports and guidance manuals.

In Scotland, the Advisory Council report on *Secondary Education* (1947) which seems to have had little help from inspectors, included a chapter on the inspectorate (without having been asked for it) and expressed a growing wish for change in the role and attitudes of Her Majesty's Inspectors. While paying some graceful compliments to the quality of the personnel, the report urged that there should be less emphasis on the 'time-wasting practice' of 'hurried, routine inspection' and more on 'guidance and encouragement', so that inspectors would become 'above all consultants and collaborators' of a profession which had matured to full stature and status.[2]

This was a widespread point of view. In an essay prefacing a UNESCO report on *The Inspection and Supervision of Schools*, Ben Morris (1956) showed that such changes were occurring in many countries. Where formerly the main emphasis in his work lay on authoritarian control, prescription and enforcement of regulations, he said, the inspector in various countries now relied on 'persuasive leadership, consultation and guidance'. One of the ministry's annual reports pointed out that the aims of the modern inspectorate 'differ hardly at all from those envisaged by Kay-Shuttleworth'.[3] This view was reiterated by a Senior Chief Inspector in 1961 (Wilson, 1961). In 1968 a select committee of Parliament investigating the functions of Her Majesty's Inspectorate in both countries reported that in England and Wales 'the statutory obligation on the Secretary of State to cause inspections of all educational establishments has for long been disregarded' and that 'Her Majesty's Inspectors regard themselves in the main as advisers' (Select Committee Report, 1968). In Scotland, the select committee were told, inspection remains 'an important part of the Inspectorate's role' but it was evident here too that the main work of the inspectors had become advisory (ibid., Part II). Far-reaching changes had occurred in the Scottish inspectorate's functions during the previous two decades.

Today there is a growing volume of opinion that no form of supervision from 'outside experts' is necessary or even valuable. Formal

---

[2] A later generation would call this the Fyfe Report, as the chairman was Sir William Hamilton Fyfe, Principal of Aberdeen University. But the writing owes much to J. J. (later Sir James) Robertson, Rector of the Grammar School, Aberdeen.

[3] *Education in 1949* (HMSO, 1950).

inspection by local officers is fast disappearing in England and Wales, though advisory services are expanding. In Scotland there is no likelihood that the quickly growing advisory services will ever take on an inspectorial function. The British educational systems are teacher-centred, and it is increasingly being recognized that the supervision of teachers is a matter for the teachers themselves. The Head of a school is responsible for the professional competence and development of his staff, and he has under his leadership a variety of others concerned with the work of supervision and advice: deputy and assistant heads, heads of departments, and teachers with pastoral and counselling duties. The teacher's autonomy in the business of transmitting knowledge is genuine, but it is not complete: the school itself places contraints upon him by means of syllabuses, internal regulations and other guidelines (King, 1973). No responsible teacher would deny the need for his work to be 'audited'; but it is not now necessary, in our mature and resourceful educational systems, for this to be done by specially appointed officials. Peer-group evaluation and other self-evaluation methods being developed in medicine and other professions can be applied with even greater assurance of success by the teaching profession. The greatest single development in the management of curricular matters in the future will undoubtedly be a huge increase in teacher-participation (Owen, 1973).

This is not to say, however, that there will be no roles for the government inspectors or local advisers to play. On the contrary, the complexity of the educational systems is such that it is more than ever necessary that the administrators and managers should have ample professional advice from officials who are closely acquainted with the schools. Also, the growth of teacher-dominated guidance agencies, such as the Schools Council in England and Wales and the General Teaching Council in Scotland, requires an adequate number of full-time professional officers to promulgate and implement their recommendations. Already more than sixty of Her Majesty's Inspectors work with or for the Schools Council, and field and development officers are being sought by other bodies. At national level, it is true to say, the inspectorate would have to be invented in some form if they did not already exist.

At local level, an advisory service is necessary to provide teachers with the resources they need if they are to evaluate and develop their own professional progress. These resources are various. Advisers are required to provide educational leadership: to foster the belief that professional development matters and to help teachers to find the means to achieve it. Advisers are needed to devise and organize various kinds of in-service educational experience—courses, workshops, conferences, working parties and other forms of cooperation which cannot be provided in school. They are needed to develop teaching materials, and to adapt teaching programmes to local conditions; to help teachers to formulate instructional goals in the particular context of the individual school; to help in the validation and implementation of innovatory schemes emanating from national and international study groups. They are required, in the national context, to represent local views and to facilitate local development of new approaches; and in the local context to plan the future educational provision required to fulfil the objectives of local and national thinking. They are a necessary 'inter-face' between the schools and the colleges of education. For primary schools and for younger teachers in particular, they are needed to help in the solution of day-to-day problems which cannot be affectively tackled at school level. Above all, they are needed to help sustain the morale of teachers struggling to cope with the ever-increasing complexity of education in modern society.

BIBLIOGRAPHY

Advisory Council Report (1947), *Secondary Education*, HMSO, Edinburgh.

Bishop, A. S. (1971), *The Rise of a Central Authority for English Education*, Cambridge University Press, London.

Blackie, John (1970), *Inspecting and the Inspectorate*, Routledge & Kegan Paul, London.

Bone, T. R. (1968), *School Inspection in Scotland 1840–1966*, University of London Press, London.

Cruickshank, Marjorie (1970), *A History of the Training of Teachers in Scotland*, University of London Press, London.

Edmonds, E. L. (1962), *The School Inspector*, Routledge & Kegan Paul, London.

James Report (1972), *Teacher Education and Training*, HMSO, London.

King, R. (1973), *School Organisation and Pupil Involvement*, Routledge & Kegan Paul, London.

Lawton, Denis (1973), *Social Change, Educational Theory and Curricular Planning*, University of London Press, London.

Lester Smith, W. O. (1968), *Government of Education*, Penguin, London.

Lester Smith, W. O. (1969), *Education*, Penguin, London.

Maclure, J. S. (1969), *Educational Documents: England and Wales 1816–1968*, Methuen, London.

Morris, Ben (1956), 'School Inspection and Supervision', UNESCO Education Abstracts, volume 7-8, *Inspection and Supervision of Schools*.

Norwood Report (1943), *Curriculum and Examinations in Secondary Schools*, HMSO, London.

Owen, J. G. (1973), *The Management of Curriculum Development*, Cambridge University Press, London.

Pilley, John (1958), 'Teacher Training in Scotland', *Universities Quarterly*, 12(3).

Robbins Report (1963), *Higher Education*, HMSO, London.

Scotland, James (1969), *The History of Scottish Education*, University of London Press, London.

Select Committee Report (1968), *Report from the Select Committee on Education and Science, 1967-1968. Part I: Her Majesty's Inspectorate (England and Wales). Part II: Her Majesty's Inspectorate (Scotland)*, HMSO, London.

Selleck, R. J. W. (1972), *English Primary Education and the Progressives*, Routledge & Kegan Paul, London.

Smith, Dennis (1971), 'Power, Ideology and the Transmission of Knowledge', *Readings in the Theory of Educational Systems*, Earl Hopper (ed), Hutchinson, London.

Wilson, Percy (1961), *Views and Prospects from Curzon Street*, Blackwell, London.

2 Local Education Authorities in Wales

T. M. MORGAN

Wales has the same local government structure as England in that both countries have basically the same types of local government units, with the same responsibilities for the same functions. Moreover the Education Acts—and that of 1944 is the most important—refer to England *and* Wales.

Following the major reorganization of local government in April 1974, Wales has eight counties. Those in South Wales have populations around the half-million mark; those in Central, West and North Wales are somewhat less populous, the most rural county of all, Powys, having not many more than 100,000 people. For local government purposes the county is governed by an elected county council. The county council is the Local Education Authority, so there are eight Local Education Authorities in Wales. One county councillor is chosen for one electoral district and, while the size and population of the electoral district is bound to vary with the nature of the district, it will give some indication of representation to say that in South Wales one county councillor is likely to represent 5,000–8,000 people. Each county councillor serves for a term of four years.

The typical Local Education Authority controls or has great influence over a vast range of educational institutions and provisions. My own county, Gwent, for example, is responsible for hundreds of schools of various types attended by pupils aged from two to nineteen. It provides and maintains technical colleges, an agricultural college, a college of education (i.e. a teacher training college), it makes grants to students at these colleges and at colleges, university and non-university, in other parts of Great Britain. It runs four field study centres and a residential adult education college. It is solely responsible for all the public libraries and for careers advice which is available to college students as well as to school pupils. It is responsible for the transport of pupils and in this as in other things it adopts more generous standards than those prescribed by the Secretary of State. It provides meals for pupils, it looks after the health of pupils. It has nearly a hundred youth clubs of its own and grant-aids many others. It initiated and operates a very imaginative and extensive leisure service, encompassing quite literally all leisure time provision from A to Z, from archaeology to zither playing, and frequently in purpose-built modern premises. Not surprisingly, considering the number of teachers, technicians, caretakers, wardens, cooks, clerks and others employed in all these places and with all these services, it is by far and away the biggest single employer in the county.

The most obvious difference between England and Wales is that Wales has a language of its own. Admittedly, only about one-quarter of the population speak it. Attitudes to the Welsh language in the schools of Wales are exceedingly diverse. Some schools teach through the medium of Welsh. Some schools include Welsh in the curriculum as a 'second' language because their Local Education Authority says that they must (and these schools could be sub-divided into those which applaud the Local Education Authority policy and those which submit to it); some schools include the teaching of Welsh in the curriculum voluntarily because they are allowed by their Local Education Authority to decide whether to teach it or not; some, given the choice, do not include Welsh in the curriculum at all.

There is nothing in the Education Acts about the teaching of Welsh, although the Secretary of State for Wales and his Office encourage its teaching, as does Her Majesty's Inspectorate of Schools, which has a department of the Inspectorate specifically for Wales. The decision is one for the Local Education Authority under the responsibility given to it in the Education Act for decisions about secular instruction. The Welsh Joint Education Committee, on which all the Welsh Local Education Authorities are represented, supports very strongly the teaching of the Welsh language, while recognizing that some of the Local Education Authorities which belong to it are passionately committed to the preservation of the Welsh language, while others are lukewarm. When it controlled primary and secondary education in Wales, i.e. up to 1970, the Department of Education and Science was anxious to have Welsh taught. For many years every publication and every utterance by the Department of Education and Science, and by its successor in primary and secondary education control, the Welsh Office, relating to the teaching of Welsh, has been sympathetic.[1] Although no direct and strong pressure has been exerted on Local Education Authorities, there has been implicit the attitude that it is more commendable to teach Welsh than not to teach it. The Central Advisory Council for Wales, a statutory body appointed by the Secretary of State, states in its report on primary education in Wales—the Gittins Report—that an ultimate educational objective in Wales should be complete bilingualism. The attitudes of the Local Education Authorities themselves are varied. Monmouthshire (now the major part of the new authority, Gwent) specifically rejected the Gittins aim of complete bilingualism, believing it to be wholly unrealistic in a county where fewer than 1 per cent of the population can speak Welsh.

As the previous paragraph notes, there has been a change in the arrangements for control at government level of primary and secondary education in Wales. Until 1970 central governmental control was exercised by the Department of Education and Science in London. Since 1970, responsibility for primary and secondary education in Wales has been transferred to the Secretary of State for Wales (DES, 1970). He works through the education section of the Welsh Office. While all matters relating to primary and secondary education in Wales come under the Secretary of State for Wales, all matters concerning other aspects of education—further and higher education, the youth service, the supply and training of teachers, the appointment of HM Inspectorate—come under the Secretary of State for Education and Science.

My personal opinion is that this 1970 change was made because it was

[1] See, for instance, Ministry of Education (1952, 1953) and Department of Education and Science (1967).

thought to be politically expedient, using 'politically' more in a nationalistic than in a party political sense. It is also my opinion that it is administrative nonsense but, like a lot of nonsense, it has its advantages. It is administrative nonsense because, despite the quality of the education personnel in the Welsh Office, without a vast increase in staff there just cannot be enough of them to give the total coverage of all the aspects of primary and secondary education which is needed for really effective control and advice at government level. It is also administrative nonsense because control of one part of education in London and of another part of education in Cardiff assumes a division in education itself which even in administrative terms ought to diminish and is diminishing. An example is seen in many of the best schemes for the reorganization of education for pupils aged between eleven and nineteen along comprehensive lines. A number of Local Education Authorities are establishing comprehensive colleges for pupils aged sixteen to nineteen. Administratively, these are part of further education and therefore under the Department of Education and Science in London. If, however, a Local Education Authority has schools taking pupils from the age of eleven right to the age of nineteen, those schools come under the Welsh Office in Cardiff.

The advantages coming to Wales from the arrangements which I have described result, I think, from Department of Education and Science sensitivity in London, although Celtic skill and cunning in Cardiff could also be a contributory factor. It seems to me that Wales does quite well when resources for things like building allocations are shared out over the whole of England and Wales.

Another fundamental difference between England and Wales is that there is in Wales a body called the Welsh Joint Education Committee, which I have already mentioned. It has a unique constitutional status[2] and exercises many functions in relation to education. Each Local Education Authority in Wales has representation on the Welsh Joint Education Committee broadly in proportion to the county's population. There is no such association, with such status and functions, in England.

The Welsh Joint Education Committee has three main roles. First, it is permanently a co-ordinator and not infrequently an initiator. In its sub-committees are discussed, by representatives of education com-

[2] The Welsh Joint Education Committee was established by Order of the Minister of Education under a provision of the 1944 Education Act, in accordance with a Working Party recommendation (1948).

mittees in Wales, a host of matters relating to all aspects of education: the teaching of Welsh, the salaries of part-time teachers in technical colleges, orchestral music, school terms, the youth service—the range is as extensive as education itself. The Welsh Joint Education Committee's policy also constitutes the Welsh view to be expressed to the Secretary of State or to various educational bodies which want to know Welsh opinion on some educational topic. Some consequences of Welsh Joint Education Committee co-ordination or initiative are the Welsh National Youth Orchestra, special arrangements for the publication of books in the Welsh language, the establishment of the Welsh Agricultural College, a Welsh College of Librarianship, a National Language Unit, and a School Museum Service based on the National Museum of Wales.

Second, the Welsh Joint Education Committee is a regional advisory council for further education. Further education has been something of a vigorous jungle growth and perhaps the healthier for that during the growing period. A rational approach and the need to use resources economically means that there must be tidying up, with consequent decisions that this course shall be situated at College A, with advanced work at College B and so on. It is the Welsh Joint Education Committee that is responsible for this rationalizing in Wales.

Third, the Welsh Joint Education Committee is an examining body. As an examining body it is responsible for three levels of school examination and for various post-school technical examinations. Again it is the only examining board in England and Wales functioning at each of these levels.

The Welsh language, the Welsh Office and the Welsh Joint Education Committee are the main administratively identifiable differences between England and Wales, as they affect education at the local authority level. There are other differences, subtler and not so easily categorized, and other features of Local Education Authority administration, in both England and Wales—such as those relating to spheres of influence—to which further attention might usefully be given.

BIBLIOGRAPHY

Department of Education and Science (1970), *Primary and Secondary Education in Wales* (D.E.S. Circular 18/70, Welsh Office Circular 108/70), HMSO, London.
Gittins Report (Advisory Council for Education, Wales) (1967), *Primary Education in Wales*, HMSO, London.

Ministry of Education Working Party (1948), *Educational Administration in Wales*, HMSO, London.
Ministry of Education Welsh Department (1952), *The Curriculum and the Community in Wales*, HMSO, London.
Ministry of Education Welsh Department (1953), *The Place of Welsh and English in the Schools of Wales*, HMSO, London.

3 The General Teaching Council for Scotland

JAMES MILLER

The General Teaching Council for Scotland is a unique body. It was set up by the Teaching Council (Scotland) Act 1965. I think that it would be helpful to explain the circumstances which led to the formation of the Council.

Before the 1939 war, Scotland had a surplus of teachers. Standards for entry to training were high and many Scottish teachers felt that it would be comparatively easy to obtain an all-graduate profession in Scotland. By the end of the war, however, there was already a shortage which became steadily more acute during the next fifteen years. It seemed to teachers that this shortage had led to a reduction in academic requirements for entrance to training and also in some respects to a reduction in the amount of training required. The shortage had also led to the employment of many uncertificated teachers; some of these people, although untrained, were well qualified academically but there were many others whose educational qualifications fell far short of those required of the trained teacher in Scotland. This increasing employment of unqualified teachers naturally caused a feeling of resentment which intensified in 1960 when the Secretary of State was known to be considering a proposal for the training of non-graduate men as teachers of general subjects in primary schools. Many teachers suspected that this proposal would be followed by proposals for the training of non-graduate teachers to teach academic subjects in secondary schools.

By 1961 there were a number of signs that relationships between the teachers' organizations and the then Secretary of State had reached a crisis. The Secretary of State, appreciating the seriousness of the situation, took a number of steps to reassure the teaching profession. The most important of these, in the present context, was his decision to set up a Committee under the chairmanship of a Scottish judge, Lord Wheatley, with the following terms of reference:

To review, in the light of the requirements of the education service and the practice in relation to other professions, the present arrangements for the award and withdrawal of certificates of competency to teach, and to make recommendations regarding any changes that are considered desirable in these arrangements and any consequential changes in the functions of teacher training authorities.

The Wheatley Committee contained twenty-two members, including teachers, Directors of Education, and representatives of the Colleges of Education, the Universities and the education authorities; a majority of the members were certificated teachers. Reporting in 1963, its central recommendation was that 'a new machinery should be devised for the teaching profession, and that there should be established a General Teaching Council for Scotland broadly similar in scope, powers and functions to the Councils in other professions'.

The 1965 Act closely followed the recommendations of the Wheatley Committee. It rejected the concept of a Council whose functions would be confined to the establishment and maintenance of a register; the Council was given wide educational responsibilities. It also recognized that the public interest must be represented on a body which was to have considerable influence on an essential social service.

The Act defined the principal duties of the Council as being—

(i) to establish and maintain a register containing the names, addresses and such qualifications and other particulars as may be prescribed of persons entitled to registration;

(ii) to keep under review standards of education, training and fitness to teach of those entering the teaching profession and to make to the Secretary of State such recommendations with respect to these standards as they might think appropriate;

(iii) to consider, and make to the Secretary of State, recommendations on matters (other than remuneration and conditions of service) relating to the supply of teachers;

(iv) to keep themselves informed of the nature of the instruction given in the Colleges of Education.

Practical Powers of the Council

Possibly the most significant power (and certainly the most easily appreciated by the teacher) is the almost complete control over the admission and removal of names from the register.

A student who is recommended by a Scottish College of Education is automatically registered on payment of the registration fee. The Council has complete control over the admission to the register of all applicants trained outside Scotland.

The Council has the power to remove names from the register (a considerable power since only registered teachers can be employed in local authority and grant-aided schools in Scotland). A name can be removed from the register if—

(i) the service of the teacher during his probationary period is unsatisfactory;

(ii) the teacher has been judged to be guilty of serious misconduct.

The ultimate power on the framing of Regulations governing the conditions of entry to Colleges of Education and the principles to be observed by the Colleges in recommending students for registration lies with the Secretary of State. Some teachers feel that this limitation on the powers of the Council makes it something of a 'paper tiger'. It seems unrealistic, however, to expect any government to relinquish the powers which govern the supply of teachers. The Secretary of State, before he makes any changes in Regulations, must consider the observations of the Council on his proposals; the Council also has the right to initiate discussions on changes in the Regulations. Where the Secretary of State is not prepared to accept the Council's recommendations, he must make public his reasons for rejecting the advice. In practice, the Secretary of State has usually accepted the advice given by the Council.[1]

The Attitude of the Profession towards the Council

It is probably true to say that Scottish teachers now accept that the Council is 'here to stay' (see Inglis, 1972). This could certainly not have been said in the tumultuous early years of the Council's existence when there were serious doubts as to whether the Council would survive. But if it can now be claimed that the Council is accepted, it cannot be

[1] He did, however, reject the Council's recommendation that the raising of the school leaving age should be postponed.

said that its functions are really understood. The present Council is well aware of this problem and has recently established a Public Relations Committee which is making a determined effort to publicise the Council's work. Open meetings of teachers are held from time to time in various parts of the country to give teachers the opportunity of meeting and questioning Council members.

The Council can fairly claim that it has played an effective role in stopping the employment of unqualified teachers in Scottish schools. It is however true to say that this has been made possible only because of a significant improvement during the last few years in the supply of teachers. There are, however, still parts of Scotland where there are serious shortages of teachers; before the existence of the Council this shortage would have led to the employment of uncertificated teachers, despite the protests of the teachers' professional organizations. Undoubtedly the representations of a statutory body such as the Council have made it more difficult for central government to maintain a policy of solving supply difficulties by the lowering of standards. There is necessarily sometimes an apparent conflict between the interests of the teachers and the public interest (the Council would of course say that in their insistence on the maintenance of standards they are the true guardians of the public interest). The existence of the Council makes it certain that the professional point of view will have at least a more effective voice.

The Council has set up an organization which deals efficiently with registration, probation and exceptional admission to the register. It has good relationships with the two largest teachers' organizations and is developing a political skill in its relations with the Scottish Education Department. Many teachers feel, however, that its relationship with the Department is rather too 'bland' and non-controversial. This type of criticism would diminish if the Council appeared to be in a state of permanent conflict with the Department. The Council's attitude, however, is that conflict should not be sought for its own sake; neither should it be avoided.

Perhaps even more delicate than the relationship between the Council and the Department is the relationship between the Council and the Colleges of Education. The Colleges are represented on the Council and their representatives have played a most important part in the Council's work; the Colleges give specialist advice to the Council and the Council increasingly helps the Colleges on admission problems.

Teachers do not understand why lecturers in the Colleges are not re-quired to register; most lecturers have in fact registered voluntarily and it is probable that all will be required to register within the next few years.

The main problem in relation to the Colleges of Education, however, is the fact that many teachers believe that the Council should have much more control over the courses of training provided in the Colleges. It is argued that the General Medical Council (and other professional Councils) have control over training schools. I would not wish to give any opinion on this claim but it is clear that if the Council were given real powers over the content and the conduct of College courses, then either the membership of the Council would have to be altered signifi-cantly so that it contained a much larger number of members who had specialized knowledge of training, or else the Council would need to appoint highly qualified officers to carry out the 'supervisory' functions. One thing is certain—there will be considerable debate in the future about the proper balance between the powers of the Council and the freedom of the Colleges.

Finally, it may be observed that, if the Council is to develop in prestige and in real influence, it will need the active support and under-standing of the profession. It will have to continue to show that it is independent of both the teachers' organizations and of the Secretary of State. It will have to show that it can anticipate problems and initiate educational discussion. It must avoid any temptation to settle for a quiet niche in the educational edifice.

BIBLIOGRAPHY

Inglis, W. B. (1972), *Towards a Self-Governing Teaching Profession*, Moray House College of Education, Edinburgh.
The Wheatley Report (1963), *The Teaching Profession in Scotland, arrangements for the award and withdrawal of certificates of competency to teach*, HMSO, Edinburgh.

12 Educational Administration and the Contemporary City

ERIC BRIAULT

The streets of a modern city form a distinctly hostile environment for the young; if you happen to be five years old the exhaust smoke hits you right in the face. We therefore begin by identifying some of the aspects of the contemporary city which affect the task of education and thus indirectly of educational administration. The hostility of the urban environment is not confined to the exhaust smoke in the streets. High blocks of flats are hard for families and unfavourable to child rearing and too often their surroundings present little of interest to the child and all too little play space. In many of the crowded hearts of our cities, grass is hard to be found and playing spaces quite insufficient and for one reason or another often insufficiently equipped. The concrete jungle is a place to escape from if you can afford it, and yet these great cities continue to be areas of steady growth. The population flows into them from the countryside and indeed, as far as we in London and many other cities in Britain are concerned, from other parts of the world as well.

The second feature of the contemporary city which we must therefore identify, and of which we must seek to work out the educational consequences, is that of continued growth. This growth itself is a matter of change and brings with it other changes, of which the most notable is probably the flight from the city centre. The older inner hearts of cities have gradually died, and in some cases have been rebuilt, rehabilitated and certainly changed. Meanwhile, families move from inner to outer areas and the city sprawl extends further and further. Difficulties of communication increase as a result, and the hostility of the city streets is increased by the resoluteness of the traffic flow. Alongside these demographic changes in the population of the growing city areas, there are significant changes in occupations. Areas which once gave plenty of work to a wide range of people, areas which once had workshops and factories, change over to different kinds of occupations, mostly the shops and offices and the service industries. Moreover, the continual pressure for housing itself tends to drive out work places and to diminish the amount of open space.

The migration changes, to which I have referred, generally result in a net migration loss out of the inner city areas. This is accompanied by a fall in the average level of attainment of the population, including the child population, even if not probably in the average intelligence of the children themselves. It is the more enterprising and able families who make the move to more salubrious outer areas, though there is some counter-tendency in the re-occupation and upgrading of some inner areas, as families in higher income groups return to reduce their travelling time.

As a result of these changes the city scene increasingly develops the contrasts of affluence and squalor: the affluence of the office blocks and the expensive shops, the theatres and cinemas and clubs, the recreations of the well-to-do, and the squalor of overcrowded dwellings, ill-kept streets and a high incidence of social misbehaviour. The riches to be made from city enterprises give rise to increasing land, as well as building, costs and the perfectly proper pressures to replace bad housing with better and at lower densities, together with the social pressures for open space and educational and recreational provision, add up to tremendous land hunger over a very great part of the contemporary city. There is, therefore, intense competition for land and planning applications become of critical importance. This land hunger intensifies the trend towards high rise building, itself so inimical to satisfying child development.

What are the special aspects of the contemporary city as far as education is concerned? The point which I have just mentioned has a direct effect on educational provision, for the shortage of land and the high cost of it, tend towards inadequate sites for schools and other educational premises. The population changes and, in particular, the movement out of the inner city, tend to leave behind old buildings in the dying heart and in the poorer streets, buildings which cannot easily be replaced because the need for them is less than it once was. It is true that this has the compensation that pressure on the space within those buildings is diminished, and indeed, some of the criticisms long heard of old Victorian schools have been reduced when the space standards they provide in an area where population is falling is compared with the space standards which would be provided in a new school building to replace them.

The lack of open space and the difficulties of transport are severe handicaps to educational provision, making it difficult to provide children with good opportunities for physical education and recreational activities which necessarily call for open space. When this open space has to be sought at a greater distance, then the always increasing problems of travel make it that much more difficult to achieve a satisfactory result. The growth of sports which do not require large areas of grass, and the relative decline in the popularity of team games, goes some way to compensate for these problems.

The contrast between affluence and squalor in terms of educational considerations give rise to what the Plowden Report (1967) came to call educational priority areas. Whether or not these areas have been given priority, it is an educational feature of the contemporary city that there are within it neighbourhoods which are deprived by reason of overcrowding, poor housing, low standards of living, broken or one-parent families, from which children come to school already deprived and have to be educated against that background—a background which at its very least amounts to lack of parental support and, far too often, amounts to total hostility from the home towards the educational enterprise.

A quite different feature of education in the contemporary city is the relatively high proportion of provision for further and higher education which the city makes. It is natural that the urban conurbation should provide a university, probably a polytechnic or college of advanced education, and also teacher training. There will also be a wide variety of vocational further education provision, designed to meet the needs for full or part-time study of those in or entering upon employment, especially in the kind of fields of occupation which occur within the city itself. The great city will therefore inevitably have a higher student population, in proportion to its total population, than the country as a whole. This may be, and indeed often is, a source of strength to the city, and it is a quite inevitable result of reasonably economic planning of such facilities. It does, however, yet again increase the pressure both on land and upon housing; the problems of student housing in some of our great cities, particularly in countries where it is not the custom for the student to live at home, are becoming severe.

Against this background of the contemporary city what should we say about its education service? First, it can almost certainly be said that the city will be able to provide for the education service a wide range of strong support services. The costs of education within the city may be in part borne nationally; but if they are wholly or entirely provided by the city itself, then fortunately the rich can be made to pay for the poor.

The ways in which the education service of a great city will take advantage of the resources available to it, will include the provision of a range of services to its schools and colleges which, by reason of the very density of provision in the city, can both be more justified and can be more effective than is probably the case in areas of less dense population. I have in mind in this connection both human and material support services; a good administration, a strong advisory or inspectorate service, ancillary support for the schools and colleges by way of educational psychologists, welfare officers and the like. In-service training is a particularly important aspect of support and here the city has some advantages. The resources of university, teachers' colleges and teachers' centres are available. It is generally practicable for teachers to take advantage of these opportunities because of relative ease of travel and courses can be provided without the need for residential provision. In-service training for other groups than teachers should not be forgotten: school caretakers, technicians, clerical staff and so on.

Similarly its physical resources enable the education service to provide the schools and colleges with learning materials in wide variety, to provide such things as coach transport for handicapped pupils, and to loan films and equipment and so forth. These are the supports which the schools in the inner city have come to expect and with which they are generally provided. We are seeing a rapid increase in the range of learning resources available, with the development of materials in a variety of media in addition to traditional print. In a dense urban area, cable television is practicable, and we in Inner London have, I believe, the largest system of closed circuit educational television in the world. Interrelated material for both pupils and teachers, in audio and visual as well as printed form, is produced in our media resources centre. Such production can of course meet the needs of a whole state as easily as those of the city itself, but it is in the city and particularly for the dense urban area, that such resources are often produced. In the city too are other special learning resources (in the broadest sense) provided by museums and art galleries, theatres and concert halls.

The task of securing the proper distribution of resources throughout the education service in the great city is by no means a simple one. The administrator will be required to secure that all schools and colleges are adequately staffed and provided with materials, equipment and buildings. At the same time he has to arrange that resources are distributed differentially so as to meet the special needs of the areas of deprivation which most require them, and also to meet the special needs which are peculiar to the urban scene. He therefore has a number of nice judgements to make or matters of policy on which to secure appropriate decisions.

As to the general distribution of resources, it is my view that the proper role of the educational administrator is to arrange for a basic resource provision, both human and material, for all the schools, colleges and other parts of the education service, below which the standards of no individual institution should fall. If then he can provide himself with an index of need, reflecting the factors which, as a matter of policy, it has been decided to take account of, the factors which give rise to educational and social deprivation, he should be able to add more resources to those institutions or areas which most need them.[1] Administration will have to be peculiarly sensitive to the problems of land hunger and to the educational difficulties and disadvantages imposed upon children and young people by the nature of the urban environment.

These resources, which include the support resources, will also have to be chosen in ways which reflect the needs of the city and thus there will be priorities in the use of finance and the use of land, which reflect the particular characteristics and problems of the contemporary city. It will be observed that this assumes the answer to a major question, namely whether the right way of dealing with educational deprivation is to pour more resources into deprived areas. This is certainly presently the assumption in this country, but it is hard to say whether there is yet adequate documentation to show that it is successful.

[1] In Inner London a policy of positive discrimination has been vigorously pursued in recent years. 'The order of schools in relation to their special needs is based upon the primary and the secondary school indices provided by the research and statistics division. The actual variable addition for each school is settled on the advice of the district inspector, who has regard to this order but may know of needs which the index does not reflect. Policy consists on the one hand in the decision that no school shall be worse off than the basic scale and on the other that more shall be given to those with greater needs. A major consideration on the part of the Authority each year, reflected in its budget, is the level of the basic minimum and the amount of resources to be put into the variable sector.' (ILEA, 1973, pp. 34–5)

I return to the differential distribution of additional resources to schools or areas where urban deprivation is greatest. Obviously, additional educational resources do not strike at the root of the problem of inner city deprivation, and other measures are needed if a real cure is to be attempted. But this is no reason for not seeking to counter its effects in some measure by enhancing the educational opportunities of children who come to school handicapped by it.

It seems to me that the most difficult problem, to which we have not yet found, at any rate in Britain, an adequate solution, is of ensuring that the additional resources made available to the individual institution because it is in a deprived area or because it has a higher proportion than others of children with special needs, are actually devoted to the individual children who most need them and not disseminated or even, I might say, dissipated across the institution as a whole. This is a matter for the internal arrangements of schools or colleges which has to be settled within the individual institution, and upon which advice may be given, but hardly the lines of detailed action laid down, from outside the institution.

This brings me to a central aspect of my understanding of the role of educational administration, namely that its task is to provide resources and support for the individual institution and then so to organize its affairs that the day to day decisions about the use of resources should take place effectively, efficiently and in a manner of positive discrimination within the institution itself. This is another way of saying that an arm of educational administration must be participation by those involved. While this participation can take place centrally in terms of advisory committees and consultative bodies and the like, the essential participation to which I am referring is that which takes place within the individual institution and on the part of those involved directly in the institution with those who are, as one might say, its customers. The institution must develop arrangements which will enable it to achieve a creative consensus upon which to deal with both problems and innovation. It must have the means of evaluating both its problems and its success or lack of it in dealing with them, and of evaluating the usefulness of innovation, whether indicated from without the institution or generated within it.

This is an essential aspect of educational administration of the institution itself and it remains a part of the task of central administration, both to make it possible for individual institutions to behave in this way and to find means of stimulating and encouraging them to do so (Briault, 1973, 1974). We must therefore consider the extent of the managerial responsibility given to the individual institution. This depends in part upon whether the institution is funded wholly or only in part from central or statutory sources. If funds are independently raised or made available from independent sources, then the school or college can take its own decisions as to how to spend at least that margin of resources, whether on buildings or equipment, teachers or non-teaching staff. On the other hand, money coming from state or local authority sources is generally earmarked in respect of particular kinds of expenditure and, in the absence of other sources, there may be little flexibility which the school can exercise. For example, a school is generally given a fixed teaching staff complement, a fixed amount of non-teaching staff and a sum of money for expenditure on books, materials and equipment. These are not interchangeable. In my view, it is the task of central administration to arrange affairs so that a greater degree of flexibility than this can be exercised by the individual school.

I referred earlier to the basic minimum staff for all and the allocation of additional resources to those with greater needs. It is a proper exercise in decentralization to allocate some resources to all schools, and more to some schools, which can be used for teachers *or* non-teaching staff or materials and equipment. At the same time it is proper for central administration to lay down basic minima especially of teachers, for every school (see Fowler, 1974). By means of arrangements for the alternative use of resources, the authority can encourage a managerial approach within a school or college, which enables it to respond to its problems and opportunities and to direct extra resources to activities most likely to benefit those children who are specially deprived.

So far we have given attention to pupils and students, schools and colleges but the responsibilities of an education service extend beyond these institutions. There are educational needs in the broadest sense which are met by less formal arrangements such as those provided in this country under the youth service and in the field of adult education. It is the responsibility of educational administration to identify the educational needs of the whole community and to seek resources to meet them as far as possible.

Both the identification of these less formal needs and the right ways of meeting them are essentially to be undertaken not centrally but in a distributed fashion. They are likely not merely to involve a distributed form of administration, such as that which provides local administrative centres and the administrative arrangements of the schools and colleges themselves, but individual workers who are in direct contact with the many small groups and communities within the community as a whole. There are, in many contemporary cities, cultural groups with their own special interests whose educational needs are particular to them but nevertheless the responsibility of an education service to meet.

There are important decisions to be made as to the way in which less formal education for young people is organized and administered. Often so called non-vocational classes are arranged as part of the responsibility of a further education college. This may result in too little regard for work often thought of as having a low professional status. The great city is capable of providing youth centres and adult education centres organized in their own right, responsive in a way which formal education cannot be to locally felt needs in these days of increasing leisure. Such centres can be in a very real sense the means by which education reaches out to the whole community. If the links with schools are good, adult education can assist parental involvement, too often lacking in inner city areas. Educational Centres of this kind also play an important social role in the urban environment, where worthwhile leisure activities are not otherwise easy to come by, especially for those with small incomes.

In developing educational provision in a large and densely populated area, administration necessarily operates through recognized structures —both the structured arrangements of the administration and of the individual institutions themselves. The responsibility for the different parts of the service is frequently carried by separate senior officers, many of whom may have their own specialism. Thus the very intensity of educational provision in the contemporary city may build a kind of separatism into educational administration and into the education service itself.

In my view, however, educational administration has a responsibility to seek to achieve a wholeness, a wholeness of the education service, a wholeness of thinking and approach to the educational needs of children and students and adults, having regard not only to their time in school or college or adult class but to its relationship to their world of home and work and leisure. In recognizing educational need, there is a further challenge to achieve a conception of the wholeness of the community itself, even though its infrastructure may be infinitely varied and essentially cellular in character.

Strong administration places responsibility in clearly defined positions within an overall structure. The links between the necessarily separate parts of the administrative structure cannot, and should not, come only at the head of the pyramid. There is a danger that the only generalist in the educational administration, either of the whole education service or of an individual educational institution, is the head of that service or the head of the institution, together probably with his deputy in each case. It is, however, the task of those immediately below him, right down to those in middle management levels, firstly, to conceive the service or the institution as a whole even though they bear responsibility directly for only part of it; and secondly, to establish effective communication and good educational links between the parts of the service or the structures within the individual school or college at the appropriate level. It is bad administration if communication always travels upwards and down again. Good administration, whether educational or any other kind, will ensure that communication travels horizontally at appropriate levels, as well as moving up or down where responsibility cannot be carried at the lower level.

In practice in an education service positive efforts on the part of administration are required to secure that those actually involved in one sector of the service, say the primary schools, directly communicate with the secondary schools and in doing so have a conception of the wholeness of the child who passes through from one stage of education to the next, some of whose activities are not in school but in a play centre or a youth centre or, later on, in some form of adult education. Too often these links between the parts of the service are so weak as to make continuity difficult for the child or the student, and sometimes so poorly informed on either side of the structural break in the service as to fail to give to the would-be students sufficient information upon which to enable him to make decisions about his future course of study.

A few years ago I had the privilege of spending some months in Australia. Towards the end of my tour I paid a visit to a secondary school in Western Australia, to which was attached a farm for teaching purposes. While my wife and I were there we were asked whether we would like to see a sheep sheared, and, of course, we very much wished to do so. A large sheep was quickly shorn by the electric cutter in the skilful hands of the instructor, and as the sheep scampered away naked there remained on the floor a great untidy pile of fleece. The instructor gathered it up in his arms and with one fling cast it smooth, entire and without a wrinkle on the great table before us.

From time to time it is the responsibility of those in charge of educational administration in a great city, or indeed anywhere else, to cast before themselves and their colleagues, in so far as they can do so, a vision of the education service as a whole, entire and unwrinkled, as was that fleece in Western Australia. From its richness and from its wholeness, the individual school or the particular teacher may spin the thread of the individual child's educational development. There will then be woven from those threads, given the resources and their right management, the educational cloth which is an essential fabric of the society of the contemporary city.

BIBLIOGRAPHY

Briault, E. W. H. (1973), 'Resources for Learning', *Educational Administration Bulletin*, 2(1), 1–10.
Briault, E. W. H. (1974), *Allocation and Management of Resources in Schools*, Council for Educational Technology Occasional Paper No. 6, Councils and Education Press, London.
Fowler, G. T. (1973), 'Resources for Education and their Management', in Ewan, E. A. (ed), *Management of Resources*, Proceedings of Second Annual Conference of British Educational Administration Society, Moray House College of Education, Edinburgh.
Inner London Educational Authority (1973), *An Education Service for the Whole Community*, ILEA, London.
Plowden Report (1967), *Children and their Primary Schools*, HMSO, London.

PART THREE

Theory into Practice

13 The Contribution of Research to the Study and Practice of Educational Administration

WILLIAM TAYLOR

This paper divides into four parts. In the first I want to argue that the research-study-practice relationship in educational administration constitutes a problem in respect to which speculative theorising and unsubstantiated assertion are much more evident than empirical enquiry, but that only through the latter are we likely to obtain fresh insights and useful new knowledge. In the second part I advocate the value of a sociology of knowledge perspective in providing the framework within which the data of empirical enquiry might be given meaning, but counsel caution in the use of such a perspective. The third part examines the context and organization of educational studies with special reference to their implications for the development of educational administration. The final part comprises some remarks about the price that might have to be paid to achieve a tighter and more direct relationship between research and practice in educational administration.

At no point in this paper do I review or attempt to evaluate the very real contributions that have been made to our understanding of the impact of research on study and practice by authors such as Havelock (1968a, 1968b, 1971), Rogers and Shoemaker (1971), Bennis, Benne and Chinn (1961), Schmuck and Miles (1971), Hoyle (1970, 1972) and Dalin (1973). Many of the things they have to say about innovation and change in education seem to me to justify the usefulness of some of the approaches that I want to discuss in the paragraphs that follow.

I

Those who make judgements on the relation of research to study and practice of educational administration can be seen as constituting three groups. Members of the first tell us that with certain honourable (but usually unspecified) exceptions, the impact of research on what features in courses in our field and what practising administrators do has been and is insignificant. Such statements attract attention, stimulate debate and inspire refutation. They also reinforce the practitioner's stereotypes about research, console him for his ignorance, and encourage researchers, erroneously, to believe that some kind of fresh start can be made, free of the errors and the methodological taints of the past. Such judgements also have the more serious weakness of being untrue.

A second group of commentators are more optimistic. They assert that research has indeed influenced what is found in courses and textbooks in educational administration, and also the kinds of things that go on in Principals' studies and administrative offices. They believe that this is a good thing, and that in so far as inadequate support for new work, poor communications and various kinds of misunderstandings get in the way of a freer flow of facts and findings, then those deficiencies should be tackled and the channels cleared.

Prudent conference organizers usually arrange for their proceedings to be opened by a member of the first group and closed by one of the second.

A third group includes those who recognize the complexity of the research-study-practice relationship and the virtual impossibility of one man grasping it fully, who see the rhetorical and ideological significance of many of the judgements that are made about it, but who none the less regard the relationship as a field not so much for assertion as for empirical enquiry. Membership of this group implies the possession of considerable knowledge about the relevant research literature, about the institutionalized means for the generation, transmission and implementation of ideas, about the content of existing study opportunities and the nature of current practice in educational administration. I certainly cannot claim such knowledge. All I can hope to do in this presentation is to identify myself with those who find discussion of the research-study-practice relationship both intellectually stimulating and potentially significant for the organization and success of all three kinds of activity.

I have already stated that it is both unhelpful and mistaken to assert that research has had *no* influence on study and practice. It is, however, a matter of great difficulty to trace the direct and indirect effects of particular research findings within complex social systems. Twenty-five years of reading, writing, teaching and examining in my own field makes me believe that I could make a reasonable job of describing and explaining how during this period one or two significant ideas originated, were disseminated to peers and students, incorporated in the literature and standard teaching materials of the subject, and, in interaction with related ideas and perceptions of events originating elsewhere, influenced the decisions of policy makers and administrators. The ability to do this even on a very limited scale depends heavily upon acquaintance with some of the people concerned, personal participation in conferences and informal discussions over a period of years, membership of the formal and informal clubs and cabals of the trade, and the experience of having acted as external examiner for a substantial number of colleges and universities. Most of us could probably do the same in respect of a few of the findings which currently serve as 'anchoring ideas' in our own specialism. Such an effort is a worth-while personal exercise. It underlines the complexities of the business and its dependence on private knowledge. It sharpens the critical sense with which we evaluate attempts to generalize about the relationships involved. Finally, and of chief importance in my present context, it makes perfectly clear that if in most forms of activity the research-study relationship is complex, obscure, and frequently baffling, it is nonetheless real.

The problem with which we are trying to grapple in disentangling the impact of new ideas and research findings on what administrators and students of administration think and feel and do is by no means unique to our own specialism. Historians have long been concerned with just such issues. Thus Ford (1968), in considering the effect on social practice of the ideas of early nineteenth-century classical economists, makes clear that research and writing that sustains, supports or is in some way perceived as relevant to one particular doctrine or set of beliefs is more likely to influence practice than a possibly more profound but less clearly focussed body of work. Many of the researchers that we might identify as the most significant in our own field became so not because of the intrinsic importance of their findings, but because these findings became attached to a movement. In so-called basic as much as in applied research, our criteria for the identification of problems and selection of research topics (especially when the latter require Foundation support) are determined by the social, political and economic circumstances and intellectual climate of the time. *Within* the field of administrative studies proper, the balance of influence in the research-practice relationship is firmly on the side of practice; the problems of practice serve to define the programmes of the researcher.

This is not, however, the case in terms of the whole *range* of researches relevant to administrative practice, which include work in sociology, social psychology, economics, philosophy and political science. The problems identified and researched into by students and professors of educational administration arise primarily from their concern with the improvement of administrative practice; the theories that they construct as a framework for further research reflect both these concerns *and* those findings they select from work in a broader range of disciplines as relevant to the development of understanding about administrative process. The ways in which criteria of relevance in problem identification and theory construction develop and change over time is itself an important area for study and reflection.

To pursue the line of enquiry suggested by Ford, and to take due account of the complexities revealed by the introspective exercise recommended in the first part of this section, requires that we be more specific about the mechanisms by means of which contact is established and maintained between activities defined as research and as practice. It may be helpful to suggest that there are effectively three main ways in which the existence and findings of research have an effect on the study and practice of administration.

First, research affects the prevailing *Zeitgeist* in a field of study, helping to formulate criteria of relevance, indicating the ideas and the concepts that are pertinent to the analysis of problems, shaping the meaning that students and participants attach to events, sustaining and legitimating the existing and emerging ideologies of the field.

Second, students taking courses in educational administration are encouraged to read books and journals which include research reports and are examined on their knowledge of these sources; put more pretentiously, research plays a part in the process by means of which entrants to the specialism are socialized. The longer-term effects of research encountered in this context are diffuse rather than specific; practitioners rarely internalize a particular finding which they later 'apply' to the solution of practical problems. What research findings do is to shape the perspectives that together constitute the appreciative system shared by groups of practitioners in a particular situational context (of which more anon) and which facilitate a subjective modification of experience on the part of the individuals concerned.

Third, research yields techniques, tools and frameworks for analysis that are directly employed by practitioners in the solution of problems.

Acquaintance with these techniques is sometimes a product of following a systematic course of study. More frequently, I suspect, it arises from some kind of search process activated by the identification of a task or difficulty, a process that can include combing through journals and other likely printed sources, attending workshop sessions, talking with peers and consultants and practitioners from other fields, raking through old notes, and listening to broadcasts.

It should be made clear that this is not a classification of kinds of research, but of the *contexts* in which research bears upon what principals and officials do in their schools and offices. A particular research finding can function in all three contexts. An evaluation of PPBS, for example, or a research-based assessment of management training needs, can affect the climate of ideas, the content of courses and the development of student attitudes, *and* add to the stock of techniques on which a practising administrator might draw in dealing with a problem encountered in the course of his work.

II

It seems to me that we shall not begin to understand how the activities that we call research, study and practice interact with one another unless we place them firmly within a single comprehensive model of the 'knowledge system' of educational administration. This requires a naturalistic, or if you like, phenomenological approach. What I would like to call 'doing Education' refers to the activities involved in producing, legitimising and disseminating knowledge about teaching and learning and administering, about schools and colleges and universities, about people as pupils, students, and teachers. Some of the headings in terms of which such a comprehensive model might be constructed were suggested by the American sociologist Louis Wirth in his preface to the first edition of Karl Mannheim's *Ideology and Utopia* (1936). What Wirth had to say was not directed specifically towards the study of education, let alone the specialism of educational administration, but it does have clear relevance for our own task. I have elsewhere employed his classification in an analysis of what is implied by doing educational research (Taylor, 1973). All I want to do here is to use some of the same headings to suggest ways in which we might obtain greater insights into the knowledge system of educational administration, and move a little closer towards understanding the research-study-practice relationship.

The first point made by Wirth is that attention has to be given to the epistemology of a subject, to the nature of the concepts and the logic that it employs, 'to the socio-psychological elaboration of the theory of knowledge itself'. This task requires that the rules of logic themselves be regarded as problematic, and, in common with the rest of our intellectual tools, as part and products of the whole of our social life. To follow Wirth's intention in our own specialism would require that we analyse its cognitive foundations, and identify the disciplines from which our concepts and theories are drawn and the manner in which theory construction takes place. Here, again, a naturalistic approach can be beneficial. Baldamus (1973) has emphasized how little we know at first hand about how those who produce theories in the social sciences go about their task. One of the implications of regarding the research-study-practice relationship as constituting an empirical problem is to devote more study to the activities of theorists, to pay more attention to books such as P. E. Hammond's *Sociologists at Work* (1964) and, in a different field, Watson's *The Double Helix* (1968). Baldamus (1973) points to the fact that ' ... the relatively most tangible characteristic of theorising points to a process through time that can best be described as sustained "*articulation*"; an initially vague and vacillating image of a complex framework is perpetually re-defined so as to produce an increasingly definite and stable structure.' This implies, of course, that the concepts and frameworks involved are sufficiently stable and imbued with adequate explanatory potential to sustain and inspire a considerable volume of empirical research. Our own field has itself thrown up, or derived from elsewhere, a number of concepts and theories which are capable of functioning in this way; organization theory, the analysis of bureaucracy, leadership studies, inter-group process, are well known examples. In examining the research literature, however, it is difficult to avoid the impression that socio-psychological mechanisms are at work that reward not so much the testing, falsification, reformulation and progressively more complex articulation of existing theories, but the invention of new speculative categorizations, few of which have a life that extends beyond a single thesis, research paper or book.

Wirth goes on to specify that need for a 'reworking of the data of intellectual history with a view to the discovery of the style and methods of thought that are dominant in certain types of historical-social situations.' This involves enquiries into the relationship between shifts in intellectual interests and attention and changes in other aspects of social structure. It is relatively easy to make a number of somewhat superficial points about the links between fashions and phases of research in educational administration and the prevailing social and economic climate. It is somewhat more difficult, and rarer, to refine these speculations by means of carefully worked out empirical studies. In the broader area of educational research there is a good deal of writing and enquiry cognate to this particular task, but it tends to be scattered and unfocussed. Some recent work in the history of education, such as that by Joan Simon and Brian Simon (1973) has contributed substantially to our understanding of the relationship of educational ideas and changes in a wider society. That this is so has much to do with the fact that the work of both these authors is informed by an explicit theoretical orientation which gives form and direction to their analyses. There is little doubt that such an explicit orientation is needed if the data of intellectual history is to be given any kind of meaning or significance. On the whole, educationists seem more anxious about the dangers of theory without data than of data without theory. Yet the latter is usually pretty useless. As Toulmin (1972) has pointed out, the collection of extensive empirical data about the physical world in the fourteenth century would have been of little use to physics, since no clear theoretical questions had at that time been formulated on which such observations could throw light. And Baldamus (1973) reminds us that ' ... the discovery of an "anomalous" event is possible only if and in so far as a new theory has been created which defines it as anomalous'. Data without theory is, however, professionally and politically 'safer', which may help to explain its popularity. The analysis of educational ideas, whether in particular specialisms such as administration, or on a more general front, has too seldom involved a sufficiently sophisticated approach to the relationships between intellectual, social and political history. It is clear that many aspects of contemporary educational ideas, such as the emphasis placed upon child centredness, the justifications put forward for various kinds of instructional grouping in schools, the ways in which the reorganization of secondary education is legitimized and—who knows—some of the presently fashionable techniques in our own specialism, are all profoundly ideological in character. Conant's saying, 'science owes more to the steam engine than the steam engine to science' has applications in our own field too.

Among other relevant headings suggested by Wirth are the motives and interests that prompt certain groups to promote and to disseminate particular educational ideas, how the interests and purposes of such groups come to find expression in specific theories, doctrines and intellectual movements, and the recognition that is accorded to different types of knowledge as evidenced by the resources devoted to their cultivation. His most immediately significant heading for our present purposes relates to the need for a 'systematic analysis of the institutional organization within the framework of which intellectual activity is carried on. This involves, among other items, the study of schools, universities, academies, learned societies, museums, libraries, research institutions, and laboratories, foundations and publishing facilities'. Wirth argues that it is important to find out how and by whom these activities and institutions are supported, their inter-relations and internal organization.

Here we are at the heart of the area of empirical enquiry to the importance of which attention has already been drawn. Some of the data for such enquiries is already available in the form of catalogues, calendars, programmes of study, prospectuses and other documents issued by the organizations which offer courses of study in our field. Yet little work of this kind has in fact been done. A study such as that by Gregg and Sims (1972) provides valuable information, focussed in this case on the assessment by faculty members of the quality of staff and programmes of graduate departments of educational administration in major universities in the United States. At a more informal level, Gibson (1972) has undertaken an impressionistic survey of what professors of educational administration regard as the most important books and articles to which their students should be referred. (A study of the titles suggested by three or more of his respondents, and of the disciplinary bases and theoretical orientations of the works represented, would be of interest. The list of authors will be a familiar one to most readers. It includes Barnard, Bennis, Benne and Chin, Benson, Bidwell, Blau, Bruner, Callahan, Campbell, Etzioni, Griffiths, Gulick, Halpin, Homans, Katz and Kahn, Machiavelli, March and Simon, McGregor, Roethlisberger and Dickson, Schmuck and Miles, Silverman, Tead, Toffler, Waller and Weber.) It is not difficult to think of some of the kinds of research that would be relevant to a better understanding of the 'institutional organization within the framework of which' research and the study of educational administration are carried on.

Finally, but not less important, Wirth believes that attention has to be given to the 'persons who are the bearers of intellectual activity'. It is members of this group who set and mark examination papers, recommend book lists, supervise and direct educational research and development activities, devise curricula, teach students, order library books, address conferences, contribute to the journals of our trade, and undertake all the other tasks that collectively add up to the activity of 'doing educational administration'. Questions have to be asked about the composition of the group, the social origins of its members and the means by which they are recruited, their class affiliations, rewards and prestige, and their internal professional organization.

The number of studies of this kind is growing, but there have been few in our own field. Work such as that by Halsey and Trow (1972) and Caplow and McGee (1958) are now quite widely known. In the United States Campbell and Newell (1973) have conducted a study of US professors of educational administration that contains little for our comfort. It appears that professors in our field are in the main part of 'middle class America'. They are the products of the education divisions of the publicly supported universities, and only a small proportion have training in one of the basic disciplines that underpin the study of administration. Although individuals holding appointments as professors of educational administration can be found in no fewer than 311 universities in North America, only 59 of these are in membership of the University Council for Educational Administration. It appears, too, that professors of educational administration have little time for or inclination towards research, and that their activities outside the classroom tend to be focussed more upon field studies and consultancies. Campbell and Newell report that a research commitment of as much as fifty per cent of an individual's time was desired by only six per cent of the entire group. They comment that 'it seems doubtful that a professional field can be appropriately developed with so little energy going into its study'. These findings confirm the impression given by earlier studies such as those by Hills (1965) and Haller (1968).

But caution is needed in the use we make of a sociology of knowledge perspective in helping to explain the research-study-practice relationship in a field such as educational administration. It is an easy step from identifying the ways in which occupational location—as administrator, professor, researcher—helps to define criteria of relevance and to shape the appreciative frameworks characteristic of particular groups, to believing that there is no sure basis of knowledge on which to stand

and that everything is relative to position and group interest. Too many people have taken this step. To do so is to travesty the intentions and insights of those who have helped to develop the analytic usefulness of the sociology of knowledge. Lukes (1973) has recently asserted the claim that 'there are no good reasons for supposing that all criteria of truth and validity are (as many have been tempted to suppose) context dependent and variable' and that 'there are good reasons for maintaining that some are not, that these are universal and fundamental, and that those criteria which *are* context dependent are parasitic upon them'. Merton (1972) sees the claims for relativity as an aspect of what he calls 'insider doctrine'.

... that doctrine assumes total coincidence between social position and individual perspectives. It thus exaggerates into error the conception of structural analysis that there is a *tendency for*, *not a full determination of*, socially patterned differences in the perspectives, preferences and behaviour of people variously located in the social structure. The theoretical emphasis on tendency, as distinct from uniformity, is basic, not casual or niggling.

We would do well to heed this warning if we are to recognize both the usefulness and the limitations of the sociology of knowledge perspective.

III

The kind of research that gets done in educational administration, and the ways in which its findings affect the climate of ideas in the field, the socialization of practitioners and the availability of tools and techniques, depends in part on the place that such research is seen as occupying within the framework of human and social studies. Educational administration usually features as one of the options or specialisms offered by a university, school or department of education. In the U K it has recently begun to feature in the programmes of university and polytechnic schools of management and administration, outside the framework of educational studies. In such management settings there is a stronger emphasis on the quantitative and planning aspects of educational administration and on its relationships with the other administrative functions of local and central authorities. At the same time the study of educational administration in university schools of education is showing signs of fragmentation, with interest and resources being directed towards educational planning, the administration of particular sectors of educational provision, such as higher education, and to economic, financial and accounting problems, rather than 'educational administration' as such. It is difficult at this time to forecast the long-term significance of these trends, especially for research and its impact on practice. What looks to be happening is a greater concern with the development of sophisticated administrative and planning procedures and techniques, at the expense of more general studies of educational leadership and organization.

Whilst not wishing to limit the study of educational administration to Schools, Departments and Institutes of Education, I would myself want to argue that these organizations have a special responsibility for work in this field. First, because as I have suggested elsewhere (Taylor, 1969), we must increasingly think not of the education and training of administrators, but of preparing a variety of educational personnel for the performance of administrative functions. Second, because professors and students of educational administration gain much from working alongside those who are concerned with the analysis of educational process from the standpoint of other disciplines. Third, because administration in the field of education has special characteristics that mark it off from administration in other fields of activity, some of which appear to be threatened by developments associated with the recent local government reorganization in England and Wales. If research and study in educational administration is to be seen as an aspect of educational studies, we need to examine the place that it occupies within this broader framework.

There have been few attempts to examine and categorise the development of educational studies in the United Kingdom. Such analyses as have been made are closely linked to histories of teacher training, for it was only when separate institutional provision began to be made for the education and training of men and women to staff the schools that there emerged courses in the theory and practice of learning and teaching. Not that the kinds of knowledge included in such courses were new. The distinction between knowledge of a subject and knowledge about how to teach it had little meaning in earlier times. As Simon (1970) has pointed out, the great works of medieval scholasticism were essentially textbooks, designed to be used for the purpose of teaching. Earlier still, it was Aristotle who averred that the surest sign of a man's wisdom was his capacity to teach what he knew. Anyone familiar with nineteenth-century accounts and analyses of European and American teacher education will know that nearly all the issues that bother contemporary teacher educators, such as certification, induction into teaching, the relationship between academic, professional and practical work in courses of teacher preparation, and the specificity of training needed by those aspiring to work with children of different age groups, were very much live issues a hundred or more years ago.

In the dominant model of educational studies in this country, educational theory is conceived as a composite body of knowledge that issues in principles for practice, and educational studies as an area in which contributions from a variety of distinctive disciplines and forms of knowledge are brought to bear upon educational problems. This model can be seen reflected in syllabuses, the organization of courses and educational research, and in staffing policies and practices in colleges and universities. It is tempting to look at it in terms of what Thomas Kuhn (1962, 1970) has called a paradigm of knowledge,[1] and the attempt has in fact been made (Musgrave, 1971).

Kuhn's ideas have received a great deal of criticial attention from philosophers of science, historians and sociologists in the thirteen years since the publication of the first edition of *Structure of Scientific Revolutions*. It has been asserted that quite apart from its not being original (Toulmin, 1972) Kuhn uses the concept of paradigm in twenty-one distinctive and inconsistent senses (Masterman, 1970), that scientific change does not take place in the way that he describes (Watkins, 1970; Pearce Williams, 1970), and that his more recent amendments, which stress the importance of many 'mini revolutions' rather than a few examples of scientific catastrophism, rob the theory of whatever

[1] Kuhn's concept of paradigm is an important part of his theory of intellectual revolutions. In any scientific field, there are for a time certain theories and methodologies which command widespread professional assent, and which suggest the 'puzzles' which practitioners will try to solve. This paradigm is never completely rigid. After a time 'a growing sense ... that an existing paradigm has ceased to function adequately in the exploration of an aspect of nature to which that paradigm has previously led the way' inaugurates a scientific revolution. Kuhn labels scientific activity during the period between the revolutions 'normal science' and argues that by 'focussing attention upon a small range of relatively esoteric problems, the paradigm forces scientists to investigate some part of nature in a detail and depth that would be otherwise unimaginable ... during the period when the paradigm is successful, the profession will have solved problems that its members could scarcely have imagined and never have undertaken without commitment to the paradigm'. (Kuhn, 1970)

explanatory value it might once have possessed (Toulmin, 1972).

Perhaps more seriously for our present purposes, it is also argued that the concept of paradigm cannot be applied to the social sciences and the humanities without distorting both the theories that it represents and the facts that it is intended to explain (Smolicz, 1970; Martins, 1972).

Whilst, therefore, there are good reasons for avoiding the use of paradigm in the present context, many aspects of what has been said by Kuhn and his critics, and by other philosophers and historians of science, remain relevant to an explanation of how changes take place in the organization and content of educational studies and to the place and importance of educational administration within this framework. Such an approach is in accordance with what Polanyi (1958) has called the 'principle of overlapping neighbourhoods', whereby the content and methods of a specialism are influenced by the functional interdependence of all the specialities in a given field (Martins, 1972).

The current model of educational studies in this country emphasises that education cannot claim to be a discipline in its own right, but what Peters has spoken of as a 'focus, or meeting place of disciplines' (Walton and Keuthe, 1963). A similar approach was taken more than ten years ago in the United States by Conant in comparing the structure of educational studies with that in medicine:

I doubt that there is or ever will be a science of medicine, yet I am sure enormous strides forward have been made in the medical sciences. Therefore I think it would be better to discuss the academic disciplines that have relevance for the labours of the teacher than to try to talk in terms of the developing science of education. In other words, I shall examine academic disciplines—what might be called educational sciences or educational disciplines—rather than the science or the discipline of education.

What Hirst (1963, 1966) has to say about the nature of educational theory has been widely, if not always accurately, interpreted as a prescription for the organization of educational studies.

The theory is not itself an autonomous 'form' of knowledge or an autonomous discipline. It involves no conceptual structure unique in its logical features and no unique tests for validity ... Educational principles are justified entirely by direct appeal to knowledge from a variety of forms, scientific, philosophical, historical, etc. ... Beyond these forms of knowledge it requires no theoretical synthesis.

If the qualities of educational judgements rest solely on the validity of the relevant knowledge contributed from the various 'forms', then it follows that we should concentrate our attention on the latter, developing research and teaching in the philosophy, history, sociology and psychology of education. In some universities, the fact that education lacks an autonomous theory, and seems incapable of attracting first-class minds, has encouraged consideration to be given to the possibility of dividing responsibility for educational studies between existing departments of psychology, philosophy, sociology and history, such education staff as *are* recruited having the task of co-ordinating these contributions and maintaining the necessary clinical relationships with the schools. The lack of a specific disciplinary affiliation as psychologists, sociologists and so forth, has in some cases become a serious impediment to obtaining a post in orthodox departments in universities and colleges, and a reason for some felt anxiety about identity among the existing ranks of such teachers.

The stress during the past ten years on the disciplines that underly educational study, the attempt to recruit staff who have respectable backgrounds in these disciplines and who are willing and able to initiate research firmly based on a knowledge of what has already been done and on the best available methodology and forms of analysis, has all had a favourable effect on the status, standing and intellectual credentials of educational study. But I do not think that those who profess Education in universities have given nearly enough thought to how the contributions made by sociologists, psychologists, philosophers and others might be related to one another in courses and programmes of study that are both personally educative and professionally relevant, in the sense that they bring about 'the gradual transformation of a person's view of children, of himself and the situation in which he is acting' (Peters, 1968). Efforts to strengthen the disciplinary bases of educational studies are only likely to be useful if they are accompanied by a parallel and equally energetic effort to explicate concepts and develop theories that will guide educational action.

There seems little doubt that the quality of the bricks that make up the edifice of educational studies has improved and is improving. Too little attention, however, has been given to producing a design for the building as a whole and a specification for the cement that holds the bricks together. It is perhaps not unfair to say that, having conceded the logical impossibility of the synthesis to which Hirst refers, university men have to some extent turned away from thinking through the kind of educational theory that might be most relevant and useful in decision-making and curriculum-building. To put the matter crudely, and perhaps unfairly, the academic educationist has become mesmerized on the one hand by the importance of disciplinary respectability, and on the other by a weight of organizational responsibility, field activity and consultancy that both seduces talent and conceals mediocrity. Students and practitioners, left to make their own synthesis, tend as a consequence to be too much open to influence by producers of educational ephemera, by those who live on the identification and discussion of 'burning issues of the day', by educational journalists, pundits and commentators and all the other creations of the media.

I am not trying to suggest that the activities of all these people are intrinsically harmful or unnecessary. Manifestly they are not. Education is a highly political activity, and educational issues must inevitably stand high on the agenda in our public concerns. But I *am* suggesting that universities have a responsibility to promote and sustain a level of intellectual effort in the field of Education that in some places seems to be lacking. By separating out the contribution of the various 'disciplines', and asserting that they are all of equal importance, and by agreeing that the range and complexity of modern knowledge about education rules out the possibility of being a successful generalist, we have made the need for a systematic debate about the nature and organization of educational studies much less pressing. This can only do harm, both to the willingness of funding agencies and others to support within universities the kind of work that is needed to throw light upon pressing educational problems, and on the availability of really first-class people willing to turn their minds and dedicate their professional efforts to some of the interpretative and applied fields of educational study, such as administration.

IV

Whilst no doubt we could readily be persuaded to agree on the desirability of more research being carried out in fields relevant to the practice of educational administration, on better means being made available for the dissemination of research findings, and on the importance of relating such findings to practical decision-making in classroom and office, it has to be recognized that what the researcher, the student of educational administration and the practising administrator respectively have to say about the research-study-practice relationship often implies conflicting claims to power and influence. The problem of theory and practice is kept alive and well and living in conference halls throughout the hemispheres by the frequently heard complaints of research workers about the refusal of practitioners to listen to them and equally forceful complaints by practitioners about the irrelevance and pointlessness of much of the research that gets funded. The appointment of new kinds of change agents (Havelock, 1968; Hoyle, 1972) such as Inspectors, Organisers, Advisers and advisory teachers ('part-time in their classrooms, part-time in other peoples'') does not solve the problem if these interstitial roles themselves become professionalized and generate their own kinds of performance imperative. Efforts to limit the ossifying effects of a rigid cognitive division of labour, by such devices as short-term secondments, sabbaticals and study leave, action and team research and so forth are all to be welcomed. There is little doubt that their more widespread use would facilitate research findings being brought to bear upon action in the field, and ensure that the problems thrown up by such action are fed back into decisions about research policy and into substantive research activity. But there is a sense in which the lack of immediate impact of research and theory upon practice is the price that has to be paid for freedom to theorise. Ernest Gellner (1973) talks about the importance of what he calls the 'entrenched clauses' in society:

I can divide the stock of my ideas and convictions into those which can be denied or replaced without significantly disturbing my total picture and composure, and those which can only be budged at the cost of a wide dislocation and disturbance ... there is no special, privileged type of basket into which all societies place their most valuable eggs. You cannot say, for instance, that in any society the world foundation story, or the rule for selecting political leaders, or theology, or the rules governing sexual behaviour, will be singled out for special reverance and cross-tied by so many firm links to all other institutions, that they cannot be shaken without everything else being shaken ... the sacred may lurk in the most unexpected quarters.

Gellner goes on to point out that an empiricist view of the world stresses its mosaic-like qualities, in which the parts are independent of one another and can be rejected and replaced without the structure of the whole being threatened; the entrenched clauses have been eroded virtually to one, namely 'the existence and nature of the mosaic's framework itself ...' In such a world, cognition enjoys some kind of diplomatic immunity.

The fact that undertaking research and theorising involves no direct threat to accepted practices means that it can be permitted with a minimum of social constraint. If the links between research and practice were immediate and direct, there would be much more interest in controlling the process and ensuring some kind of doctrinal uniformity. Similarly, courses of study that lead to recognized professional qualifications, and which are pre-requisites for the performance of professional roles, are much more likely to be open to criticism, comment and sometimes even to direct intervention than those offered on an open market or voluntary basis. There are costs attached to everything. The research worker and the professor who want to extend their influence over what goes on in classroom and administrative office need to recognize the price that they may have to pay.

All this said, there is growing recognition of the need to improve opportunities for in-service education that enable practitioners to come into contact with the findings of research and with those who undertake it; to involve in our field specialists in the basic social science disciplines who know what the relevant work is, where it is to be found and how its results are to be interpreted; to encourage the development of digests, reviews, abstracting services and all the other means of diffusion and dissemination that enable information to be made available to those who need it, when and where it is required; to provide incentives (higher degrees, salary increments, promotion opportunities) for practitioners to continue their studies; to furnish appropriate levels of support for an adequate range of new work on topics and themes in the selection of which those in the field have played a full part, and to create and sustain an appropriate institutional structure for the support of research and study in educational administration, including national and international bodies such as BEAS, UCEA and CCEA, that transcend frontiers created by national histories, specialist roles and the division of cognitive labour.

All these are steps in a piecemeal process that has no readily definable end or objective, which leads to no final reconciliation of theory and practice, no eventual integration of professorial, practitioner and research roles, no Nirvana in which the problems no longer exist. Our progress is like that of the pedestrian on a crowded pavement, where each move is taken with reference to a complex series of predictions about how other people will behave and with the object of ensuring that the point reached by the next step, and the one after that, will maximize the possibility of dealing with unforeseen events

To achieve a satisfactory accommodation of research, study and practice requires a recognition of the complexities and contingencies that characterize the knowledge system of educational administration, a willingness patiently to disentangle, by means of empirical enquiry, its connections and constraints, and an appreciation of the importance for the nature and direction of our efforts of the social and institutional contexts within which they are carried out.

BIBLIOGRAPHY

Baldamus, W. (1973), 'The Role of Discoveries in Social Science', in Shanin, T. (ed), *The Rules of the Game: Cross-Disciplinary Essays on Modes in Scholarly Thought*, Tavistock, London.

Bennis, W. G., Benne, K. and Chin. R. (1961), *The Planning of Change*, Holt Rinehart, New York.

Campbell, R. F. and Newell, L. J. (1973), 'A Study of Professors of Educational Administration', *Educational Administration Quarterly*, Autumn.

Caplow, T. and McGee, R. C. (1958), *The American Academic Market Place*, Basic Books, New York.

Conant, J. B. (1964), *The Education of American Teachers*, McGraw-Hill, New York.

Dalin, P. (1973), *Strategies for Innovation in Education*, OECD, Paris.

Ford, P. (1968), *Social Theory and Social Practice*, Irish University Press, Shannon.

Gellner, E. (1973), 'The Savage and the Modern Mind', in Horton, R. and Finnegan, R. (eds), *Modes of Thought*, Faber and Faber, London.

Gibson, R. O. (1972), *Educational Administration Readings Survey* (Mimeo), State University of New York, Buffalo.

Gregg, R. T. and Sims, P. O. (1972), 'Quality of Faculties and Programmes of Graduate Departments of Educational Administration', *Educational Administration Quarterly*, Autumn.

Haller, E. J. (1968), 'The Interdisciplinary Ideology in Educational Administration', *Educational Administration Quarterly*, Spring.

Halsey, A. H. and Trow, M. (1972), *The British Academics*, Faber and Faber, London.

Hammond, P. E. (ed) (1964), *Sociologists at Work*, Basic Books, New York.

Havelock, R. G. (1968a), *Bibliography on Knowledge Utilization and Dissemination*, Centre for Research on Utilization of Scientific Knowledge, Ann Arbor, Michigan.

Havelock, R. G. (1968b), 'Dissemination and Translation Roles', in Eidell, T. L. and Kitchel, J. M. (eds), *Knowledge Production and Utilization in Educational*

Administration, University Council for Educational Administration, Columbus, Ohio.

Havelock, R. G. (1971), 'The Utilization of Educational Research and Development', *British Journal of Educational Technology*, 2(2).

Hills, J. (1965), 'Social Science, Ideology and the Professor of Educational Administration', *Educational Administration Quarterly*, Autumn.

Hirst, P. H. (1963), 'Philosophy and the Study of Education', *British Journal of Educational Studies*.

Hirst, P. H. (1966), 'Educational Theory', in Tibble, J. W. (ed), *The Study of Education*, Routledge & Kegan Paul, London.

Hoyle, E. (1970), 'Planned Organizational Change in Education', *Research in Education*, 3, May.

Hoyle, E. (1972), 'The Role of the Change Agent in Educational Innovation', in Walton, J. (ed), *Curriculum Organization and Design*, Ward Lock, London.

Kuhn, T. S. (1962, 1970), *Structure of Scientific Revolutions*, University of Chicago Press, Chicago.

Lukes, S. (1973), 'On the Social Determinants of Truth', in Horton, R. and Finnegan, R. (eds), *Modes of Thought*, Faber and Faber, London.

Mannheim, K. (1936), *Ideology and Utopia*, Kegan Paul, London.

Martins, H. (1972), ' "The Khunian Revolution" and its implications for Sociology', in Nossiter, T. J., Hanson, A. H. and Rokkan, S. (eds), *Imagination and Precision in the Social Sciences*, Faber and Faber, London.

Masterman, M. (1970), 'The Nature of a Paradigm', in Lakatos, I. and Musgrave, A. (eds), *Criticism and the Growth of Knowledge*, Cambridge University Press, London.

Merton, R. K. (1972), 'Insiders and Outsiders: A Chapter in the Sociology of Knowledge', in American Journal of Sociology, *Varieties of Political Expression in Sociology*, University of Chicago Press, Chicago.

Musgrave, P. W. (1971), 'Some Social Functions of Theory in Teaching', *Australian Journal of Education*, 15(2), June.

Pearce Williams, L. (1970), 'Normal Science, Scientific Revolutions and the History of Science', in Lakatos, I. and Musgrave, A., *Criticism and the Growth of Knowledge*, Cambridge University Press, London.

Peters, R. S. (1968), 'Theory and Practice in Teacher Training', in *Trends in Education*, 9.

Polanyi, M. (1958), *Personal Knowledge*, London.

Rogers, E. M. and Shoemaker, F. F. (1971), *Communication of Innovations: A Cross-Cultural Approach*, Free Press, New York.

Schmuck, R. and Miles, M. (1971), *Organizational Development in Schools*, National Press Books, Palo Alto, California.

Simon, B. (1973), 'Research in the History of Education', in Taylor, W. (ed), op. cit.

Simon, J. (1970), *The Social Origins of English Education*, Routledge & Kegan Paul, London.

Smolicz, J. J. (1970), 'Paradigms and Models: A Comparison of Intellectual Frameworks in Natural Sciences and Sociology', *Australian and New Zealand Journal of Sociology*, (2).

Taylor, W. (1969), 'Issues and Problems in Training the School Administrator', in Baron, G. and Taylor, W. (eds), *Educational Administration and the Social Sciences*, Athlone Press, London.

Taylor, W. (ed) (1973), *Research Perspectives in Education*, Routledge & Kegan Paul, London.

Toulmin, S. (1972), *Human Understanding*, Clarendon Press, Oxford.

Walton, J. and Keuthe, J. L. (eds) (1963), *The Disciplines of Education*, University of Wisconsin Press, Wisconsin.

Watkins, J. W. N. (1970), 'Against "Normal Science" ', in Lakatos, I. and Musgrave, A., *Criticism and the Growth of Knowledge*, Cambridge/London, University Press.

Watson, J. D. (1968), *The Double Helix: A Personal Account of the Discovery of the Structure of DNA*, Weidenfeld and Nicolson, London.

Wirth, L. (1936), Preface to Mannheim, K., op. cit.

14 Educational Administration Research: Progress Reports

1 Research Trends in the United States

R. OLIVER GIBSON

Research in the field of education is so varied and the criteria applied to its evaluation are so dependent upon differing perspectives and upon the role of knowledge that any general assessment is an extremely hazardous undertaking at best. There are problems of conscious selection of materials, unconscious omissions of results, bias stemming from perspective and limitations in the nature and use of the existing information systems. Consequently, this review is presented in a highly tentative mode.

PROPOSED ANALYTIC FRAMEWORK

In recent years analysis of the nature of scientific development has been pursued by such writers as Northrop (1947) and Kuhn (1970). Northrop's analysis of stages of inquiry tends to focus the study of particular problems by identification of (1) problem statement, (2) the natural history stage and (3) the stage of deductively formulated theory. Kuhn has identified a pre-paradigm period followed by the paradigm period which may in turn become a pre-period for the emergence of other paradigms. In the Postscript to the second edition (pp. 174–210) Kuhn identifies what he calls the 'disciplinary matrix' which includes certain symbolic generalizations, certain beliefs, values and exemplars. It appears that the matrix is a broadly shared set of beliefs about the field and, as such, might be called an ideology of the field. Such beliefs are distinguished from the more restricted theory, model or paradigm that serves to guide scientific investigation of scholars in the field. Kuhn also distinguishes among emergence of *community, transition* and the period of *consensus on 'paradigms'* of the field. Clearly Kuhn has in mind a continuous social process in which ideas flow and ebb. Periods are useful for analytic purposes but the process itself is in no way segmented.

It may be that the basic process involved here is one of maturation of a profession, field or discipline. Usage of the words 'research' and 'science' appears to involve a transition from simple descriptive experience to a stage where observed facts are 'systematically classified' through the use of 'intellectual techniques', 'schemes of abstraction', or 'paradigms'. It seems useful, then, to distinguish among (1) the period of emergence of community, (2) the transition period and (3) the period of maturity. It appears that those stages (they are bound, as already pointed out, to be analytically arbitrary to a degree without clear demarcations in real time) may be characterized along the following lines:

COMMUNITY DEVELOPMENT	TRANSITION	MATURITY
Emergence of groupings	Reduction of groups approaching one	Recognized intellectual techniques
Variety of groupings	Increasing consensus	Conscious transmission to students
Lack of consensus on generalizations, beliefs, values, etc.	Development of community media	Community validation through community media
Emphasis upon direct observation, cases, etc.	Reduction of diversity in definition, etc.	Intellectual technique replacement
	Growing emphasis upon intellectual techniques	

Research in educational administration may be recognized as a basically contemporary phenomenon that mirrors trends already apparent in a larger field. The emergence of a research community in education in the United States occurred in the second quarter of the present century. From this there emerged the basis for a research community in educational administration that took shape by the end of that period, signalled by the organization of the National Conference of Professors of Educational Administration. It was organized initially at a meeting of the American Association of School Administrators, indicative of a tradition of association with the practice of school administration. The *Review of Educational Research* already provided a form of community research synthesis under the control of a larger grouping. For rough analytic purposes it is assumed that the pre-1950 period can usefully be designated as the community development period. The transition period is seen as that since 1950 to the present. It will be contended that current developments are in some ways indicative of growing readiness for a stage of maturity.

TRANSITION PERIOD (1950—PRESENT AND BEYOND)

The transitory nature of affairs in educational administration in the period immediately after 1950 has been widely recognized. In the Introduction to the 1955 *Review of Educational Research* the new trend was identified and some of the concomitant conditions cited. Gregg, writing on 'Preparation of Administrators' in the 1969 Fourth Edition of the *Encyclopedia of Educational Research* wrote, 'The decade of the 1950s, particularly, was one of much ferment in the study of administration' (p. 994). In the same article Gregg went on to say, 'The field of educational administration has not been distinguished by its research, whether done by students or by professors.'

In this early stage of maturation it could be expected that there would be a relatively strong emphasis upon data collection for descriptive purposes. Two such modes might be cases and field studies. The use of cases has been broadened greatly during the transition period; however, the emphasis has been almost exclusively on use for teaching rather than for research purposes. *Case Studies in Educational Administration: An Information Storage and Retrieval System*, published in 1965 by the University Council for Educational Administration, suggests a move toward research potential; however, the Introduction continues the teaching emphasis: 'We believe that this system will provide the professor of educational administration with the necessary tools for locating, in a reasonable period of time, case studies useful in a particular teaching situation' (Horvat, 1965, p. i). Field studies have also been used primarily for teaching purposes with a strong emphasis upon service to the field. Thus there was a major element of factual-normative data collection directed toward the practicalities of decision making. Illustrative of efforts at a more research oriented analysis are Griffiths *et al.*, 'Teacher Mobility in New York City' (1965) and Willower, 'Hypotheses on the School as a Social System' (1965). On the whole, however, cases and field studies have not emphasized empirical data for research purposes.

At the same time there was emerging a concern for the use of theory in research. For the first time the Review of 1958 contained a chapter on administrative theory. In 1956 the *Administrative Science Quarterly* commenced publication. At about the same time publications on theory by Coladarci and Getzels (1955), Halpin (1958) and Griffiths (1959) indicated an emergent trend toward use of intellectual techniques within the field. As such, the set of events could be viewed as a bell-wether in the transition from the early stage toward a more mature scientific status. The Review again in 1961 included a chapter on the relationship of theory to research. This trend emerged again in the Review of 1964 in a chapter on the 'science of administration' in which the straightforward claim was made, 'A science of administration is emerging' (34 (4), Oct. 1964, p. 485).

The last Review (1967) to appear did not include a chapter with a title that dealt with theory or science. In the Foreword, Ericson contended, 'The erstwhile search for "administrative theory", for example, seems virtually abandoned today ...' (37 (4), October 1967, p. 376). In the 1964 Review, Lipham had already sensed a change in the theory movement and had cast it in rather more positive terms, 'It is probably accurate to conclude that during the past several years there has been substantially less theorizing about theory and considerably more application of existing behavioral science theories, particularly social systems theory, to the problems of educational administration' (1964, p. 450). However, in 1970 Halpin contended that the theory movement had fizzled (p. 2). In the absence of reviews of research in educational administration since 1967 the trend is somewhat obscure. It is still moot whether the theory movement has been incorporated into the fabric of research or whether it has aborted. Probably the answer is somewhere in between.

Each of the reviews of research during this transition period has registered dismay at the quality of research being undertaken in educational administration, particularly the theoretical shortcomings and lack of consensus on definition. It has been pointed out that Gregg reiterated that position in 1969. The recent study by Campbell and Newell reaches a similar conclusion, 'Professors of educational administration engage in many activities, but they appear to have little time for, or inclination toward research' (1973, p. 138).

Much of the above alludes to an immature but maturing field. One of the indicators of transition toward maturity has been noted as the development of media of communication within the research field. The University Council for Educational Administration emerged in the later fifties and took on increasing vigour in the sixties. Also during the sixties, educational administration took on a clearer research identity through becoming a Division within the American Educational Research Association. In 1965, UCEA commenced publication of the *Educational Administration Quarterly* and started publishing *Educational Administration Abstracts* the following year. These developments may be seen as further maturing of the research community. At the 1974 annual meeting of the educational administration division of AERA the decision was made to reinstitute regular reviews of research in educational administration. In the Presidential Address at the 1974 annual meeting of UCEA, Willower stated that during recent years, roughly that characterized here as the transition period, ' ... we got what science commonly confers: some frameworks that varied in scope and coherence but were at least directed toward explanation, some tentative conclusions that denied the quest for certainty and remained open to correction and revision, and a greater incidence, if not a wide acceptance, of a probing, critical stance devoted to the question, why?!' (p. 1). He went on to call for an initiative through UCEA to further the development of knowledge. The study by Campbell and Newell reports a clearly identifiable group of professors whom they designate as purist-researchers (1973, p. 99) who are part of a larger research-oriented group of 'cosmopolitans' that make up about one-fifth of professors. In sum, the above seems to indicate that media have been institutionalized, that further thrusts are being initiated and that there is a core of professors with commitment to maturing of the field.

CURRENT RESEARCH EMPHASES

Recent policy priorities have tended to be reflected in the research that has appeared. Concern for equal educational opportunity has been associated with studies of financing, productivity and ways of equalizing financing and benefits. The following are illustrative of this emphasis: research applications in budgeting (programmed budgeting, PPBS), in person-organization relationships (Organizational Development), planning and accountability together with performance appraisal. There continues to be a number of studies that treat variables in person-organization relationships particularly in relation to bureaucratic status and degree of participation in decision making. Some attention has been given to belief systems (ideologies) as a way of explaining organizational behaviour.

For a field in which administrative courses of action are bound to be of critical importance, the absence of longitudinal studies is noticeable. Related, perhaps, is the relative absence of systematic analysis of policy and planning processes. The University Council for Educational Administration, however, is publishing a book of 'analytics', *Futurism in Education* (Stephen Hencley and James Yates, eds), which provides various techniques which lend themselves to forecasting and longitudinal analysis. One indicator of maturation, it has been suggested, is the attention given to intellectual techniques for purposes of analysis.

It is also noteworthy that, in a recent analysis of studies reported in the *Educational Administration Quarterly* and *Administrator's Notebook*, Brown (1972) distinguished between those which use 'hard' and 'soft' theory and those using 'hard' and 'soft' data. He came to the conclusion that 96 out of 175 studies (55 per cent) fell in the category of soft data and soft theory while two studies (1 per cent) could be placed in the hard data-hard theory classification. Perhaps of more significance within the present analysis is the fact that the next frequency (28 or 17 per cent) was soft theory-hard data. Such a pattern would seem to be consistent with a transitional field where theory is emerging and will increasingly be available to be tested against data.

In this paper research trends in educational administration have been conceptualized in terms of categories growing out of the work of Kuhn and others. The field of educational administration is seen as having gone through the stage of community development; it is now well into a transition stage, and is moving towards a future status of research which will be characterized by the use of intellectual techniques for the analysis of interesting problems. The trends perceived, though lacking the rigour of quantification, suggest that, in the field of research in educational administration in the United States, some of the critical components necessary for the emergence of an early stage of maturity are in the process of development.

BIBLIOGRAPHY

American Educational Research Association, *Review of Educational Research*, various issues, published since 1931.

Brown, Daniel J. (1972), *The Poverty of Educational Administration: A Case for Mathematical Modelling*, Paper presented at AERA.

Campbell, Roald F. and Newell, L. Jackson (1973), *A Study of Professors of Educational Administration*, University Council for Educational Administration, Columbus, Ohio.

Coladarci, Arthur P. and Getzels, Jacob W. (1955), *The Use of Theory in Educational Administration*, Stanford University Press, Stanford.

Gregg, Russell T. (1969), 'Preparation of Administrators', *Encyclopedia of Educational Research*, 4th edn, Robert L. Ebel (ed), Macmillan, New York.

Griffiths, Daniel E. (1959), *Administrative Theory*, Appleton-Century-Crofts, New York.

Griffiths, Daniel E. *et al.* (1965), 'Teacher Mobility in New York City', *Educational Administration Quarterly*, 1(1), 15–31.

Halpin, Andrew W. (1958), *Administrative Theory in Education*, Midwest Administration Center, University of Chicago, Chicago.

Halpin, Andrew W. (1970), 'Administrative Theory: The Fumbled Torch', in Kroll, Arthur M. (ed), *Issues in American Education*, Oxford University Press, New York, pp. 156–83.

Hills, Jean (1965), 'Social Science, Ideology and the Professor of Educational Administration', *Educational Administration Quarterly*, 1(3), 23–39.

Horvat, John J. *et al.* (1965), *Case Studies in Educational Administration: An Information Storage and Retrieval System*, University Council for Educational Administration, Columbus, Ohio.

Kuhn, Thomas S. (1970), *Structure of Scientific Revolutions*, 2nd edn, University of Chicago Press, Chicago.

Northrop, F. S. C. (1947), *The Logic of the Sciences and the Humanities*, Macmillan, New York.

Shibles, Mark R. (1973), *Significant Educational Research During the Past Ten Years*, Paper presented at AASA.

University Council for Educational Administration (1974), *Newsletter*, 15(4), 1–5.

Willower, Donald J. (1965), 'Hypotheses on the School as a Social System', *Educational Administration Quarterly*, 1(3), 40–51.

2 Research and Development in Canada

E. A. HOLDAWAY

The main purpose of this paper is to present some information and opinions concerning research and development (R & D) in educational administration in Canada. Because I am more familiar with research and development at the University of Alberta than elsewhere, the content largely draws from that experience. Some information based on correspondence and publications from other sources has also been incorporated.[1]

The relevant OECD definitions (OECD, 1970) have been adopted, even though they tend to overlap. In paraphrased form they are:

1. *Research*—systematic inquiry to increase knowledge or to understand a subject.
2. *Basic Research*—original inquiry to provide more complete knowledge or understanding.
   (a) *Pure basic research*—generated by pure scientific curiosity;
   (b) *Oriented basic research*—undertaken to identify principles necessary to help solve practical problems.
3. *Applied Research*—investigation to solve recognized practical problems.
4. *Development*—systematic use of research results to introduce new processes or products, or to improve existing processes or products.

EDUCATIONAL RESEARCH AND DEVELOPMENT IN CANADA

Although many types of organizations are involved in educational research, by far the greatest amount is conducted by staff and students in the universities. The amount conducted in a faculty of education at a particular university depends upon several factors other than size—teaching load, interest in research, supporting services, availability of funds, and encouragement by colleagues are all involved, as is the presence or absence of a thesis requirement for a graduate degree.

[1]The assistance provided by Dr C. S. Bumbarger in reviewing a draft of this paper is acknowledged with thanks. Drs T. R. Williams, P. Dupuis, C. Bjarnason, R. O'Reilly, and K. W. Wallace provided information—this is also gratefully acknowledged.

Most provincial *departments of education* in Canada also have research divisions which vary considerably in size. The topics which they examine also show variety, but they normally tend to relate to practical problems. The *larger school districts* have research divisions: most of these seem to be organizers and facilitators of research, rather than conductors of research. Some provinces have *research institutes*, for example, the Educational Research Institute of British Columbia, which is an independent cooperative agency whose board members include representatives from many educational organizations.

Some provincial and national organizations also conduct and/or sponsor research, especially the teachers associations. The Canadian Educational Association is involved in research through (1) conducting some studies, (2) preparing research registers, and (3) organizing seminars for research officers of school districts. The fledgling Canadian Society for the Study of Education (established in 1972) consists of university and other personnel interested in educational research—its 800 members belong to CSSE and to at least one of seven constituent associations. The main CSSE functions are to represent educational research nationally, to conduct conferences, and to prepare publications.

A fundamental difference between Canada and other federal states such as Australia and the USA must be recognized. Constitutional and cultural differences will probably prevent the Canadian federal government from becoming involved in a national educational research effort, at least for the foreseeable future.

General Difficulties

Some general major difficulties can be identified in educational research conducted in Canada, particularly in research performed by university personnel. No doubt some of these difficulties are also experienced in other countries.

Structure. The over-riding structural difficulty appears to be the lack of formal integration, co-ordination and communication among agencies. Universities, school districts, and departments of education, even within one province, show little awareness of each other's research. Even within one university, research conducted by individual departments in a faculty of education is commonly unknown to other departments, although different departments may be tackling aspects of the same general problem. Another structural problem involves the lack of a unified educational research lobby at the federal and provincial government levels—without this voice, politicians remain uninformed about the needs and potential of research. The relationships between funding agencies and researchers and their institutions provides a third type of structural difficulty.

Functions and Types of Research. Some of the more commonly mentioned functional difficulties are the following.

(1) The universities are insufficiently involved in experimentation with new programmes and procedures, that is, they do not participate sufficiently in applied research and development.

(2) Researchers do not concentrate sufficiently upon the formulation of research problems nor do they try to identify problems of national importance. Getzels (1974, p. 5) quotes Einstein on this matter, 'The formulation of a problem is often more essential than its solution ...'. Getzels notes that solutions may be transitory, and urges that universities must continue to be involved in asking questions and obtaining information, and not merely deliver technical services or advocate policies.

(3) Because the United States performs most of the world's educational research, Canadian researchers must examine the need for duplication of US work and the opportunities and priorities for research into Canadian education.

(4) The adjudication of research proposals provides many difficulties with respect to assessment, the time involved (up to a year if over $5,000 is involved), and the usual inability to modify a proposal through meaningful interaction with knowledgeable fellow scholars. This particular difficulty makes contract research more desirable to some university staff.

(5) Research projects are too often 'one-shot affairs'. Long-term longitudinal projects, in which a series of individual studies can be incorporated, are rarely attempted.

(6) Insufficient attention is paid to the developmental phase of R & D—some university staff feel that it is not their responsibility, while those who attempt it often encounter considerable difficulty.

Resources. The most commonly mentioned difficulties relate to the numbers and skills of staff in a position to conduct research, and to the shortage of necessary finance. Staff shortages are particularly noticeable in the larger school districts.

Climate of Support. Educational research does not yet appear to be credible. Researchers face negative attitudes because (1) the usefulness of research is not always clearly explained, (2) universities sometimes impose what are seen to be heavy demands for involvement, (3) promised feedback is not always forthcoming, and (4) practitioners often expect immediately applicable results, and do not realize how much research is often required to find 'solutions'. Senior administrators seldom consider research findings when making decisions: perhaps this occurs because we have not been able to answer this question convincingly: 'What has educational research contributed to practice?'

Evaluative Criteria. All educational researchers face the difficulty of establishing criteria by which particular results obtained from their research can be judged.

UNIVERSITY RESEARCH IN EDUCATIONAL ADMINISTRATION IN CANADA

Establishment of the Division of Educational Administration at the University of Alberta in 1956 marked the beginning of organized teaching and research in educational administration in Canada. By 1972–3 the major universities in Canada all had graduate programmes in educational administration (Miklos, 1973). The consequent growth of departments of educational administration has meant an overall increase in research production. This increase was not accompanied by a corresponding development of a formal communication network, so staff in different universities were not really aware of each other's research. Formation of The Canadian Association for the Study of Educational Administration (CASEA) was partly in response to this need for better formal communication, not only with respect to research, but also in programme development.

Some Trends

Some general trends in research topics have been discerned in the Department of Educational Administration at the University of Alberta. With respect to *thesis subject matter*, the following sequence was identified by Dr E. D. Hodgson.

1. Role studies—of superintendents, principals, vice-principals, supervisors.
2. Leadership studies.
3. Organization studies—bureaucracy, professionalism, interaction analysis, organizational climate, etc.
4. As staff increased in size and in variety of interests, the above three

kinds of studies continued, but they tended to be overshadowed by
studies related to the following:
(a) Finance and Planning;
(b) Post-Secondary Education;
(c) History, Political Science, Law;
(d) Cultures and Acculturation.
5. Our present thesis topics appear to deal very largely with operational questions about schools and school systems (administrative
staff ratios, personnel utilization, expenditures and achievement,
administrator-faculty conflict, salaries and working conditions,
teacher evaluation, comparison of innovative high schools, etc.).

A trend to some *longitudinal research* has also occurred, e.g. in studying administrative ratios and innovation. Although such longitudinal
emphasis is desirable and recommended, planning of long-term continuing research is not easy—problems of continuity of staff and funding, and foresight in seeing how one phase can lead to another, are some
examples of difficulties.

The organization of research is likewise undergoing some evolutionary changes. More *project* work is now being conducted. Some of
this is in teams of staff and students, frequently in response to a problem
identified by a school system, a department of education, or a post-
secondary college. This may involve contract research, as in the case of
a current major evaluation of the system of Regional Offices of Education in Alberta, or individual non-funded studies. These projects also
include some research activities undertaken as requirements for
particular graduate level project courses.

Five other Canadian universities supplied information about their
educational administration research, particularly with respect to these
two questions:
(a) Do you have any policies (explicit or implicit) concerning the
basic-applied emphasis which is acceptable for thesis research?
(b) Has any trend occurred in the relative amounts of each of con-
tractural and scholar-generated research undertaken by your staff?
The following briefly summarizes the responses of these universities.

BASIC-APPLIED EMPHASIS ACCEPTABLE FOR THESES
University 1   Research should have practical use, i.e. provide information on actual operational educational problems:
whether this always occurs is questionable.

University 2 Both basic and applied research are acceptable: the criteria are rigorous methodology and educational significance.

University 3 A substantial theoretical base is required, and theses are theoretical rather than applied. More emphasis on investigating practical problems is desirable, but we lack knowledge of appropriate methodology.

University 4 Even if a thesis deals with actual problems, it must be presented within a theoretical framework.

University 5 All research must have a substantial theoretical base, but students are encouraged to provide information dealing with actual problems of educational systems. Such systems are granting increased access provided that a feedback mechanism is incorporated in the proposal.

TRENDS IN RELATIVE AMOUNTS OF CONTRACTUAL AND SCHOLAR-GENERATED RESEARCH

University 1 Very little contractual research: a university cannot be heavily involved in both research and teaching functions.

University 2 Mostly staff-generated.

University 3 Because the provincial government now grants substantial research contracts, most staff research has been of this type. However, teaching occupies much more staff time than does research.

University 4 Some very substantial contracts have been placed by school districts and the principals' federation. However, these research contracts are only accepted when they do not interfere with regular university instruction and other activities.

University 5 The amount of contractual research is continuing to increase. Joint research involving school districts may see the districts requesting provincial funds. However, control by the provincial government over release of reports from projects they have funded causes concern.

SUGGESTIONS FOR CONDUCTING R & D IN EDUCATIONAL ADMINISTRATION

The following suggestions are based upon the literature, our experience at the University of Alberta, and opinions of researchers in other Canadian organizations. They are thought to be generally applicable, regardless of the length of time for which R & D in educational administration has been conducted in any particular country or region. Most of these suggestions are applicable to all educational research, and not merely that in administration. The classification of suggestions under (1) structure, (2) functions and types of research, (3) resources, and (4) climate of support is that used earlier in describing some general difficulties.

Structure

1. Institutions involved in conducting R & D should ensure that their *internal structures* (e.g. time allocations, communications) are adequate—this applies to universities, departments of education, school districts, and research institutes.
2. Such institutions should ensure that the *structural links* among themselves are adequate: such links may be strengthened by the formation of national and state/provincial research associations. Particular attention should be paid to inter-university communication.

Functions and Types of Research

1. *Universities.* (a) University staff should concentrate upon scholar-generated research, should try to identify and tackle research problems on a longitudinal basis, and endeavour to incorporate some thesis research into their overall research activity.
(b) University staff should be free to work on both pure and oriented basic research without governments or granting agencies expecting immediately applicable results.
(c) University staff should be free to undertake some contract research.
(d) University staff should investigate proposed new programmes and procedures prior to implementation, and conduct follow-up studies.
(e) University staff should undertake more multi-disciplinary R & D: those in educational administration should particularly consider joint projects with economists, geographers, political scientists, sociologists, and social psychologists, as well as those in other faculty of education departments.
(f) University staff should be actively involved in precise identification and statement of R & D problems.

2. *Departments of Education* should be primarily concerned with R & D functions related to:

(a) provision of financial support to R & D;

(b) identifying major problems related to a country/state/province and initiating appropriate R & D activity, preferably in conjunction with other researchers;

(c) obtaining information necessary for planning and resource allocation.

3. *Larger school districts* should be primarily concerned with:

(a) coordination of research activities involving their personnel;

(b) sponsoring action research by teachers;

(c) identifying major problems related to their district operations and initiating appropriate R & D activity, preferably in conjunction with other researchers;

(d) obtaining information necessary for planning and resource allocation.

4. *All institutions* should concentrate more upon the developmental aspects of R & D—the developmental activities should be considered in the initial planning of a project. They should also carefully examine successful educational operations, and not continually be researching problems concerned with operational difficulties.

Resources

1. Adequate staff, finance and facilities should be provided in the different types of organizations.

Climate of Support

1. R & D staff should endeavour to change the attitudes of teachers, administrators and politicians towards educational research by demonstrating the positive contributions that R & D can make, and by involving some or all of these groups in planning R & D. An effort should be made to demonstrate to practitioners that any *single* basic research project is not usually amenable to developmental activities— several or even many may be required.

2. R & D staff should integrate some of their demands for data collection, and build in appropriate feedback and developmental activities.

To conclude, I feel that by following some or all of these suggestions, we may be able to answer the question of what R & D has contributed to education in a more convincing way than we can at present. Never-theless, in the field of educational administration research we should not be too negative—our R & D base has developed well in the past twenty years and is currently expanding. We may need now to begin serious developmental activity using this knowledge.

BIBLIOGRAPHY

Getzels, J. W. (1974), 'Problem Finding: This Distinctive University Role', *Educational Research*, February, 5–6.
Miklos, E. (1973), *Preparation Programs for Educational Administrators in Canada*, Canadian Association for the Study of Educational Administration.
Organization for Economic Co-operation and Development (1970), *Frascati Manual—The Measurement of Scientific and Technical Activities*, O E C D, Paris.

15 Speculations on Teaching in the Field of Educational Administration

G. E. WHEELER

This paper invites consideration of the following questions:

Should teaching in the field of Educational Administration be different from teaching in other fields, whether closely related, e.g. health administration, or perhaps more distant—industrial administration— or even different in category—science, language or philosophy?

What are the special problems of teaching educational administration?

Are there varying categories of need amongst students which themselves affect teaching?

What purposes might our teaching be expected to fulfil—does it, or even can it, fulfil the expectations of the taught? i.e. how great is the gap between what we know and want to teach and what we don't know and what the student wants to learn?

Lastly—though a negative answer renders some of the other questions irrelevant—is educational administration a useful subject, i.e. a subject which, when learned has relevance to the actions of the administrator?

In considering these questions, we must necessarily turn our attention to the teacher and to the student. For the sake of simplicity I will use the word 'student', to include both the young man and the young woman absorbing something of the idea of educational administration in a degree or diploma course and, at the other end of the scale, the Head Teacher or Director of Education, or Senior Administrator seeking some help in the labyrinth of actual decision-making. All students are likely to have wants that can never be satisfied. Students and teachers of educational administration can be categorized as including (i) those who know much of the theory and arts of administration but who want to know more; (ii) those who are in trouble or difficulty and therefore want knowledge and ideas which are different from those which they have at the present time (yet simple and easily digestible);

(iii) those whose natural or induced discontent is such that they seek change and innovation even for the worst, and (iv) those who simply want to know what it is all about and are possibly hostile to the formalized study of educational administration.

The critical question is whether teaching in the field of educational administration either should be, or is, different from teaching in other fields of managerial or administrative activity, or indeed teaching of any other kind of knowledge, skill or technique. If there is a difference then we must try to discover what is distinctive and develop teaching methods which reflect uniqueness. We seem already to have identified special problems as indicated by the adoption of the case method and the in-basket as peculiarly relevant to the problems of teaching educational administration. But these techniques derive from other fields of activity and are themselves being widely used in this country for engineering craft students on the one hand and on the other for the initiation of Justices of the Peace in their duties. We also have to consider what special qualities the educational administrator needs to acquire, bearing in mind that these qualities and skills may be dependent upon the cultural and social background of the community in which he practises. George Eliot reminds us that 'That's a bad sort of eddication as makes folks unreasonable'. What is the reasonably good sort of education for the administrator of education?

There have been problems certainly deriving from the lack of a body of knowledge to teach—the practice of administration outpacing the theory. Education is itself fickle of definition and shy of measurement. Further, since the activity of administration is necessarily partly problem-centred and with problems deriving from the community, we are forced to teach in a manner bordering on the prophetic. Here we have the problem of all the social sciences; we could follow some of our sociology colleagues in attempting to create destructive societies in which analysis would merely precede damnation, but our students who have to deal with today's problems would not thank us.

In many other fields of study, as in educational administration, we are easily possessed of a great deal of knowledge and technique which is no longer useful, save in historic studies or in the preservation of the archaic. The teacher who has a responsibility for determining what he teaches has the perpetual problem of choosing what may be useful and relevant. His yearning for some general theory which will explain all phenomena in his field or even a dozen such general theories (which will at least provide him with a complete course) is understandable. Such a want, and indeed the search for the satisfaction of such a want, derives from a mechanistic view of our area of concern, and this is only sustainable if we can make our world stand still. So it may not be the subject matter which is special to educational administration and different; it may be the needs among the students themselves which affect our teaching and have a uniqueness. Certainly, many of our students are professionals, or quasi-professionals, whose axiom is that the right to decide on what is correct (or educationally desirable) is their own. As professionals they must have derived this capacity, either inherently or from the educational processes which we (or others) have given them. If the education profession, or the profession of educational administration is different from others, it must somehow be discerned by a distillation of what we teach. In A. J. Balfour's view, 'Our ideals are framed, not according to the measure of our performance, but according to the measure of our thoughts' (Balfour, 1895).

The student of educational administration is probably like most other students at times, requiring no more than the certainty that he has acquired some form of prescribed knowledge which ratifies his professionalism, his application for a job, his self-confidence. On other occasions, he seeks counselling, guidance, sympathy, inspiration and creativity. If our student is a practising administrator, he may feel that these real needs are unlikely to be satisfied elsewhere than in the confessional of the tutorial. Our student too, if he is a practising administrator, always knows that he has tomorrow's or next week's or next month's actual real problems to come and both he and we are naive if we anticipate that those real problems will always draw largely upon his experience, his knowledge, or those techniques which he already possesses.

In so far as we can rely upon our prophetic capacities, or a general and composite theory of educational administration, we can point the way—even our analytic frameworks have utility only in so far as we can postulate ways of action deriving from the use of the analysis. Only then can we help, for example, the Principal of a college who suddenly finds that he is required to chair a tribunal of enquiry into matters concerning students and staff in his college, where students and staff are likely to be represented by Counsel, and although this tribunal is independent of the legal system of the country in which he operates, appeal to the courts is possible and indeed, ultimately to the head of state. Here indeed is a situation where rapid learning plays its part. No experience he can acquire after the problem has arisen will be useful. It is unlikely that we, as teachers, would have dealt with this unusual situation in our standard approaches to the problems of being Head, yet for him, the problem is likely to be the most critical in a decade. If this kind of situation becomes common, we research it, include it in our syllabus—if not, we would be accused of a genetic esotericism by including it!

In a technique orientated society, students seek rapid knowledge of techniques and their application. In this country, we see efforts to use techniques of planned programmed budgeting systems, corporate planning, management by objectives, and staff re-education, amongst many. There are no special problems in teaching the nature of these techniques (though perhaps planned programmed budgeting systems is a long name for a very limited technique); rather that one is expected to try to teach how a new technique might affect existing administrative situations, how such benefits as may be derivable from the use of the technique can be achieved and how circumstances can be created in which the technique will be utilized. We may, as teachers, additionally have to provide knowledge which acts as the antidote to the fever of enthusiasm and soft-soap with which the sacerdotal consultant proclaims his 'mytho-systems'. Sad experience leaves no room for doubt in the question of techniques that many educational administrators regretfully believe that it is:

> Safer with multitudes to stray,
> Than tread alone a fairer way—
> To mingle with the erring throng
> Than boldly speak ten million wrong
>
> (Nugent, 1739)

If not techniques alone, or history and description, can concepts and analysis provide fulfilment of our objectives, or do we play the academic game which consists of creating the syllabus and examination, inviting students to fulfil the entry qualifications and lay down their deposit, hypothesizing the varying chances of success and giving the Diploma prize at the completion! Where the prize is high enough, where the gift of it is within our own command, we may be able to create a high correlation between the syllabus, the teaching and the taught's requirement. This is a rather special case, having both utility and respectability, and although part of the educational game which has to be administered, not I hope the sport with which we are concerned.

The growth of literature related to educational administration is a study in itself. How far our contributions are pollutive and using the world's natural resources unnecessarily is a question we should ask since we are in an activity so similar to packaging. There seems to be no limit to the number of packages which can be made to surround the simplest products. Indeed, the simpler the product, the more ornate and deceiving are the imprisoning packages with which it may be embellished. Is educational administration so complicated that it needs growing professorial academic attention—let alone consultancy and advisory intervention—to help the practitioner?

A pessimistic view of the situation is that we are as uncontributive to the process of educational administration as are academics to the nature of music, or art, that we have joined the cacophony of commentators who are seemingly characteristic of human activity. If we are optimistic, we should remind ourselves of a few of the reasons for the growth of the study of educational administration, on such a world-wide basis and the implications for us as teachers. We should note that the growth has been contemporaneous to our growing awareness of an environmental ignorance. We should note that education in the last half-century has ceased to be regarded as an elitist activity. It is something, together with good health and good food which has come to be regarded as a right. It may be worth noting that in other areas of human activity, e.g. the arts, sport and even government, concern with administration grows as patronage and privilege decline. As systematic provision replaces philanthropic courtly encouragement, demands for management and administration grow. The total growth in our knowledge and skills of all kinds, increases the problems of managerial choice. There is decision, therefore, not only in what the process of education is about or what the curriculum or the particular syllabus shall be, but also in the choice of what collection of resources and technology shall be applied to the educational process and what particular limitations shall be placed upon what the educator is attempting to do.

As our range of choices increases, so does our total volume of activity. In Britain, at the moment, we are energetically developing curricula, sponsoring counselling, encouraging nursery education, widening the opportunities for higher education, removing institutional idiosyncrasies and hence concerned in managing all of these activities. Whilst we are increasing the capacity to educate, we are not necessarily increasing the capacity to learn and therefore the managerial and administrative problem of deciding what should go into the pint pot, even though the pot is made of stretchable plastic rather than glass, remains a problem. We should not imagine that if we could find a big enough plastic pot all our problems would be taken away!

Change and growth amplified administrative problems at the logistic level—getting the 'right' mix of resources creates problems of administrative choice where precedents equip us poorly and theory has yet to catch up with the data upon which hypothesis can be made. We rush ahead to the innovative and creative ideal leaving a trail of administrative hoops to trip up the unwary student, teacher or politician. The existence of a general resource problem, i.e. a general economic problem, leads to the attitude which may now have become instinctive in economic man, that better use of resources must result from more effective administration, and since resources seem to be inevitably scarce or squandered, an increase in managerial or administrative competence and activity is clearly critical.

Even more significantly, economic man may hold the belief that good management, either bureaucratic or entrepreneurial, will somehow conjure up even more resources. (This is not a belief supported by all teachers. The educational administrator is still seen as a predator.) Since educational systems (at least in the UK) are as profligate in the use of resources, material and human, as in the use of other forms of power, we have come to accept low utilization of rooms and buildings, of students' and teachers' time and failure, as a natural part of the educational activity. We allow the ignorant to experiment, the naive to control, the stupid to demand, what our educational system shall provide. In this country, at least, there is no shortage of educational resources in terms of the imaginable needs of students, whether nursery or adult.

The shortage which *does* exist is that of administrative creativity and determination to deal with problems, both at national and institutional level. This same shortage appears to pervade the world of business which we so often emulate. The problem of value is central to administrators and we may wish we had the deceptive simplicity of the business world. The problem is avoided neatly when one is able to confine concern to the cost of some product which is real and measurable, or by submission to the idea of profitability. The fact that profitability may come from luck or judgement, the inability to calculate the risks rather than the ability to do so, inflation rather than investment, tax avoidance rather than tax payment, does not entirely destroy a feeling that some objectivity lurks around the corner which enables the teaching process to continue. Admittedly, when it comes to practicalities, one is never quite sure, where one's students are concerned with business administration, whether one should help the students to understand:

(i) what the law is
(ii) what the law is ... and how to avoid it—or
(iii) what the law is, how to break it and not get caught.

In the area of educational administration, the concept of a value, at least in the British educational system, is central, and that value so ill-defined as to make almost any educational activity valuable! We are able to deny that training is education, unable positively to avow that children be brought to any specific and particular idea of the democratic community within which they live, let alone set and assure standards of literacy and numeracy. The growing challenge to this openness leads the educational administrator to questions such as—what impact does education have upon technology, or technological or economic well-being, on social equality or the development of the under-privileged, either in schools or as inhabitants of this specific area. Once objectives such as these have been identified, the administrative processes become more subject to evaluation and the charismatic type of education is more usefully and readily challenged. We are still left with the problem that we are helping educational administrators to fulfil roles in value-dominated situations, where too little has been done to quantify or identify the nature of the values to be achieved.

Our confused acceptance of open-endedness as nefarious is a challenge to the concept of administrative competence, unless we believe it competent to create a situation of indefiniteness and inconclusiveness. As staff and students within our education system become more critical of paternalistic or nonparticipative processes, administrative situations of greater complexity are created. It is not self-evident that higher motivation amongst the educational labour force compensates for the resources involved in participative processes or for the frictions created in an attempt to solve every educational problem at local level. The tension between an 'educational service' concept and educational self-management is a tension which we are hardly able to deal with as yet.

These are but a few of the changes which have come upon us in the last decade. We must add the great surge of interest in management of all things, a surge of interest which originated in the USA and has spread through the United Nations and its various agencies, with the belief that management and administrative education is a necessary part of the package-deal embracing economic growth, social well-being and community development. Learning through the processes of example, evolution, experiment, can still be found in the infant school. It is the temper of our society—our world society I think—that technology which can train a man to go to the moon, ought to be expanded to allow him to stay on earth and enjoy it and be educated upon it. We might for a moment debate the relevant interaction of knowledge and its teaching. The growth for example, in knowledge about teaching economics preceded any great utilization of economists in our business and national life. Currently, the same is probably true of sociologists. In other fields, however, the demand for learning, or to be taught has preceded research, conceptualization, theorization and the creation of the discipline. This has certainly been true in the teaching of industrial management, and it would appear to have been largely true in educational administration so that there may now be many teachers ready to teach what they believe they know to those credulous enough to believe that that is what they should learn! We can also notice that in the world of administration which is always full of problems, there is a ready creation of myths to cure managerial maladies and techniques to try and further managerial expectations, and thus we come to the beginning of the teaching situation and full cycle in our argument.

Speaking of the talents of an economist, J. M. Keynes (1933) remarks that the study of economics does not appear to require gifts of a very high order, and it is not regarded as an intellectually taxing subject. Yet, he points out, good, or even competent economists are rare. He explains this paradox by listing the rare combination of qualities that the economist needs. He must be mathematician, historian, statesman and philosopher. He must understand symbols and speak in words. He must contemplate the particular in terms of the general, and touch abstract and concrete in the same flight of thought. He must study the present in the light of the past for the purposes of the future. No part of man's nature or his institutions must lie outside his regard. He must be purposeful and disinterested in a simultaneous move—as aloof and incorruptible as an artist, yet sometimes as near to earth as a politician. Surely this description applies perfectly to the educational administrator.

I think for economists we might substitute educational administrators and then begin to notice how in the absence of a central discipline, the vagaries of either multi-disciplinary or multi-ethological, or even multi-logical approaches to the idea of educational administration emerge. I have already hypothesized that there is no satisfactory composite theory, let alone practice of educational administration, which meets the problems if not the demands of the practising administrator. The needs of the student on an academic course can be determined by us, whilst the needs of the administrator are determined by his environment, which is in itself determined by the complete 'us'—the complete community. We are unable to provide a complete model of the environment, though when we are dealing with institutions, it is quite likely that we can prepare models which will help Heads and others to understand something of the dynamics of the institution in which they work.

If we go along with Professor Revans' hypothesis that administrators face needs of understanding the environment in which they work, of understanding their own perceptions and attitudes and of understanding the techniques which can be applied to the alteration of the situation in which they live (Revans, 1973), we can begin to see the nature of teaching in educational administration, the nature of the content of the syllabus and the nature of a methodology. Since perception is acquired by experience, teaching methods, even if not giving real experiences, can provide simulations which have reality. What the Head Teacher learns in order to act in a simulated situation, he cannot unlearn, however much he under-values the actual simulation. The technique which he learns in order to carry out an exercise is a technique which, if he gains enough confidence to practise it, he can attempt to use in a real situation. We can widen his managerial vocabulary, we can diminish the mythology and we can enhance his skills and technology. We need not dwell on the methods which we can use to do this, the case study, the in-basket, the project, the piece of academic work, the counselling process, the exchange of experience—all of these are teaching methods and all of these we must use, together with the aids to learning from computers and the other derivations from the plasto-metallic educational revolution.

CONCLUSION

I have touched upon many uncertainties and doubts, yet there are propositions about which we should have a high degree of certainty and which may help us in the design of our teaching programmes:

1. the vast majority of occupants of senior posts in educational institutions or administrative services have no formal training before or after appointment in educational management.
2. major operational problems continue to arise for which even trained personnel need support and training.
3. a large range of techniques and skills could be acquired by principals, heads of department, administrators in general—the problem is identifying those which may be useful or worthwhile.
4. most senior staffs are lamentably unaware of the managerial, educational, and social environment in which they operate—the university professor is likely to be unaware of the nature of technical education, 'higher' education is divorced from nursery education.
5. there is no satisfactory composite theory, let alone practice, of educational administration which can match the problems being faced.
6. what and whether training and support are necessary is largely dependent on the degree of effectiveness with which educationalists are expected to manage educational institutions.
7. if there is a need to learn, other than by the accident or necessity of experience, then the problems of curriculum content, student motivation, and teaching methods become significant and most significant when the perceived needs of the student, i.e. the educational administrator, his employer, or staff, and the teacher or designer of the curriculum, are different. It is worthwhile exploring some of these differences and of asking the question whether, for example, the learning needs—and therefore teaching methods, need to be different when what we are teaching is concerned with a managerial activity which is:
   (i) Policy making—at institutional or system level.
   (ii) Policy making at departmental or functional level.
   (iii) Organization building.
   (iv) Operational—at system, institution or functional level.
   (v) Technique centred—especially where new techniques are developed or where techniques new to education are introduced into it.

(vi) Problem or 'crisis' centred.

Again, our teaching methods will probably need refinement so that a differentiation of method, let alone curricula, is practised when we are concerned with, for example, the 'complete' training of a Headteacher for that role, rather than an activity which is one of 'sensitising' Headteachers to knowledge, attitudes and problems, or of giving an appreciation of a technique. Again, *timing* is significant, for if we are teaching youthful enthusiastic men and women before their first appointment to a significant post of responsibility in administration, the methods and their urgent demands will be different from on-appointment training or post-appointment training, when very soon the active experience of any group of 'students' rapidly comes to exceed that of the 'teachers'.

So, there is much teaching which seems worthwhile—providing we remember that:

It is not explanations which survive but the things which are explained, not theories but the things about which we theorise. (Balfour, 1895)

BIBLIOGRAPHY

Balfour, A. J. (1895), *The Foundations of Belief*, Longmans, Green, London.
Eliot, G. (1857), *Scenes of Clerical Life*.
Keynes, J. M. (1933), *Essays in Biography*, Macmillan, London.
Nugent, Robert (1793), *Epistle to a Lady*.
Revans, R. W. (1973), 'The response of the manager to change: contents of address', *Management Education and Development*, 4(2).

16 International Management Training for Educational Change

PER DALIN

The concept of educational change is not an easy one, because the term means so many things to different individuals. Even the same innovation in a given culture is looked upon quite differently by different interest groups. For some, a certain change is an innovation or improvement, for others it is a change, but not an improvement, and for others, 'the more things change, the more they stay the same'. If one expands the notion and discusses educational change among individuals from different countries, one adds another significant complication to the discussion. This may be possible, however, if one discusses a given phenomenon inside a particular, rather homogeneous group (e.g. a discussion of the individualization of instruction among Headmasters from several countries), but it would probably be very difficult to discuss the whole range of educational changes among different interest groups from various countries. This is often what international programmes try to do.

If one is more concerned with the process by which educational innovations come about than with the characteristics of the innovation itself, one adds another complication to an international discussion. The way in which a particular country deals with the change process is rooted in tradition and styles of operation. The existing decision-making structure, e.g., the degree of centralization and decentralization, the question of *who* is in charge, the assumptions participants in the change make about roles and role relationships, and the level of training and sophistication of the people who have to implement the change, are some key factors that will influence understanding about educational change and its management.

AN INTERNATIONAL PROGRAMME: A RATIONALE

My introductory comments may suggest that it is rather foolhardy to start a programme on the management of educational change and to give training in this area at an international level. Arguments against such a programme may be adduced on political, economic and educational grounds, and these were carefully considered before IMTEC (International Management Training for Educational Change) was established. The main reasons for establishing such a programme were as follows:

1. The educational systems in all member countries of the Organisation of European Cooperation and Development (OECD) are undergoing change. By no means are these changes identical, but there are several common trends.

2. All member countries are experiencing problems in planning, developing, or implementing educational change. Though the problems differ, attempts to solve them are similar.

3. Most member countries are looking for assistance to increase their capacity to manage educational change. Increasingly it is understood that the process by which change takes place is crucial to its success.

4. The knowledge base, the state of the art in terms of our understanding of the change process, is limited. Most research has been done in America, mainly by psychologists and sociologists. The type of research that has been done in Europe, differs considerably from most of the American work. Little has been done to bring the various research traditions in different countries together to get a deeper understanding of the change process. It is a concern in several countries that we need to build the resources together to get a better base for the management of educational change.

5. Individuals who are involved in a national educational system are often 'locked in' to particular assumptions and practices regarding the way in which educational change should take place. It is often very hard to be conscious of one's own assumptions and values. The way we look at learning, education, its governance or financing, is deeply rooted in national traditions and practices. International activities provide opportunities for individuals and institutions to challenge assumptions that we usually take for granted.

These are some of the arguments behind the organization of the IMTEC project. Nevertheless, several problems were recognized as constraints and barriers, problems that need further clarification: *How* can different individuals from so many countries learn from each other, given the differences in cultural, political, economic and educational conditions? What role will the language play in intensive training sessions? *Who* should benefit from training? Should the existing 'establishment' benefit, or should there be a new organization trying to identify and develop new talents? How can potential candidates for the course be properly selected? How can the international training be properly linked to educational change priorities in the different countries? How can an international training programme be more than an 'external' training situation without links to the practical situation? If training should be more than isolated training, but have consequences for implementation, how can one capitalize on a beginning network of trained individuals? How can knowledge be disseminated, taking into account that there are around two and a half million administrators and eleven million teachers in the educational systems of the OECD countries?

THE IMTEC PROJECT

The OECD in Paris, in 1968, created an organization called 'Center for Educational Research and Innovation' (CERI)[1] under the leadership of Ron Gass. The purpose of this new organization was to assist member countries in their innovative efforts. During the first three years of CERI's existence, several projects were initiated to get a clearer understanding of the process of change in education. The first initiative was taken at a conference organized in Cambridge, England, in 1969, on the subject of the management of educational innovation (CERI, 1971). As a follow-up to that conference, seventeen case studies of innovations were undertaken in nine different countries. These case studies, under a general analysis entitled 'Strategies for Innovation in Education', were published in 1973 by CERI.

The Cambridge Workshop recommended that CERI develop an international training activity on the management of educational change. The planning of this project, International Management Training for Educational Change, started in the second half of 1971. Several countries indicated their interest and throughout 1972 several planning meetings were held. Altogether, seventeen countries[2] committed themselves to the project which is financed by grants from their governments

[1] CERI, OECD, 2 rue André-Pascal, Paris 16e, France.

[2] Austria, Belgium, Canada, Denmark, Finland, France, The Federal Republic of Germany, Ireland, Italy, The Netherlands, Norway, Portugal, Sweden, Switzerland, Turkey, the United Kingdom and the United States of America.

and by a private grant from the Ford Foundation. In addition, the US Government provided a voluntary planning grant, and the Norwegian Government a voluntary contribution that covers the costs connected with the Headquarters based in Oslo.[3] An office coordinating the French-speaking activities is located in the OECD in Paris. Altogether seven staff members (professional and technical) are engaged in the project, in addition to part-time consultants from many countries.

A project like IMTEC cannot operate successfully without a reference point in each country. Most countries have, therefore, organized what is called an IMTEC National Reference Group. These groups are 'systemic' in their membership, i.e., they are made up of individuals who represent various roles in the national system, such as teachers, local and central administrators, researchers, representatives of teacher organizations and others.

Concepts

The work so far has led us to a systemic view in studying educational change. This has resulted in a systematic approach to the analysis by participants of innovations in other cultures (e.g. Sweden and the UK). The development of the programme has also resulted in a better understanding of the *management function* in educational change, and the degree to which this function is shared at various levels in the school system. Finally, concepts have been developed regarding *training approaches* to the management of change. These concepts are only tentative and based on the four training courses offered thus far. Owing to the rather comprehensive feed-back system that is designed into the project (external evaluation, Secretariat assessment, country evaluation, etc.), considerable learning has taken place that will be important for the further development of such concepts.

Training results

The training needs of member countries differ considerably. IMTEC has designed a series of different, but related instructional activities. The first effort was a general seminar on the management of change that was presented in June, 1973, at Hankø, Norway. This course was built largely around the analysis of case studies of innovation that were included in the CERI case study series cited above. The three-week course was attended by individuals considered by the countries as being

[3] IMTEC/OECD, Post Box 79, Blindern, Oslo 3, Norway.

influential in change efforts in their countries. During the last few days, each country sent individuals who held top leadership positions in the educational system, the rationale being that a dialogue between the 'innovators' and the top political and administrative leadership is necessary for a systematic change process to take place.

The second training activity focussed on the management of change in secondary education. The course was divided into two parts, the first one being a more 'theoretical' training session of ten days (in Spåtind, Norway), the last part being field visits to study the innovation process in Sweden or England. In the first part of the course, a 'living case study' of a secondary innovation in Norway and a secondary innovation in England was presented. In the second part of the course, each group visited secondary school innovations in the countries, interviewed a large number of individuals in the schools as well as in the various administrative units and organizations at a local and central level, and at the end prepared an analysis of the change process in the country that was presented to a panel of leading educators from the host country.

A third training activity on the management of change in elementary education was held in May, 1974, near Bergen, Norway. The design of this course differed somewhat from the two earlier described above. First of all, the course was designed to meet learning needs of *project groups* and not individuals. These groups were asked to bring a description of on-going innovation in elementary education in their country. These descriptions had been written around a common outline proposed by the I M T E C staff to highlight the process and problems of managing educational change. The course started with a dramatization of a history of an innovation (Smith and Keith, 1971). All discussions took place in small groups and after the dramatization, the first of three projects was presented and discussed. The purpose of the first part of the course was to increase the awareness of participants about the comprehensive problems of managing educational change. The second part of the course was a series of presentations, lectures, discussion sessions, films and other activities designed to increase the individual choice in the course. This part of the course was called the 'Mini-University'. The last part of the course was designed to assist the project groups in identifying critical factors in the process of change in their project and to facilitate communication among the various project groups. Altogether nineteen projects were presented during the course.

In June of this year a ten-day course on the management of change was also presented in the French language and held in Sèvres outside Paris. The design of this course was basically case-oriented with field site visits and a panel discussion with French authorities. Cases were presented from Canada, Belgium, Portugal and France. The field visits in France concentrated on a discussion of strategies for change in the French educational system. In particular the role of research and development in the system and the centralized nature of decision-making was in focus.

So far about two hundred and fifty individuals from seventeen countries have had their first training in an international setting of the management of change. These individuals represent various roles, including high level administrators, researchers, developers, teachers, union representatives and opinion leaders. I M T E C has so far involved about one hundred advisers and consultants in the planning, development and implementation of the programme.

Network building

More important, sometimes, than the direct training result is the development of national and international networks that facilitate continual cooperation and learning after the training course. The Secretariat has a number of examples of such developments already. In an informal way ideas and products have been shared, study visits have been organized and direct bilateral cooperation between individuals and institutions are being implemented. In this connection it is important to note that about ten countries have organized national reference groups. Increasingly these groups will have access to information from other countries and from within their own country. This is an important network building programme that presently involves hundreds of 'key' individuals, and will probably have consequences for many more.

Material

A priority in 1973 was to gather and analyze learning material relevant for I M T E C training. These materials include recent articles, books on the management of change, games and simulations. It has been important for the staff to develop a network that could provide the project with up-to-date materials as developed in different countries. The following are already available:

(a) An annotated bibliography on the management of change that will be updated periodically.
(b) A substantial number of articles that have not yet been published.
(c) Materials from member countries (including 'status papers' and 'management analysis papers') from the beginning of 'national files' on the management of change.
(d) Position papers, evaluation reports and other IMTEC material on management training.

Further publications are in preparation on the concept of management, on case-analysis, and on training approaches.

National follow-up activites

Many countries have already organized seminars, started research projects, initiated training or encouraged discussions about the management of educational change. It is anticipated that these activities will be expanded with the assistance of IMTEC staff, and institutions and individuals from the 'IMTEC network'. IMTEC also has a Fellow Programme that is designed to help member countries to follow up the international activities. In most cases the governments pay the salary of these Fellows to work on particular projects to be implemented when the Fellow returns to his country.

THE IMTEC FUTURE

IMTEC is a decentralized project in the CERI Programme of work, which is likely to continue at least to the end of 1976. Only preliminary discussions have taken place in relation to its *long term* future, but a certain shift in priorities over the next three years is considered desirable. In general the following tasks are looked upon as necessary:

1. *The Further Development of Concepts*. The systemic view of educational change needs further clarification and development. A series of small seminars on the critical processes involved will be organised, to be attended both by researchers from different disciplines and by practitioners with key responsibilities in the change process.
2. *International Training Courses*. Several countries have offered to be hosts for international training courses in the next two years. The courses will concentrate on specific educational reforms in the host country, and case studies from other countries illustrating similar problems will be used.

3. *The Development of National Follow-up Activities.* Since national resources are limited in several countries, the network developed through IMTEC should be the basis for systematic international cooperation in the field. The national activities may range from small improvements of existing training programmes, which are already developed, to the creation of completely new programmes and institutions.

4. *The Development of a Management Curriculum.* Training individuals and institutions to cope with educational change is a complex task. It is an important goal for IMTEC to facilitate international co-operation in this field and pull knowledge and resources together. Training for certain groups might take the form of formal courses up to the Ph.D. level. In other cases more informal training sessions of short duration might be appropriate. It is expected that the next two or three years of development will clarify the options available for training the various groups involved in the change process in education.

IMTEC is thus a short term project to assist Member countries in analyzing their capacity for educational change and help train a core of individuals who can be instrumental in improving the management of educational change. It is hoped that the project will plant some seeds that will grow and mature and be of significance in the various countries which have helped in its development.

BIBLIOGRAPHY

CERI (1971), *The Management of Innovation in Education*, CERI/OECD, Paris.
CERI (1973), *Case Studies of Educational Innovation.* Vol. I: *At the Central Level*, Vol. II: *At the Regional Level*, Vol. III: *At the School Level*, CERI/OECD, Paris.
Per Dalin (1973), *Case Studies of Educational Innovation*, Vol. IV: *Strategies of Innovation in Education*, CERI/OECD, Paris.
Smith, L. M. and Keith, P. M. (1971), *Anatomy of Educational Innovation: An Organizational Analysis of an Elementary School*, Wiley, New York.

17 Competency/Performance-Based Administrator Education (C/PBAE): Recent Developments in the United States

JAMES M. LIPHAM

Competency/performance-based administrator education (C/PBAE) is currently viewed as a significant new thrust on the American educational scene. As a major innovation, C/PBAE may be appropriately analyzed in terms of extant typologies of social change. For example, Thelen's three-phase typology of educational change includes the following stages: (1) enthusiasm or initiation, the period during which the innovators and their disciples are actively working to develop and establish the new technique or process; (2) vulgarization or spread, during which time the innovation is taken up by people other than the innovators, the general public is encouraged to form unrealistic illusions about the change, and otherwise competent educators suddenly develop into conceptual lemmings; and (3) institutionalization or ritualization, at which time the change, or some watered-down imitation thereof, is incorporated through training in the new technique into the operation of the school (Thelen, 1964). In my view C/PBAE is currently at the enthusiasm stage in the United States and is rapidly moving into the vulgarization stage.

To place the C/PBAE movement in an appropriate historical context, its origins and antecedent theoretical foundations are traced briefly as a prelude to determining the meaning of the concept.[1] Then, C/PBAE is defined and described in terms of general systems theory. Next, the current status of the diffusion of the concept is documented in terms of several contemporary efforts toward the implementation of C/PBAE. The paper concludes with an enumeration of some basic objections to the approach and with a brief discussion of future institutionalization of the concept.

[1] For an extended discussion of four major historical approaches to the preparation of educational administrators, see Lipham and Hoeh (1974, pp. 19-30).

ORIGIN OF C/PBAE

Basically, the present emphasis on competency or performance does not represent a drastic or dramatic departure from the thrust of very early programmes for preparing educational personnel. In fact, the current C/PBAE movement appears to represent a throwback to the World War I era of the scientific management or 'efficiency' approach to administration wherein it was assumed that there was 'one best way' to do a job, as well as to administer the doing of a job.[2] Moreover, C/PBAE undoubtedly appeals to many administrators who were educated in the 'efficiency' tradition (Callahan, 1962) during the period from 1915 to 1945 when the approach to administration was highly prescriptive.[3]

In essence, this traditional view was atheoretical, if not antitheoretical, in that it is assumed that if one were first told 'what' should be done, shown 'how' it should be done, and given the appropriate resources to do it, then undoubtedly one would be productive. Without belabouring the point, suffice it to observe that this earlier simplistic view was found to be lacking in many respects, such as 'who' is to decide what should be done, 'how' people should relate to one another in the process, and 'why' some solutions are somehow better than others. Thus, in the 1940s the emphasis in administration shifted from an organizational, 'autocratic', or 'efficiency' orientation to a personalistic, 'democratic', or human relations point of view which prevailed in preparation programmes for educational administrators in the United States until the mid-1950s, when the behavioural science approach emerged.[4]

The Behavioural Science Approach to Administration

The social or behavioural science approach to administration and leadership incorporated elements of both the traditional orientation, which stressed the formal organization, and the human relations view, which stressed interpersonal relationships. In the social science approach, emphasis was placed on theories of both organizational and individual behaviour.[5]

[2] See Taylor (1911), Gilbreth (1911), Gantt (1916), and Bobbitt (1913).
[3] See Cubberley (1916) and Reeder (1931).
[4] See Follett (1940), Mayo (1933), Roethlisberger and Dickson (1939), and Yauch (1949).
[5] See Coladarci and Getzels (1955), Argyris (1957), Halpin (1958), Campbell and Lipham (1960), Presthus (1962), March (1965), Scott (1967) and Thompson (1967).

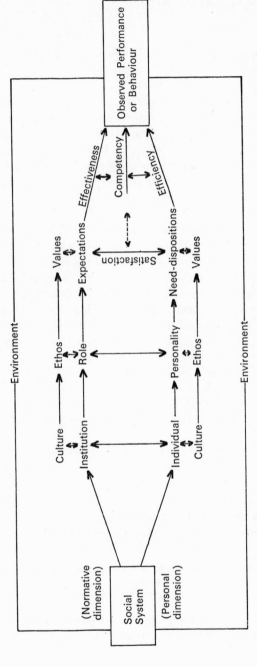

Figure 3. Social Systems Model of C/PBAE. Adapted from Getzels and Guba (1957, p. 430), and Getzels, Lipham and Campbell (1968, p. 105)

One of the powerful behavioural theories of administration which undoubtedly served as an unwitting progenitor of the current C/PBAE effort was the model of educational administration as a social process.[6] As may be seen in Figure 3, according to this theory the observed performance or behaviour of people within an organization may be analyzed and understood as deriving from both the normative and the personal dimensions within a context of cultural values. Effectiveness in terms of this model is defined as the extent to which one's observed performance or behaviour meets the expectations held for the organizational role (represented in Figure 3 along the diagonal between role-expectations and observed performance). At the present time, many C/PBAE proponents have tended erroneously to equate competency with only this measure of effectiveness. This model, however, directs attention to two other significant variables: individual efficiency, the extent to which one's performance is congruent with one's need-dispositions; and satisfaction, the extent to which the expectations of the role are congruent with the need-disposition of the individual. In the future, competency must be understood and treated within the C/PBAE approach as a function of the direct interaction of effectiveness and efficiency, along with the indirect contribution of the satisfaction of individuals within the organization.

Throughout the era of the behavioural science approach to administration substantial progress was made in delineating, describing, and assessing administrative competence in three domains: role performance, decision-making behaviour, and leadership behaviour. Regarding role performance, literally thousands of studies based on social systems theory were conducted concerning the roles of school board members, school superintendents, central office personnel, school principals and assistant principals, department heads and unit or team leaders, teachers, and students.[7] In all of these empirical studies a requisite basic consideration was that of delineating operationally the basic content—the tasks, functions, processes, or behaviours—of the focal role being examined. In most of the studies, moreover, systematic attention was paid to the assessment of competency in terms of

[6] See Getzels and Guba (1957), Getzels and Thelen (1960), and Getzels, Lipham and Campbell (1968).

[7] For an integrated treatment of empirical research utilizing social systems theory in educational administration, see Getzels, Lipham and Campbell (1968).

effectiveness, efficiency, and satisfaction, as well as other measures of organizational and individual achievement.

Particularly congruent with the current C/PBAE emphasis was the work of the Southern States Cooperative Program in Educational Administration wherein analysis of the administrator's role included consideration of the following:

1. Job analysis and identification of critical tasks.
2. Categorization of tasks and identification of knowledge and skills to perform in each category.
3. Theory definition, to provide the 'cognitive maps' needed to understand the tasks, and selection of appropriate procedures and courses of action for their completion. (Graff and Street, 1956)

Theory-based research regarding decision-making behaviour in education was directed more toward the personal than toward the normative dimension of behaviour. In a seminal analysis of the relationship between personality and administrative performance, Hemphill, Griffiths, and Frederiksen devised the first comprehensive set of simulation exercises which were designed to isolate the dimensions of effective performance in the administration role (Hemphill, Griffiths and Frederiksen, 1962). This project, sponsored in part by a grant from the United States Office of Education, not only stimulated the subsequent development of many simulations useful in administrator selection and training,[8] but also derived alternative factors for scoring and analyzing the decision-making behaviour of educational administrators. Certain of these categories of decision-making behaviour are still widely utilized in C/PBAE programmes for analyzing administrative performance.

The research on leadership emphasized equally the sociological and the psychological dimensions—situational and individual factors—in examining the effective performance of leaders. Considerable theory based research has been conducted concerning the behaviour of the leader-in-situation. Methodologically, the research procedures have required the following: selection of a target population of putative leaders (often based on formal position held); assessment of leadership behaviour utilizing rating scales, interviews, and observations; measurement of individual, group, and organizational variables believed to be

---

[8] See University Council for Educational Administration (1973).

related to either general or specific leadership behaviours; and examination of the interrelationships among the variables.[9]

Two basic formulations, one developed at the Ohio State University (Halpin, 1956) and the other at the University of Chicago (Getzels and Guba, 1957), provided the conceptual frameworks and assessment procedures for analyzing competent leadership behaviour. The Ohio State formulation isolated the dimensions of 'initiating structure' and 'consideration'; the Chicago formulation delineated the 'nomothetic', 'transactional', and 'idiographic' dimensions of leadership behaviour. These formulations, which continue to be widely utilized, examine leadership behaviour within the context of the school as a system.[10]

The General Systems Approach to Administration

General systems theory represents the most recent foundational approach to administration to emerge in this century. The general systems view—holistic, interdisciplinary, methodical, and analytic—is concerned with organizational boundaries, environments, structures, inputs, processes, outputs, and feedback (Immegart, 1969). Systems theory is particularly basic to C/P B A E, wherein particular attention is paid to the identification of objectives and the development and utilization of materials and procedures that affect both the processes and outputs of training programmes in administration.

The systems model presented in Figure 4 provides a useful construct for examining C/P B A E. At the left of the model, the students (operands), professors (operators), facilities, and material constitute the basic inputs to the system which is the university or training institution. Through the use of systematic procedures, the structured subsystems within the university process the inputs—hopefully in a cost-effective manner. The prime output of the system is professionally prepared personnel who possess the understandings, skills, and attitudes required for effective performance in administrative positions in the field of education.

As Andrews (1974) recently observed, current C/P B A E programmes have to their detriment ignored three aspects of the general systems model: (1) the quality of the inputs (particularly students) to the system, (2) the feedback processes between and among the subsystems of

[9] For a comprehensive analysis of multiple approaches to the study of leadership see James M. Lipham. (1973, pp. 1–15 and 26–43).
[10] See James M. Lipham (1971, pp. 77–81).

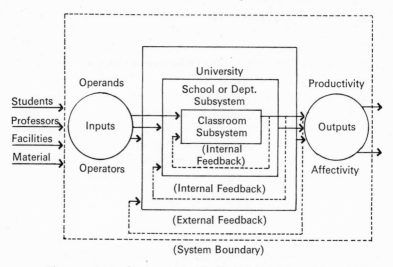

Figure 4. General Systems Model of C/PBAE. Adapted from Lipham and Hoeh (1974, p. 34)

the university, and (3) the relationship of the university to the larger environment which provides the legitimacy for the administrator training programme. Proponents of C/PBAE have, however, devoted sustained attention, both to the processes utilized within the classroom subsystem and to the outputs of this subsystem, and it is to these emphases that we now turn for an operational definition of the concept.

DEFINITION OF C/PBAE

C/PBAE is here defined as a process for preparing persons that are competent to perform an administrative role in education because systematic attention in their training has been given to: (1) identifying the requisite inputs; (2) specifying the domains of role behaviour and assigning priorities to them; (3) developing measures of competent performance; (4) providing individualized, reality-centred learning experiences, (5) evaluating the acquisition of understandings, skills, and attitudes; and (6) certifying competence to perform as an educational administrator. The major stages in this process, displayed graphically in the simplified systems diagram in Figure 5, deserve further elaboration since there has been a tendency erroneously to equate C/PBAE with only one or two of its component parts.

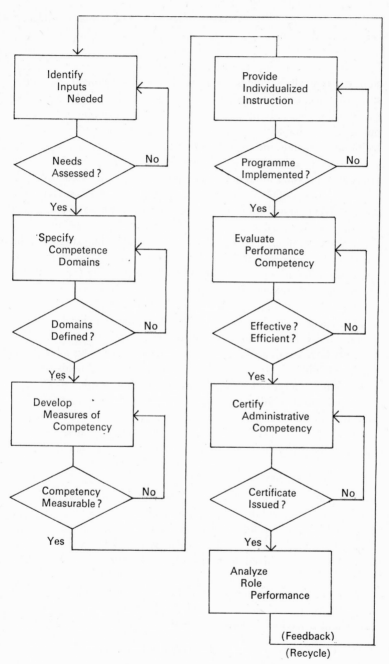

Figure 5. Flow Diagram of C/PBAE

Input Assessment

Identification of the inputs required for C/PBAE is an essential initial step that typically includes a systematic needs assessment. Recently, such assessment of the needed competencies has involved widespread participation, not only by professors and practitioners, but also by the public, since ultimately training programme products must meet the legitimate demands and expectation of the society.

At the national level, several alternative beginning points have been utilized in assessing the requisite inputs. Regarding the 'ends' or goals of educational administration, for example, the UCEA systematically analyzes, revises, and projects its programme and purposes every five years (UCEA, 1974). Regarding the quality of the 'means' in educational administration, scholars have conducted revealing studies of the adequacy of university training programmes, the nature of the professorship (operators), and the quality of the students (operands) in preparatory programmes.[11]

A major strength of C/PBAE is that it requires a systematic assessment of needs, not only at national, but also at state and local levels. In cooperation with many groups, faculties in educational administration typically have conducted systematic studies of the various administrative specialities offered, examined other disciplines and fields for relevant content, surveyed the field for requisite emerging skills, and examined through follow-up studies the performance of those previously trained. The purpose of such baseline data, of course, is to depict the actual state of administrative competence—'where we are'—as a basis for projecting the idealized state—'where we should be'.

Domain Definition

An adequate needs assessment provides considerable insight in delimiting, defining, and describing the domains of competence required in the administrative role. Yet some of the greatest disagreements, even among proponents of C/PBAE, occur over which taxonomic schemata should be utilized to define the major behavioural domains. Using the social systems model in Figure 4, some prefer to describe competent behaviour in terms of the stereotypic personalistic syndrome required for the administrative role. Others, however, characterize competent behaviour in more conventional role terms—administrative

[11] See Gregg and Sims (1972), and Campbell and Newell (1973).

tasks, administrative processes, or foundational theories of administration, as shown in Table 6.

Table 6. Administrative Role Domains in C/PBAE

Administrative Functions	Administrative Process	Administrative Theories
Instructional	Planning	Systems Theory
Programme	Organizing	Social Systems Theory
Staff Personnel	Stimulating	Values Theory
Pupil Personnel	Communicating	Role Theory
Finance and Business	Coordinating	Organization Theory
Management	Evaluating	Decision Theory
Educational Facilities		Leadership Theory
School-Community		
Relations		

Nor is disagreement limited to the nature of the domains; it also concerns such matters as the viability and independence of the basic content categories within each domain. In this regard, a prime advantage
of the C/PBAE approach must be cited: it serves to raise programme
planning issues from an implicit to an explicit level.

In C/PBAE, as contrasted with a less systematic approach, the
description of the competency domains is basic, since it is at this stage
that priorities must be set. Once such priorities are established there is
set in motion a whole series of subsequent steps requiring a considerable investment of time, energy, and resources.

Competency Measurement

Identifying the procedures that will be utilized to attain specific competencies is a crucial stage in C/PBAE. At this stage, each competency
must be defined in terms of three basic elements: commonality or
variability of objectives, acceptable levels of attainment of the objectives, and variance in the sequencing of the content within and across
the domains (Klausmeier, 1974). Regarding the objectives, whereas
some are common to all administrative roles, others are unique both to
particular roles and to particular students preparing for those roles.
Concerning the acceptable level of attainment, full mastery, to include
understanding and application, may be expected of some students but

only limited mastery, perhaps at the familiarity level, may be expected of others. Regarding sequencing of the content, some concepts in administration may be understood only if previous knowledge is assimilated, whereas other concepts appear to stand alone and may be presented in a variable sequence. Six viable types of instruction which combine these three elements are as follows:

Type I   Common objectives, full attainment, invariant sequence across domains

Type II   Common objectives, full attainment, variable sequence across domains

Type III   Common objectives, variable attainment, invariant sequence across domains

Type IV   Common objectives, variable attainment, variable sequence across domains

Type V   Variable objectives, variable attainment, invariant sequence across domains

Type VI   Variable objectives, variable attainment, variable sequence across domains.

These basic variables may be used to depict alternative programme designs. The C/PBAE approach may best be described as being that of Type I wherein (1) consensus has been reached concerning the common objectives of administrator training programmes; (2) the expectation is that students will master fully the objectives; and (3) the content domains are presented in a sequential pattern wherein the requisite understandings, skills, and attitudes are developed methodically and cumulatively. By contrast, traditional preparatory programmes in educational administration have permitted, if not encouraged, wide variance in the instructional objectives to be attained; have acknowledged that individuals vary considerably in their ability to reach acceptable levels of attainment, and have permitted students to elect course content in any order (the possible exception being the requirements of an undergraduate degree and a basic introductory course in administration).

Instructional Programming

Instructional programming in C/PBAE poses particular problems within the typical semester-hour pattern of course offerings for several reasons. First, the emphasis in C/PBAE programmes is on instructional objectives, hence the classical 'pretest-teach-posttest' model is often posed as the ideal—particularly by pedagogues in such ordered fields as reading, mathematics, and science education. While this classical approach may be appropriate for both the familiarity and understanding levels of attainment, it becomes less useful at the application level wherein several skills may be operative simultaneously. And even though curricular purists may decry this circumstance—even railing against any objective that is not stated in behavioural terms—the time comes when preoccupation with detailed and prescriptive objectives is counterproductive. In this regard, one is reminded of the faculty that developed over 2,000 explicit behavioural objectives, only to find that little time was left to achieve them. At best, compromises must be made—particularly concerning objectives in the affective domain—and at the present time, these compromises tend to break traditional courses into several modules of varying type and duration among which student choices can be elected.

A second major focus in C/PBAE is the use of a wide variety of instructional methodologies at different junctures in a trainee's preparation programme. McCleary and McIntyre have addressed this issue by inventorying the different instructional methodologies currently utilized in educational administration and classifying them in terms of both the levels of learning and the competencies to be learned (McCleary and McIntyre, 1972). Whereas reading, lectures, and discussion might be appropriate at early levels of attainment when familiarity with a broad array of content is desirable, at higher attainment levels other methodologies may be more appropriate.

A final major emphasis in C/PBAE instructional programming is that of utilizing reality-centred experiences—whether in simulation exercises, apprenticeships, internships, or externships. The C/PBAE instructional programming model places particular stress on such experiences in that it highlights the evaluation of competent performance in the administrative role.

Performance Evaluation

Krathwol (1973), who vigorously supports performance-based education, has stated that the approach 'is certain to fail to reach its ultimate objective if it continues on its present course. This failure will be caused by the almost complete lack of attention given to the assessment of competencies'.

From an insightful analysis of over 200 instructional modules in teacher education, Lawrence recently identified the following weaknesses which undoubtedly apply to learning modules in administrator education as well:

1. Measurement procedures and criteria were inconsistent with competency statements in some substantial way. The most frequent inconsistency was between the objective and the type of competency measurement. For example, a paper-and-pencil test of information or memory outcomes was often taken as a measure of performance when the competency statement implied performance in the sense of making, leading, experimenting, etc.
2. Specific evaluative criteria were not given. The student was given specifications for a task, but the evaluation was to be accomplished by a test or some other measure outside the module, the criteria for which were not named in the module.
3. The measurement procedure did not cover the range of outcomes implied in the competency statement.
4. Activities required or suggested were judged not likely to generate the kind of evidence of competency indicated by the competency objective.
5. 'Command performance'—performance that the student knew was being watched for certain effects—was taken as evidence that the student had incorporated a competency into his behaviour system.

Lawrence (1974)

To improve the evaluation of performance in the future, Lawrence (1974, p. 302) suggested the following: (1) that competencies be selected on a conceptual base rather than eclectically, (2) that change in performance be used as the criterion for validating competencies, (3) that research be built into designs for testing training procedures and materials, (4) that low-inference evaluative measures be utilized, and (5) that greater consistency be obtained between competency objectives, measurement procedures, and evaluative criteria. Attention to these suggestions concerning evaluation would simplify the certification of competency.

Competency Certification

Certification, in terms of licensing to practise administration, traditionally has been granted by state departments of education acting on recommendations of universities. In C/PBAE, however, two certification trends are worthy of note. First, as Drummond (1974) has observed, controversies over the movement toward mandated programmes of competency-based education reflect a basic change in the

sharing of power over professional education. Whereas university professors traditionally have controlled the content, procedures, methodology, and, ultimately, the entry of persons into the profession, in
competency-based programmes this power must be shared among
school board members, administrators, teachers, and, in some states,
citizens.

Another trend in C/PBAE certification is that the demand for
accountability extant within the nation at large has now hit the education professions full force. As Andrews (1974, pp. 311-12) has aptly
shown, within the systems approach (presented in the model in Figure
4), the output of C/PBAE programmes becomes the basis for legiti-
mation of the programmes. He stated, 'Given the added dimension of
legitimacy, it seems clear that we will have to build a sense of programme worth in order to avoid entropy and, in the end, extinction'.
This sense of urgency currently pervades the profession of educational
administration.

DIFFUSION OF C/PBAE

As indicated at outset in this paper, C/PBAE has generated considerable enthusiasm in educational administration circles both within the
major associations of professors and at several major colleges and universities throughout the United States.

Association Activities

The University Council for Educational Administration (UCEA), the
National Conference of Professors of Educational Administration
(NCPEA), and the Professors of Secondary School Administration
and Supervision (PSSAS) of the National Association of Secondary
School Principals (NASSP) have all devoted sustained attention to
C/PBAE. The UCEA effort, funded in part by a grant from the
United States Office of Information to the Atlanta, Georgia, Public
Schools, brought theoreticians from major colleges and universities
together with practitioners from the schools to identify, analyze, and
assess the areas of competence required for effective performance in
the school principalship. In the Atlanta project, the following competence domains were delineated and described: initiating and responding
to social change, preparing the organization for effective response,
making effective decisions, achieving effective human relations and

morale, administering and improving the instructional programme, and evaluating school processes and products. This work is summarized in a recent book, *Performance Objectives for School Principals* (Culbertson, Henson and Morrison, 1974).

The NCPEA effort was spearheaded in 1971 by Lloyd E. McCleary, Professor of Educational Administration at the University of Utah, who initiated the call for interested professors to conceptualize, examine, and experiment with C/PBAE. An enthusiastic response to this leadership resulted in several substantial outcomes: a C/PBAE interest group was established within NCPEA; the *CCBC Notebook*[12] was founded to serve as a vehicle for the communication of new ideas, research findings, and practical approaches to C/PBAE; and over fifty learning modules were subsequently produced for individualized instruction in educational administration.[13] The format of these learning modules includes the identification of required competencies, an individualized sequence of study, group learning experiences where appropriate, and the development of performance products that carry each competence to the application level.

The PSSAS Committee, initially concerned with the administrative internship as a vehicle for preparing school administrators (NASSP, 1970), sponsored an invitational conference in 1971 concerning ways to improve the preparation of secondary school administrators. From this conference a proposed programme model was developed to include the following dimensions: the functional areas of role content, the administrative processes, the domains of administrative behaviour, and the instructional variables (methods, personnel, and assessment) involved in developing and providing continuous progress training programmes in educational administration (Brandewine, Johnson and Trump, 1972). When systematic feedback concerning this model was received, it revealed a strongly favourable reaction in colleges and universities to the emphasis on behavioural objectives in programmes for preparing school administrators.

The emphasis on competency-based education has also been strong

---

[12] CCBC Notebook, published quarterly, is available from The University of Utah, Department of Educational Administration, 339 Milton Bennion Hall, Salt Lake City, Utah 84112.

[13] Individualized Learning Modules for Principals, Teachers and other Central Office Staff are available from: ILM Publishers, 1470 Wilton Way, Salt Lake City, Utah 84108.

among teachers' associations. If only as a footnote, five developments in teacher education should be mentioned. First, recognizing the need for improving the education of teachers for work in urban areas, the United States Office of Education inaugurated in 1968 a nationwide programme for the Training of Teacher Trainers (TTT) which provided funding for several exemplary programmes utilizing performance-based models in teacher education. Second, in 1970 the National Council for the Accreditation of Teacher Education (NCATE), which accredits institutions that produce 80 per cent of the teachers in the United States, gave its approval to a new set of standards which emphasized the competency-based approach. Third, the National Education Association (NEA) fostered the establishment of Instruction and Professional Development (IPD) committees in a continuing effort to improve the professional standards in teacher education. Fourth, the American Association of Colleges for Teacher Education (AACTE) established a Committee on Performance-Based Teacher Education which has sponsored several significant publications.[14] Finally, and most recently, the Educational Testing Service (ETS) has conducted a pilot project designed to: (1) develop a taxonomy of teaching behaviour, (2) develop systems for measuring teaching behaviour, (3) evaluate the effectiveness of training systems which educate for teaching competence, and (4) develop systems for evaluating the performance of graduates of competency-based programmes (McDonald, 1974). From this effort, a Commission on Performance Based Education is proposed as holding considerable promise for involving institutions in a wide variety of research and development activities to improve education.

University Activities

It is probably conservative to estimate that as many as one-third of the Divisions or Departments of Educational Administration in colleges and universities throughout the nation are directing efforts toward reconceptualizing and recasting certain components of their training programmes in ways congruent with C/PBAE. This emphasis is particularly marked in those institutions where there is a strong emphasis on competency-based programmes for undergraduate teachers and in those states where close working relationships exist between and among professional educators in teacher training departments, in

---

[14] See Elam (1971), Elfenbein (1971), Andrews (1971), Burke (1971), Giles and Foster (1971), Wever and Cooper (1971), Browdy (1971).

educational administration departments, and in state departments of education. Only a sampling, and by no means an exhaustive, enumeration of current C/PBAE programmes may be cited as illustrative of the major lines of emphasis and endeavour.

Typical of the efforts to identify competency needs and to specify competency domains in administration are programmes at the Universities of Georgia, Minnesota, Tennessee, and Texas. Under a grant from the United States Office of Education, the University of Georgia is conducting a statewide analysis of the competencies required of school principals. This programme has brought together consultants, professors, and practitioners in regional meetings designed not only to identify basic competencies, but also to enhance the effective role performance of school principals.

The University of Minnesota's Division of Educational Administration initially examined the status of programmes for preparing school principals (Nickerson, 1972) and subsequently developed a programme matrix of skill categories and competency clusters required of administrators (University of Minnesota, 1973). In the State of Minnesota, effective 1 July 1974, the certification of all school superintendents, elementary school principals, and secondary school principals requires a minimum of forty-five quarter credits beyond a master's degree or a specialist or higher degree, and requires that all applicants have competencies in all of the following areas: school administration, supervision, curriculum, and instruction. Moreover, those colleges and universities responsible for the training must show that competency-based programmes submitted for approval have been developed with appropriate participation from school administrators, teachers, school board members, and citizens.[15] The University of Minnesota programme is designed to meet this mandate.

Tennessee, for over two decades a leader in the competency-based approach, was the first state to require that the certification of administrators be based on demonstrated competence. At the University of Tennessee-Knoxville strong emphasis traditionally has been placed on the use of internship and simulation experiences to identify, develop, and assess effective administrative performance (Rasmussen and Hughes, 1972). The elusive yet pervasive content domain of effective

---

[15] Educ 330, School Administrators, Teacher Certification Regulations, State of Minnesota, Department of Education, St Paul, Adopted 16 April 1973.

interpersonal relationships in administration is given systematic attention in the Tennessee programme (Hughes, 1974).

Texas, also a leader in competency-based education, has mandated performance-based programmes in all of that state's sixty-six institutions which prepare teachers for certification. Despite a major struggle which ensued concerning both the tenets of the performance-based approach and the control of professional education,[16] the movement there toward C/PBAE is strong. Particularly noteworthy is the work at the University of Texas-Austin by McIntyre who, in cooperation with McCleary, initially devised a general planning framework for competency development, wherein the type and level of learning are matched with the effective training processes in university programmes in educational administration (McCleary and McIntyre, 1972). In the Texas programme, particular emphasis has been placed on the competency content domain of administering and improving the instructional programme of the school (McIntyre, 1974).

Typical of the efforts to prepare C/PBAE training packages and materials are programmes at Kansas State University and the University of Utah. At Kansas State, Van Meter developed a number of procedural, topic, and author modules for the teaching of theory in educational administration (Van Meter, 1973). C/PBAE modules developed by McCleary and others at the University of Utah treat the following theories in administration: social systems theory, organizational theory, learning theory, and decision theory. As indicated earlier, individualized learning modules also are available concerning exemplary programmes at preschool, elementary, middle, secondary, and community college levels.

The assessment or evaluation of competency attainment in C/PBAE is emphasized at the University of Washington-Seattle and the University of Wisconsin-Madison. At Washington, Bolton (1971) has for several years been concerned with the use of simulation techniques for preparing educational administrators. Recently, he has developed several useful models for the evaluation of performance in education (Bolton, 1974).

At Wisconsin, the emphasis traditionally has been on assessing the adequacy of administrative theories in terms of the following criteria: clarity, vitality, utility, generality, complexity, and currency (Lipham,

[16] See Houston and Howsam (1974), Sandoz (1974) and Maxwell (1974).

1973). Currently at Wisconsin, laboratory based, computer controlled experimental research is being conducted concerning competence in information utilization in administrative decision making (Lipham and Spuck, 1974). Empirical studies to isolate the critical decision-making skills of the school principals are also being conducted in urban schools (Lipham, 1974) and in schools that have adopted and implemented the Wisconsin system of individually guided education (IGE).[17]

As these national and state efforts reveal, C/PBAE is rapidly moving toward institutionalization.

INSTITUTIONALIZATION OF C/PBAE

In considering the extent to which C/PBAE will permeate the field of educational administration, one first must examine the basic reasons for criticism of the concept. Opposition to the competency-based approach derives from multiple sources, not the least of which is an antisystems orientation wherein administration is viewed more as an art than a science. At the present time, however, the main objections are the following:

1. Philosophical objections—too much emphasis is placed on consensus, orderliness, assessment, efficiency, and accountability which can be antithetical to the essence of human life, freedom, and creativity.

2. Objections to power sharing—the expertise of the professor is challenged by practitioners, and even citizens, and the professor's power to control entry to and promotion in the profession is eroded.

3. Objections to objectives—the practice of educational administration is more situationally and personalistically unique than it is common across specializations.

4. Objections to the content domains—some domains (particularly in any given professor's specialization) are considered more important than others.

5. Objections to content mastery—phenomenological perceptivity is more important than practical performance.

6. Objections to measurement—some learning outcomes not only are

[17] James M. Lipham and Marvin J. Fruth, *The Principalship of an IGE School*, Addison-Wesley, in press.

not measurable, but emphasis on their assessment may destroy those very outcomes—e.g., the professor-student relationship.

7. Objections to measurement criteria—greater emphasis is placed on objectives that can be measured, to the neglect of those that are difficult to assess quantitatively. Moreover, weak measures may be substituted as evidence of goal attainment, thereby distorting the goals themselves.

8. Objections to 'excessive' activity and change—present systems of university instruction have evolved as more cost-efficient than individually-monitored, continuous progress programmes.

9. Objections to a behavioural emphasis—authentic thinkers, scholars, and leaders are needed more than trained management technicians.

10. Objections to fractionalization—the whole is greater than the sum of its parts; moreover, the greater the number of parts identified then the less likely it is that they will constitute a viable gestalt.

Without belabouring the opposition with obvious counterclaims to each of the aforementioned, suffice it to observe that in terms of Thelen's model of educational change (Thelen, 1964), already many associations, institutions, and individual professors are hustling to be included among the innovators—or at least among the early adopters of C/PBAE. The power and utility of the new approach probably is irreversible and ultimately will be diffused, not only throughout the United States, but in other nations as well. If the historically cyclical theory of social change prevails, however, one might even predict that eventually in the future there will emerge another, perhaps 'new humanistic' approach to the preparation of educational administrators—possibly in our time.

BIBLIOGRAPHY

Andrews, R. L. (1974), 'How Sound Are the Assumptions of Competency-Based Programs?', *Educational Leadership*, 31 (January), 310–12.

Andrews, T. E. (1971), *Manchester Interview: Competency-Based Teacher Education/Certification*, AACTE, Washington, D.C.

Argyris, C. (1957), *Personality and Organization*, Harper and Row, New York.

Bobbitt, F. (1913), 'Some General Principles of Management Applied to the problems of City School Systems', in *The Supervision of City Schools*, University of Chicago, Chicago.

Bolton, D. E. (1971), *The Use of Simulation in Educational Administration*, Merrill, Columbus, Ohio.

Bolton, D. E. (1974), 'Evaluating School Processes and Products', in Culbertson, J. A., Henson, C. and Morrison, R. (eds), op. cit.

Brandewine, D., Johnson, T. and Trump, J. L. (1972), 'The Preparation and Development of Secondary School Administrators: A Summary', *Bulletin of The National Association of Secondary School Principals*, 55 (March), 24-41.

Broudy, H. S. (1971), *A Critique of Performance-Based Teacher Education*, AACTE, Washington, D.C.

Burke, C. (1971), *The Individualized, Competency-Based System of Teacher Education at Weber State College*, AACTE, Washington, D.C.

Callahan, R. E. (1962), *Education and The Cult of Efficiency*, University of Chicago, Chicago.

Campbell, R. F. and Newell, L. J. (1973), 'A Study of Professors of Educational Administration: A Summary', *Educational Administration Quarterly*, 9 (Autumn), 3-27.

Campbell, R. F. and Lipham, J. M. (eds) (1960), *Administrative Theory as a Guide to Action*, University of Chicago, Chicago.

CCBC Notebook, University of Utah, Salt Lake City, Utah.

Colardarci, A. P. and Getzels, J. W. (1955), *The Use of Theory in Educational Administration*, Stanford University School of Education, Stanford, California.

Cubberley, E. P. (1916), *Public School Administration*, Houghton, Mifflin, Boston.

Culbertson, J. A., Henson, C. and Morrison, R. (eds) (1974), *Performance Objectives for School Principals*, McCutchan, Berkeley, California.

Drummond, W. M. (1974), 'Does PBTE Mean Reform?', *Educational Leadership*, 34 (January), 291-3.

Elam, S. (1971), *Performance-Based Teacher Education: What is the State of the Art?*, AACTE, Washington, D.C.

Elfenbein, J. M. (1971), *Performance-Based Teacher Education Programs: A Comparative Description*, AACTE, Washington, D.C.

Gantt, H. L. (1916), *Industrial Leadership*, Yale University Press, New Haven, Connecticut.

Getzels, J. W., Lipham, J. M. and Campbell, R. F. (1968), *Educational Administration as a Social Process*, Harper and Row, New York.

Getzels, J. W. and Guba, E. G. (1957), 'Social Behavior and the Administrative Process', *School Review*, 65 (Winter), 423-41.

Getzels, J. W. and Thelen, H. A. (1960), 'The Classroom as a Unique Social System', in Henry, N. B. (ed), *The Dynamics of Instructional Groups*, NSSE, University of Chicago, Chicago, pp. 53-62.

Gilbreth, F. B. (1911), *Motion Study*, Van Nostrand Reinhold, New York.

Giles, F. T. and Foster, C. D. (1971), *Changing Teacher Education in a Large Urban University*, AACTE, Washington, D.C.

Graff, O. B. and Street, C. (1956), *Improving Competence in Educational Administration*, Harper and Row, New York.

Gregg, R. T. and Sims, P. D. (1972), 'Quality of Faculties and Programs of Graduate Departments of Educational Administration', *Educational Administration Quarterly* 8 (Autumn), 67-92.

Halpin, A. W. (1958), *Administrative Theory in Education*, University of Chicago, Chicago.

Halpin, A.W. (1956), *The Leadership Behavior of School Superintendents*, Ohio State University, Columbus, Ohio.

Hemphill, J. K., Griffiths, D. E., and Frederiksen, N. (1962), *Administrative Performance and Personality*, Columbia University, New York.

Houston, R. and Howsam, R. B. (1974), 'CBTE: The Ayes of Texas', *Phi Delta Kappan*, 55 (January), 299–303.

Hughes, L. W. (1974), 'Achieving Effective Human Relations and Morale', in Culbertson, J. A., Henson, C. and Morrison, R. (eds), op. cit.

Immegart, G. L. (1969), 'Systems Theory and Taxonomic Inquiry Into Organizational Behavior in Education', in Griffiths, D. E. (ed), *Developing Taxonomies of Organizational Behavior in Education*, Rand McNally, Skokie, Illinois.

Individualized Learning Modules, ILM Publishers, Salt Lake City, Utah.

Klausmeier, H. J. (1974), '*Instructional Programming for the Individual Student*', Working Paper, University of Wisconsin, Research and Development Center for Cognitive Learning, Madison, Wisconsin.

Krathwol, D. (1973), 'Introductory Note', in Merwin, J. C. *Performance-Based Teacher Education: Some Measurement and Decision-Making Considerations*, American Association of Colleges for Teacher Education, Washington, D.C.

Lawrence, G. (1974), 'Delineating and Measuring Professional Competencies', *Educational Leadership*, 31 (January), 298–302.

Lipham, J. M. and Hoeh, J. A., Jr. (1974), *The Principalship: Foundations and Functions*, Harper and Row, New York.

Lipham, J. M. (1973), 'Leadership: General Theory and Research', in Cunningham, L. L. and Gephart, W. J. (eds), *Leadership: The Science and The Art Today*, Peacock, Itaska, Illinois.

Lipham, J. M. (1971), 'Leadership in Education', *Encyclopedia of Education*, Macmillan, New York.

Lipham, J. M. (1973), 'Content Selection in Organizational Theory and Behavior in Education', in Culbertson, J. A., *et al.* (eds), *Social Science Content for Preparing Educational Leaders*, Merrill, Columbus, Ohio, Ch. 12.

Lipham, J. M. and Spuck, D. W. (1974), '*Experimental Analysis of Information Utilization in Administrative Decision Making*', Working Paper, Dept. of Educational Administration, University of Wisconsin, Madison, Wisconsin.

Lipham, J. M. (1974), 'Improving the Decision-Making Skills of the Principal', in Culbertson, J. A., Henson, C. and Morrison, R. (eds), op. cit.

Lipham, J. M. and Fruth, M. J., *The Principalship of an IGE School*, Addison-Wesley, Reading, Mass., in press.

McCleary, L. E. and McIntyre, K. E. (1972), 'Competency Development and University Methodology', *Bulletin of The National Association of Secondary School Principals*, 56 (March), 53–68.

Mcdonald, F. J. (1974), 'The National Commission on Performance-Based Education', *Phi Delta Kappan*, 55 (January), 296–8.

McIntyre, K. E. (1974), 'Administering and Improving the Instructional Program', in Culbertson, J. A., Henson, C. and Morrison, R. (eds), op. cit.

March, J. G. (1965), *Handbook of Organizations*, Rand McNally, Skokie, Illinois.

Maxwell, W. D. (1974), 'PBTE: The Case of The Emperor's New Clothes', *Phi Delta Kappan*, 55 (January), 306–11.

Mayo, E. (1933), *The Human Problems of an Industrial Civilization*, Macmillan, New York.

Metcalf, H. C. and Urwick, L. F. (eds) (1940), *Dynamic Administration: The Collected Papers of Mary Parker Follett*, Harper and Row, New York.

Minnesota Department of Education, Educ. 330, School Administrators (1973) Teacher Certification Regulations, St Paul, Minnesota.

National Association of Secondary School Principals (1970), *Experience in Leadership*, NASSP, Washington, D.C.

Nickerson, N. C. (1972), 'Status of Programs for Principals', *Bulletin of The National Association of Secondary School Principals*, 56 (March), 10–23.

Presthus, R. (1962), *The Organizational Society*, Knopf, New York.

Rasmussen, G. R. and Hughes, L. W. (1972), 'Simulation: It's the Real Thing' *Bulletin of The National Association of Secondary School Principals*, 56 (March), 76–81.

Reeder, W. G. (1931), *The Fundamentals of Public School Administration*, Macmillan, New York.

Roethlisberger, F. J. and Dickson, W. J. (1939), *Management and The Worker*, Harvard University Press, Cambridge, Mass.

Sandoz, E. (1974), 'CBTE: The Nays of Texas', *Phi Delta Kappan*, 55 (January), 304–6.

Scott, W. G. (1967), *Organization Theory*, Irwin, Homewood, Illinois.

Taylor, F. W. (1911), *Scientific Management*, Harper and Row, New York.

Thelen, H. A. (1964), 'New Practices on the Firing Line', *Administrator's Notebook*, 12 (January), 1.

Thompson, J. D. (1967), *Organizations in Action*, McGraw-Hill, New York.

UCEA Five Year Plan (1974–9), University Council for Educational Administration, Columbus, Ohio.

University Council for Educational Administration (1973), *Instructional Materials Catalog*, Columbus, Ohio.

University of Minnesota, *Competency Program Development Plan*, Working Paper 1973.

Van Meter, E. J. (1973), 'Theory in Educational Administration: An Instructional Module Teaching Approach', *Educational Administration Quarterly*, 9 (Autumn), 81–95.

Wever, W. A. and Cooper, J. M. (1971), *Competency-Based Teacher Education, A Scenario*, AACTE, Washington, D.C.

Yauch, W. A. (1949), *Improving Human Relations in School Administration*, Harper and Row, New York.

18 The Future in Educational Administration as a Field of Study, Teaching and Research

W. G. WALKER

It is perhaps significant that the final paper of the Third International Intervisitation Programme, where the emphasis has largely been upon the *practice* of educational administration, should concern itself with educational administration as a field of *study*. Such a concern would have been treated with derision in most of our home countries as recently as a few decades ago. Today we take this concern for granted, and this is a sure sign that the practice of educational administration as a professional enterprise rather than as a technical vocation, is coming of age. It is a sure sign that the practitioners of educational administration, like those of engineering, medicine and law, for example, recognize that there is a body of knowledge which is worth preserving, probing and prodding, that the body of knowledge is built upon theoretical bases whose understanding depends upon intellectual capacities of a high order and that the utilization of that knowledge calls for an advanced level of training on the part of its practitioners. As Professor Baron pointed out in his opening paper (Chapter 2), the prerequisite for this development, a well comprehended body of custom, theory and practice about educational administration is now beginning to emerge. The key correlates of this emergence are the conducting of research into educational administration and the teaching of courses in programmes for the professional preparation or training of educational administrators.

Before proceeding, I cannot resist the temptation to emphasize that schools and school systems, as such, are here to stay, in spite of the attacks by Illich and his ilk. Schools of the future might well take on different forms, perhaps as implied by the Fauré Report, but *schools there will be*. The obvious corollary, of course, is that school system administration is also here to stay—and that if more intensive study of the field is long overdue, as the Sixth Commonwealth Education Conference in Jamaica on the theme 'Managing Education' suggested—

then how much more urgent is such study if traditional forms and structures are to be revised or even replaced!

Perhaps I should also make the point at this stage that for the purposes of this paper 'educational administration' refers to the policies, practices and procedures carried out by all administrators or managers who are responsible for the control of personnel in a school or school system. 'Educational administration' thus refers to the duties of officers ranging from Permanent Secretary or Director General to Principal of a school or Head of a department in a school.

I have expressly avoided referring to administrators of higher education institutions: in the interests of simplicity of presentation my concern must necessarily be with schools and school systems.

SOME ASSUMPTIONS ABOUT EDUCATIONAL ADMINISTRATION

Before going on to refer specifically to the two target areas of teaching and research I wish to present some basic assumptions about educational administration (Walker, 1970) which might profoundly affect our attitudes towards teaching and research in the field. The assumptions are:

1. Educational administration in schools and school systems is primarily concerned with individual children. Any policy, practice or procedure which cannot be seen as contributing to the growth, development and welfare of the individual child is indefensible. Of course, it will always be argued that such a statement is unrealistic: this thoroughly unsatisfactory teacher *must* be kept on because fighting the teachers' union is too time and energy-consuming, or, the next new school *must* be built in a particular politician's electorate because he is a powerful lobbyist. I recognize that there will always be problems of politics, economics and resource allocation, but our professional commitment demands that the child must remain 'at the centre'.

2. Educational administration is concerned with contributing not only to the growth and development of individual children, but also to the growth and development of the other key human links in the educative process—the parent and the teacher.

3. Educational administration is crucially concerned with leadership, with the capacity to produce and nourish ideas, to stimulate thought,

to introduce and manage change, to add the magic of the visionary to the customary stolidity of the actuary.

4. Educational administration is an organizational phenomenon. Its processes take place within formal and informal organizational environments, which are at once political and economic in nature and whose participants' behaviour can only be properly understood through the eyes of the philosopher and the social scientist.

5. Educational administration takes place within a framework of national goals. In the countries of the old Commonwealth such goals may find little explicit presentation in school system rules, regulations and curricula; in many countries of the new Commonwealth there may be much explicit attention to detail, including administrative modes of procedure, syllabus content and even methods of teaching.

6. Educational administration is not a process for which simplistic, easy 'how-to-do-it' paths can be spelt out. It is essentially a human interaction process which takes place in complex organizations. Effective administrative action depends upon a combination of the unique characteristics of the individual and the organization at a given time in a particular social setting.

I have presented these six assumptions to show that educational administration is a demanding field of human endeavour which goes far beyond the financial and managerial routines which are described as 'administration' in some quarters.

I have cited these assumptions because I believe that they are of great importance for the discussion which follows. The reasons for my belief I will not have time to develop, but I hope that they will become obvious as the paper progresses.

TEACHING IN EDUCATIONAL ADMINISTRATION

Teaching in the area of educational administration could refer to teaching *about* educational administration, perhaps as one might describe educational structures in a given country to undergraduate tyros. On the other hand it could refer to teaching relating to the *process* or *practice* of educational administration as one might describe structures or discuss theories of managerial behaviour to provide insights for school Heads employed in a system. It is the latter interpretation which I have employed in this paper: 'teaching' here refers only to teaching in the context of professional preparation.

It is obvious from the six points made above that administration is above all a practical phenomenon. It is something we *do*. It is equally obvious, however, that what we do calls for high levels of intellectual ability, insights into alternative modes of action, capacities to weigh up and arrive at decisions and abilities to carry out those decisions within complex organizational and political frameworks. It calls for a high level of sensitivity if the needs of children and of society are to be met to the satisfaction of the administrator.

I wish to emphasize here the concept of *high level* insights and abilities. It is the development of these which is the peculiar domain of the university or other institution of higher education. (For simplicity all institutions of higher education will be referred to as universities in this paper.) It is not the task of the university to concern itself with 'administrivia', or with homilies about 'how to do it'. On the contrary it is the task of the university to provide insights which will allow the administrator sensitively to ask the most appropriate questions, diagnose the dynamics of the situation in which he operates, make a choice among alternative modes of action and put the chosen mode into operation (Eidell and Kitchel, 1968). It is also its task to provide the administrator with insights into leader and follower behaviour involving both groups and individuals, to suggest methods of presenting and following up innovative ideas, to provide familiarity with ideas and concepts from other systems and countries and to interpret and explain the economic, political and legal framework within which he must work.

It is crucial, I repeat, that the university concern itself centrally with practice but not with the 'administrivia' associated with practice. It is when universities concern themselves with administrivia that the tension between the practitioner and the university to which Professor Baron refers in his paper, is likely to occur.

Here I must place my cards clearly on the table for all to see. With John Dewey I take the point of view that theory is in the end the most practical of all things, that we do not act independently of our motives, that the real gap, if any, is not between theory and practice, but between good theory and poor theory (Walker, 1970). Any university course or programme which cannot and does not clearly and explicitly relate theory to practice and present its theories as providing guides to alternative modes of action, is not only selling its students short and claiming more expertise than it has the right to claim, but is providing a rich source of the tension to which Professor Baron refers.

What then, should be taught in these courses? In the main the guides to administrator behaviour are to be found in the individual administrator's value system, in the value systems of the society and institution in which he works. The explanations of his behaviour in the light of these are chiefly to be found in the social sciences (Baron and Taylor, 1969). One might grossly oversimplify the situation by saying that the work of the administrator is understood not only through the concepts of politics, economics, social psychology, psychology, sociology and anthropology, but also through the too often ignored concepts of religion, ethics, values, history and literature (Crane and Walker, 1973).

Just which aspects of these disciplines will be brought to the attention of the student will depend upon his experience, academic background, level of responsibility and a number of other variables, but if he is not brought face to face with the intellectual foundations of at least some of these, his contribution as a practitioner will be all the poorer. As I have pointed out elsewhere, the administrator needs the intellectual stimulation of theory in the life of the mind; he also needs it in the buzzing confusion of the administrative day, if there is any validity in the six assumptions presented earlier.

Where should such teaching take place? In my view, in the light of the desperate shortage of information and the vast demand for relevant knowledge, anywhere and everywhere possible. Offerings might range from a one or two day meeting arranged by an inspector of schools, through a two week vacation course at a teachers' college or a six week programme at a staff college to a full masters' or doctoral programme at a university.

Who should attend such courses? Surely anyone and everyone qualified either by experience or previous academic qualifications or both, to attend the appropriate programme or institution. It is not asking too much, in view of the key role of the administrator in the efficient use of resource, for governments and other employing agencies to meet at least part of the costs incurred by individuals in attending such courses. Such 'seed money' is likely to be repaid many times in terms of administrator interest, commitment, morale and efficiency.

What should be the level of experience and maturity of participants? Throughout most of the Commonwealth and USA persons are appointed to administrative positions in educational systems only after they have successfully completed several years of professional experience, usually as a teacher, but occasionally in other occupations such as accountancy. Almost invariably, then, the educational administrator, or the budding educational administrator, already possesses a previous qualification and some years of experience. It is these qualified, experienced people who in my view constitute the most important target for our teaching effort.

In some countries, courses in 'educational administration' are offered to undergraduates in universities and teachers' colleges. While it is *possible* to mount a limited range of such courses, and while it is *possible* that in the future a first degree in educational administration might develop somewhere in the world (perhaps not such an unusual step when one considers the availability of first degrees for business managers and army officers, for example) it seems to me a great pity to expend resource on such students when no more than perhaps ten per cent of existing educational administrators in the English-speaking world outside the USA have undertaken any kind of formal, disciplined course in their area of professional concern. For many years to come we must, in my view, concentrate upon training the men or women about to enter administrative positions and on retraining and refreshing those already in such positions.

How might our teaching be most effective? I am convinced, after many years of experience and observation, that the crucial element in such teaching is *relevance*. I hasten to repeat, however, that relevance does not mean concern with trivia. What is does mean is a constant emphasis in teaching and discussion, no matter how 'theoretical', upon organizational reality so far as the recipients of the teaching are concerned. Such reality might be achieved by sheer excellence in lecturing, choice of tutorial group members, careful selection of course participants, internship arrangements, visits to other institutions and simulations of various kinds.

Perhaps I could briefly comment on the last two of these. Over the years I have found a great deal of interest and enthusiasm among my own students, all of whom are graduates and already employed in administrative positions, for visits to and discussions with administrators in a wide range of institutions ranging from government departments through semi-governmental commissions, hospitals, gaols and mutual service organizations to private enterprise in its most traditional form. This kind of informal cross-organizational teaching seems to have at least as profound an effect upon some students as does cross-disciplinary 'academic' study upon others.

With regard to simulations, those relatively inexpensive and non-threatening games of which most of us make far too little use in our teaching, one has only to mention in passing the case studies (Taylor, 1973) inbaskets, computer-based decision games and audio- and video-taped situations (Walker, 1974) now becoming available to see that such devices promise much in the way of helping to keep our feet on the ground in the future.

Who should teach such courses? Here one can only plead for a range of background and experience. For many years institutions concerned with training administrators took care to employ only long-experienced, indeed, 'long-in-the-tooth' administrators, to teach their courses. Today, it is almost universally recognized that such lecturers, on their own, tend to provide insufficient growing points. After all, it is the future, rather than the past, or even the present, which is the prime concern of budding educational administrators today.

At the same time, anyone with knowledge of the world scene in educational administrator preparation can point to institutions in which young, bright, specialists in the social sciences, but with no administrative experience in school systems, have wrought havoc through their teaching. Clearly, what is needed is a combination of experience and academic insights, ideally in single individuals, but at least in the form of a balanced teaching staff (Campbell and Newell, 1973).

Perhaps a comment upon short courses is apposite at this stage. Too often these courses are staffed by old timers from within the organization. Instead of providing a cacophony of ideas, the growing point of dynamic administration, they tend to provide an introduction to the stereotypes of the organization within which they are employed. This short-sighted staffing pattern, usually supported by those who wish to economize on funds and who too often, seek not to 'rock the boat', can also, if not firmly scotched, seriously impede the innovative potential of staff colleges run by single institutions or organizations. It is for this reason more than any other than I would avoid the establishment of single organization staff colleges as such, especially for senior administrators, and attempt to find outside programmes in which those administrators might interact with colleagues from other organizations.

RESEARCH IN EDUCATIONAL ADMINISTRATION

In the previous section I have discussed teaching in educational administration and have suggested that this might take place on a wide spectrum ranging from short, inservice courses to long, disciplined periods of university study. It would be unwise of me to suggest that research of a worthwhile nature can also be carried out as readily at all levels. I am not saying that research of various levels of difficulty and sophistication cannot be carried out at most levels, but I am sounding a warning bell that the pitfalls of research work are more numerous and more serious than are those of teaching. After all, we administrators have developed a core of knowledge and understanding through long-experience which permits us to make some reasonably confident predictions and offer explanations about human behaviour in organizational settings; outside the universities and a few specialist institutes we have no comparable core of understanding of research into *process* beyond the most elementary data-gathering level. Of course, many of us with academic training have done some minor research in comparative education or perhaps politics of education, but this is just not true of the over-whelming majority of educational administrators in the English-speaking world.

And yet without research the world stands still and none of us would wish the world to pass us by. Will the world of the twenty-first century look with confidence to educational administrators whose concepts of research, if any, are firmly based in the philosophical or historical studies of the early nineteenth century? Of course, it will not, and this is one reason why educational administrators are increasingly turning to the universities and other special foundations for assistance. We can only wish them luck, for the difficulties are horrific.

Perhaps I should emphasize at this stage that I am referring to research in the area of *educational administration*, not to research in education in general. I am often concerned, in observing research scholars in various parts of the world, that there seems to be no generally accepted idea of conducting research in the specific area, no matter how loosely defined, of educational administration *per se*. One finds administration students undertaking studies which could just as readily be carried out by students of education generally—and this at a time when very little indeed in the way of 'hard' data about educational administration is available to us. Surely it would not be too much to ask such students to 'zero in' on not just studies of staff morale, but the relationship between morale and Principal behaviour; not just the adoption of a new reading programme, but the role of the Chief Education Officer in suggesting or supporting the programme; not just the introduction of a new policy on higher school organization, but the role of the Vice-president of the teachers' union in influencing governmental policy.

It is, of course, not hard to demonstrate the difficulties facing the researcher in the field of organization and administration. These were expressed only too clearly by Schwab (1964) in his now classic description of but one school as an object of research:

> In brief, as an object of research, a school as an administered entity is an animal, a stochastic series of an especially complicated kind. Each given moment of its tenure is in large part the consequence of previous moments of that tenure; each given moment may be filled by a vast number of alternative actions or inactions, each one of which will modify in a different way the character of the next moment. If, for simplicity's sake, we freeze the flight of time's arrow, we are still faced with the same high order of complexity that faces the physiologist who attempts to study the complex interactions of parts which constitute a living organism in a relatively steady state.

In the face of such difficulties, research of a detailed, disciplinary type will doubtless remain chiefly the responsibility of the universities and slowly a data base gleaned from masters' and doctors' studies will develop. At my own university we have adopted the principle of requiring our Master of Educational Administration students to carry out research work in certain narrow, specific areas in an attempt to build up a substantial data base in at least a few fields. Thus, at one time we might have as many as twenty students in various parts of Australia working on each of Organizational Climate, Staff Morale and Pupil Control Ideology as areas of study. I believe that we shall adhere to this policy for some years to come, and I would hope that universities in other countries would join us in cooperative studies of this type.

For the bulk of budding educational administrators in the Commonwealth, however, the possibility of undertaking anything like the studies just described or even much watered-down 'field studies' is remote. Nonetheless, it seems to me that in all countries, 'new' and 'old', it behoves educational administrators to develop in their colleagues a receptivity to what might be termed 'research-mindedness'. This characteristic is typified by:

1. A readiness to seek definitions for terms in common usage, and having arrived at definitions to use them only in that sense. For example, the words 'educational administrator' cry out for definition to anyone who, at a Commonwealth Education Conference notes the differences in usage among delegates from, for example, Britain, Australia, Canada and Nigeria. Another term which causes much difficulty is 'decentralization' which can be used in either a political/governmental or administrative/devolution sense. The lack of definition of this term is causing serious misunderstandings among educators in Australia at present. No doubt glossaries like *Education in Five English Speaking Countries* (Walker, 1973) will lead to improvements here, but inevitably change will be slow.

2. A readiness to accept the existence of theory both as a guide to action and as an explanation of action taken. Once one accepts that theory serves these purposes for the practitioner, it is not too big a jump to accepting the fact that researchers use theory, too, though primarily as a source of predictions about behaviour which can then be tested, usually by disciplined modes of enquiry. It would do no harm for practitioners to realise that theory can be just as frustrating for researchers, and, indeed, for theorists themselves! (Griffiths, 1969).

3. A readiness to subscribe to (and read) journals like *Educational Administration Bulletin*, *Canadian Administrator*, *Educational Administration Quarterly* and *Journal of Educational Administration*. It might be objected that some of the material in these publications is too research oriented for many practitioners, especially in the new Commonwealth. This is probably true, and although in time journals will emerge, perhaps under the auspices of CCEA, to interpret the reported findings for practitioners, it is nonetheless important that practitioners, like medical practitioners reading their journals, at least make an *effort* to understand research reports.
In this regard special attention might be drawn to abstracting journals like *Educational Administration Abstracts* and to the services offered by national and international data banks like the ERIC Centre for Educational Management at the University of Oregon, which is now abstracting certain materials under contract to CCEA specifically to serve Commonwealth Countries.

4. A readiness to co-operate in research projects proposed by local, regional, national and international agencies. One of the major

problems faced by researchers in the area of educational administration is the fear on the part of many officials that under the scrutiny of the researcher too many skeletons will begin rattling in the officials' respective closets.

Fortunately, the emphasis in research today is away from outsiders coming in to carry out research *in* or *for* the institution and towards researchers seeking to carry out projects of an 'action' type in cooperation with those within the institution. Astute administrators these days are aware that research of this type has important connotations for organizational development. Indeed, administrators are increasingly recognizing the value to practitioners of the new 'research and development' movement and the advantages which it promises for children in schools.

5. A readiness to seek financial support for and write up research projects, 'action' or otherwise, carried out in one's school or school systems. Only when practitioners write (in association with a professional researcher, if they wish) will the great mass of practitioners be prepared to read. The problem is cyclical, but it is not impossible to break into the cycle, assuming 'research-mindedness' on the part of practitioners.

CONCLUSION

A paper of this length could not hope to achieve more than a broad overview of Educational Administration as a field of study. Nor could it do more than gloss over questions of teaching and research which relate to that field of study.

Interestingly enough, most of the issues raised here were discussed in the final session of the first International Intervisitation Programme held at the University of Alberta in 1966. One has only to read Professor Enns' summary of that discussion to see what great strides we have taken internationally in less than a decade—and yet what small steps we have taken on a few of the important issues raised today.

Still, we can indubitably conclude with confidence in the very words used by Enns in 1966, 'Interest and enthusiasm once aroused should not be permitted to relapse' (Enns, 1969).

BIBLIOGRAPHY

Baron, George and Taylor, William (eds) (1969), *Educational Administration and the Social Sciences*, Athlone Press, London.

Campbell, R. F. and Newell, L. J. (1973), *A Study of Professors of Educational Administration*, UCEA, Columbus, Ohio.

Crane, A. R. and Walker, W. G. (1973), 'The Selection of Content for a Theory-Based Perspective', Chap. 16 in Culbertson, J. *et al. Social Science Content for Preparing Educational Leaders*, Merrill, Columbus, Ohio.

Eidell, T. L. and Kitchel, J. M. (eds) (1968), *Knowledge Production and Utilization in Educational Administration*, UCEA, Columbus, Ohio and CASEA, Eugene, Oregon.

Enns, Fred. (1969), 'The Promise of International Cooperation in the Preparation of Educational Administrators', Chap. XVI in Baron G., Cooper, D. and Walker, W. G. (eds), *Educational Administration: International Perspectives*, Rand McNally, Chicago, p. 320.

Farquhar, R. H. and Piele, P. K. (1972), *Preparing Educational Leaders: A Review of Recent Literature*, ERIC/CEM, Eugene, Oregon and UCEA, Columbus, Ohio.

Fauré, Edgar *et al.* (1972), *Learning to Be*, UNESCO, Paris.

Griffiths, D. E. (ed) (1969), *Developing Taxonomies of Organizational Behavior in Education Administration*, Rand McNally, Chicago, 261.

Schwab, J. J. (1964), 'The Professorship in Educational Administration: Theory—Art—Practice', Chap. IV in Willower, D. J. and Culbertson, Jack, *The Professorship in Educational Administration*, UCEA, Columbus, Ohio and Pennsylvania State University, University Park, pp. 54–55.

Taylor, William (1973), *Heading for Change: The Management of Innovation in the Large Secondary School*, Routledge & Kegan Paul, London.

Walker, W. G. (ed) (1974), *Educational Administration on Tape*, University of Queensland Press, St Lucia.

Walker, W. G. (1970), *Theory and Practice in Educational Administration*, University of Queensland Press, St Lucia.

Walker, W. G., Mumford, J. E. and Steel, Carolyn (1973), *A Glossary of Educational Terms: Usage in Five English-Speaking Countries*, University of Queensland Press, St Lucia.

Appendix 1
Extracts from Responses to IIP papers

The following passages are taken from summaries kindly made available by respondents to some of the papers.

Chapter 3 (Eric Hoyle)

I have two general comments: firstly, that the shift from Hoyle's Model A to a Model B type of organization, i.e. from the severely bureaucratic to the open, informal and collaborative kind, has a long history that reaches back at least to the nineteen twenties, so that considerable progress has been made in some countries along this continuum; secondly, that Professor Hoyle, in pointing up the problems of leadership in organizations moving towards the open type, makes a strong case for courses of study in educational administration at the tertiary level.

Bernstein's comment that 'roles are no longer made, but have to be made' is particularly applicable to some of the problems that are inevitable in the shift towards openness and informality. In the first place, as teachers' professionality grows, so does their demand for participation in decisions that affect them. What is their role in participation? Is it consultative, collaborative or collegial? Much confusion results if this is not clear. Secondly, an outcome of 'the impact of the environment' is the demand for community involvement in educational decision-making. Here again the roles of those who represent the community on boards, councils or committees should be carefully defined.

Finally, the influence of other external pressures on educational institutions are being, as they should be, carefully examined. I have in mind, for example, the external examination of students and the external supervision or inspection of the professional work of teachers. These supervisory techniques are also gradually changing, for they cannot escape the effects of the general movement towards Model B organizations.

Dr J. O. Ewing, CCEA Executive Director
(1973–1975)

Chapter 5 (T. Barr Greenfield)

It is now almost ten years since Andrew Halpin looked down from his Olympus upon the state of research and theory in educational administration and found only a 'foggy view'.[1] 'The air of our profession is still unruffled by any fresh intellectual breeze, and the time is now propitious for the emergence of a new Messiah, with a rhetoric and a new banner.' That was said in 1967 when the whispers of a new rhetoric were faintly discernible and a new banner was appearing above the fog, but few scholars in our field recognized these signs in the appearance in 1966 of Berger and Luckmann's *The Social Construction of Reality: A Treatise in the Sociology of Knowledge* (Doubleday, New York).

Barr Greenfield's paper is one of the first clear statements of this 'new rhetoric' which argues that organizations exist not in the world 'out there' but in the minds of men who, by their very nature, strive to make their own meanings out of the world as they confront it and interact with it. From this starting point, Greenfield presents a dichotomy in theories of organization in terms of the 'old' natural systems view and the 'new' phenomenology view. As a rhetoric this is an acceptable tactic, but in fact he himself shows that there has long existed a substantial corpus of organizational theory which concentrated attention upon attempts to discover and define the modes of adaptation of individuals to organizational membership. The work of Getzels and Presthus are but two notable examples.

The paper presents a vigorous case for the development of research which attempts to develop an understanding of what membership of an organization means to the individual within it. He has left us to draw the implications for educational administration.[2] While we are doing this, let us not forget that the pupils or students are members of the educational organization and that we need to know more about *their* perceptions. So much of what passes for theory in educational administration stops at the classroom door.

A. R. Crane, University Fellow,
University of New England, Australia

[1] See *Journal of Educational Administration,* 7(1), 1969, 3–18.
[2] This refers to the original version of the paper. *(Editor)*

Chapter 6 (B. O. Ukeje)

Three symposium addresses provided contrasting responses. In the first of them, India is cited as a further example of three-tier government of education.

The Role of Central Government. According to the Indian Constitution, education is essentially a State matter, but with certain reservations. The Constitution gives to Central Government sole executive responsibility for the Central Universities and other institutions of national importance, and also the coordination and determination of standards in institutions of higher learning. In actual practice, Central Government has been a dominant partner in education ever since the planning era started in 1950–51, so much so that the national targets for all sectors of education are determined by the Centre in consultation with the State Governments. This trend seems to be in the best interest of developing a national system of education for India.

The Role of State Governments. All important decisions at the school level are taken by the State Governments, and even in higher education, colleges are set up with their approval. Some specific functions of State Governments in education are:
1. to find the financial resources;
2. to legislate for education;
3. to conduct the supervision and inspection of schools and colleges;
4. to prescribe curricula and textbooks for the elementary stage;
5. to arrange the training of teachers.

The Role of Local Bodies. With a view to encouraging local initiative and participation in educational development, a number of States, accepting a recommendation of the Balwantrai Mehta Committee Report (1957), have introduced the experiment of democratic decentralization and the transfer of elementary education to local bodies (and even secondary education in the case of Andhra Pradesh and Maharashtra States). The experience of the last fifteen years shows, however, that this experiment has not been an unqualified success.

C. L. Sapra, Reader, National Council of Educational
Research and Training, New Delhi, India

The major problem, according to Professor Ukeje, is to devise an organizational structure for making education more relevant, efficient and effective within the context of a particular culture. But how can this be done in developing countries when administration has no fixed body of dogma? The structure is necessarily influenced by variable factors of a psychological, political, economic, socio-cultural and individual nature, coupled with factors relating to a colonial past.

In Malawi decision-making is highly centralized in order to correct deficiencies in existing school programmes, and also because of the non-availability of high-level personnel. At the top is general policy making and direction, in the middle policy specification, and at the lower end actual work performance, thus making the organization an efficient tool for taking and implementing decisions.

It may be argued that centralization works in Malawi because:

1. the channel of communication from the central authority downwards is clear-cut and operational;
2. the organization of education is secure in relation to the social forces in its environment;
3. there is stability in the lines of authority upwards and downwards;
4. there is stability in the informal relations within the organization;
5. there is continuity of policy and of the sources of its determination; and finally,
6. there is a homogeneity of outlook with respect to the role of the educational organization.

> P. H. Chiwona, Lecturer, University of Malawi
> Chancellor College, Zomba, Malawi

While Professor Ukeje has stressed the importance of ideology in the determination of the respective roles of central, regional and local authorities in decision-making, he has recognized that other factors are also at work. It is this point which I wish to emphasise further. The degree of local or central control in a particular country or state or province at any particular time is more a means to an end than the term 'ideology' suggests. The point may be clarified by reference to decision-making in the area of programme development.

I would argue that the determination of broad educational goals should be done by central bodies in response to national, provincial or state needs as defined by a body with the resources required to do a neutral assessment of the gap between *what is* and *what is desired*; that the specification of curricula and decisions of instructional planning and management are properly those of professional educators; and that programme evaluation decisions ought to be undertaken by a body or bodies not constrained by conflict of interest problems.[3] To decide, on the basis of political theory or ideology alone, to make programme development in all its phases a matter of local, or of central, concern, is to prevent curriculum design activities, instructional planning and management activities, and programme evaluation activities, from being more, rather than less, rational in serving the needs of pupils on the one hand and, on the other, the welfare of the larger community.

Dr I. E. Housego, Professor of Educational Administration, University of British Columbia, Vancouver, Canada

Chapter 8 (Jinapala Alles)

Dr Alles's paper rightly begins with a statement on the heterogeneous nature of the developing countries, which is easily overlooked or insufficiently appreciated by the developed countries. Broad aims and even objectives may be common but there are differences in geographical conditions, socio-cultural traditions and economic levels which are worth noting.

The use of curriculum change in science and mathematics to illustrate 'the broad strategies of initiation, development and consolidation of curriculum change in general' may be matched by reference to developments through other sources which had different strategies. Examples are the African universities in which research into African history, languages and studies provided materials which were used in curriculum development in primary and secondary schools.

Curriculum change in the nineteen sixties was significant, but nonetheless there were changes in the preceding decades. Take the Nigerian schools in the nineteen twenties with slates and pencils, and see how they have progressively changed for the better. The lesson of continual

[3] See McIntosh, R. G. and Housego, I. E., 'Policy Issues in Program Development', in Blaney, J. *et al.* (eds), *Program Development in Education*, Centre for Continuing Education, University of British Columbia, Vancouver, 1974.

change is the need for a stable but flexible educational system, which can accommodate rapid changes for improvement. It is envisaged that the next phase will be an increased emphasis on relevance to the respective environments in developing countries and a greater awareness of the differences between one country and another, which are usually blurred or ignored when the emphasis is on international considerations.

The position of experts in the diffusion, implementation and evaluation of curriculum change is accepted, but the cooperation of the teachers is also vitally important. The teachers should therefore be involved at every stage of the development and be strengthened through in-service training. Curriculum development should be encouraged as a field of postgraduate study and research, and its elements and practice taught at undergraduate and diploma levels. It is those who appreciate the problems and the process leading to the solutions who can act as catalysts in a desirable curriculum change.

> Professor C. O. Taiwo, Provost, University of Lagos
> College of Education, Lagos, Nigeria

Chapter 10 (T. R. Bone)

My major concern with Dr Bone's clear and authoritative paper is not what is in it, but what is missing. While the problems presented are undoubtedly Scottish, they are not peculiar to Scotland. All free industrialized nations are changing in the same ways, and their common major problems are external to their own institutions rather than internal. Solutions, therefore, in my opinion, must be sought in the larger context, with special attention to deteriorating regional situations. A recourse to solely parochial solutions flies in the face of the appropriate remedy: the corporate approach to planning, with each sector contributing to the establishment and implementation of long-range goals.

Educationists the world over must accept the fact that education cannot prosper apart from all other governmental services. As research on health and environment mount, the role of formal education is recognized as a contributing rather than as a dominant factor in human development. The proposed reorganization of local government and the ending of the quasi-autonomous position of the education authority directs the resources of the entire region toward the educational growth of its people. Here the Education Officer can sit together equally with other officers concerned with the totality of living, influencing the standard of living to improve chances of academic success.

Teacher shortage, curriculum and methods, and the structure of secondary schools should be viewed only partially as matters internal to the educational establishment, and suggestions for their improvement can be gleaned also from general social contexts. In my view, teacher discontent and the concomitant shortage will not be resolved by the 'sterner measures' Dr Bone mentions, or by forcing teachers to take difficult posts. Rather, recognition of teachers as professionals, ejection of administrators from teachers' unions, reorganization of the schools, and enlightened personnel practices would improve an intolerable situation. The essence of administration is to accomplish the goals of the formal organization while, at the same time, meeting the needs of the members.

The solution to the problem of teaching recalcitrant teenagers might also rest with the new regional management team. Again, the underlying problem of truancy and discipline is present in the general society, and only a society-wide systems approach can make headway.

Daniel E. Griffiths, Dean of the School of Education,
New York University, New York, USA

Chapter 17 (James M. Lipham)

Dr Lipham's paper provides a detailed guide to a movement in administrative education, whose ripples have, as yet, scarcely lapped these shores. Ten years ago the celebrated 63rd Year Book of the National Society for the Study of Education[4] chronicled the incorporation of the behavioural science approach into the study of educational administration, and described this process as a 'ferment'. Does the competency-based approach represent yet another 'ferment', and one that is as significant in its implications as were the earlier shifts in the focus of administrative studies in the USA which Dr Lipham summarizes in the first part of his paper? I suggest that it does not of itself represent a

[4] *Behavioral Science and Educational Administration*, Griffiths, D. E. (ed), University of Chicago Press, Chicago, 1964.

major shift, but that it is one consequence of a wider and more far-reaching ferment that has major implications for administrative education in Britain and perhaps elsewhere as well.

It seems clear from Dr Lipham's paper and from several other sources that training programmes all over North America have come under intensive scrutiny over the past four years. Only those close to the situation will be able to say whether this examination has led to wide-spread improvement, or even change. The competency-based approach appears to be one outcome of the concern over the effectiveness of programmes. Another, and in many ways diametrically opposite, type of approach is that which focuses on developing the system rather than the individual, e.g. the Organizational Development (O D) approach. Here the problem of effectiveness is viewed not as resulting from a failure to specify objectives for the training of individuals but from the fact that the individual's scope for applying what he has learnt during his course is determined to a large extent by the nature of the social system to which he returns. It is interesting that two such contrasting approaches should have developed from the same set of original concerns.

The competency-based approach has arisen partly, as Dr Lipham points out, as a response to the political pressure for accountability. Its claim to be able to measure effectiveness is likely to make it far more acceptable politically than the O D kind of approach, whose implication of meddling with the social dynamics of a situation is, in contrast, likely to be perceived as highly threatening by many practitioners. In spite of this I think that system-focussed approaches such as O D have the greater potential for giving help and support to educators in dealing with administrative problems. Still, I would not want to be too dis-missive of the competency-based approach: if it serves to trigger off some searching questioning of the purposes and procedures of training programmes, it could lead to some valuable improvements.

One might add that another developing approach, the phenomenolo-gical perspective discussed in Dr Greenfield's paper, though founded on a very different position from the O D-type approach, has somewhat similar implications for training programmes, particularly regarding the emphasis on a strong clinical base involving both theoretician and practitioner.

Ron Glatter, Reader in Educational Administration,
University of London Institute of Education, England

Appendix 2
Discussion in Small Groups: Conference Feedback

A feature of IIP 1974 was the provision made for the participants, representatives of a variety of academic and administrative systems in many countries, to come together in groups of diverse membership to interchange ideas and study common problems. Extracts are given below from reports supplied by group rapporteurs.

Several groups began by discussing the advantages and disadvantages of theoretical perspectives and models in seeking to advance the *practice* of educational administration:

Although some argued to the contrary, the majority regarded philosophy, theory and practice as inter-dependent. Practice can hardly follow a logical pattern unless it is theory-based.

The group agreed that theoretical models are valid *beginning* points for the analysis and assessment of real-life administrative situations and conflicts—but that they may not always provide the answer. Prudential judgements, based upon political, economic or personal considerations, are often critical.

It was agreed that administrators need theory and operate from a theory base, implicitly or explicitly.

One group sought clarification as to what should be the primary concern of the educational administrator:

There was a consensus that what is needed is less attention to compartmentalization within the top echelons of educational systems, but much more effort being given over to how best to *integrate* in both the fields of policy development and policy implementation. ... To continue to argue that one activity is purely administrative but that another is policy development, and hence of a higher status, is to disregard the importance of the former to the success of the latter.

Another, after discussing 'accountability' and 'acceptability', took a more pessimistic view of the administrator's role:

Educational administrators are wondering whether they have become redundant, the expendable middle of the community-political sandwich.

The centralization/decentralization issue was much discussed in different national contexts, and appears in two group reports as an unresolved dilemma:

Trends towards both centralization and decentralization can exist concurrently; the growing professionalization of teachers is leading to decentralization, while the need for central planning of the total economy means centralizing tendencies. In many countries central government is increasing the amount of control through broad policies, while decreasing some of its operational responsibilities.

Centralization seems to be increasing in most countries, particularly where the federal or state government holds the purse strings and controls resources, despite the fact that much publicity is generally given to the merit of decentralization and that some powers have been delegated to regional/local areas.

Various aspects of the corporate management model of local government, found to be in operation in some of the English and Welsh local authorities visited, and also about to be introduced in Scotland, came under scrutiny in a number of groups:

The advantages of educational planning being coordinated with other essential community services was clearly recognized. It was felt, however, that education could suffer from this arrangement in times of financial stringency. It may be necessary for the educational administrators to develop political expertise to function effectively in a corporate management situation.

The recommended restructuring of Scottish local government seemed promising, especially in regard to corporate management. ... There was a feeling that lumping education in with other social services in a corporate management situation would force education to justify its expenditure more realistically.

While the concept of corporate management is generally acceptable, it is possible that it will serve as a means by the non-educational part of the management to restrain or contain the educationists.

Overseas participants, returning from visits to educational institutions, found difficulty in unravelling some of the more esoteric mysteries of education in Britain, such as the *accountability* of the Heads of schools in Britain:

Was the Headmaster responsible to the Governing Body, to the Education Officer, to the Education Committee, or to none of these—or to all? A feeling emerged that there was not a definite answer, or perhaps that the answer could only be arrived at if you first knew what was the issue in question.

The way in which educational leadership is exercised attracted some shrewd comments:

The keystone of the system is 'suggestion' all the way down the line. There is an intricate network of interaction between administrators and teachers. Heads and Principals know just how far they can go. Though little is written down, there is a subtle balancing and interplay of power.

The policy in Britain of appointing Heads with differing personalities and styles results in freedom and diversity, but also produces a wide range of schools, some very good, some very bad. It is easy to innovate, difficult to diffuse.

Teacher involvement in decision-making generally received approval, but manipulative overtones seemed implicit in one comment:

Participatory situations must surely be one of the best ways of overcoming resistance to change, and this should include the students as well as the staff.

The word 'phenomenology' did not occur in any group report, but interest was expressed in Organizational Development, albeit with some misgiving about the readiness as yet of teachers generally in many of the countries represented to be involved in participatory schemes. There were contrasting views as to the extent to which teachers should be left to make their own professional judgements:

Some teachers do not want the autonomy which everyone is wishing to give them—they are in need of guidance from a Headteacher or an Inspector.

'Open plan' should not be presented as a *fait accompli* and teachers forced unwillingly into it. The Glasgow approach to open plan primary schools impressed us because of its flexibility. When teachers begin to feel that the existence of four walls is an obstacle, 'open plan' becomes appropriate. But this realization will come at different times.

The 'open' or 'Model B' type of education, as described by Professor Hoyle, could be another form of closure: if it were simply imposed by administrators, it might destroy the flexibility which should exist in teaching. Groups of teachers should have the responsibility of deciding *themselves* how they should work.

A further aspect of the British educational scene which did not escape comment was the extent to which the community is able to make its voice heard in educational matters:

Even with a system of local governing and managing bodies, some participants wondered if parents really had a very adequate means through which they might seek redress of grievances.

The British seem to believe in the myth that in their system there is local participation in decision-making. Whether this is true may be less important than the fact that it is believed.

Finally, many groups expressed a belief in the desirability of specific training experiences in preparation for administrative roles in education, and noted the steps being taken, with the encouragement of bodies such as the British Educational Administration Society, to develop systematic study of educational administration in Britain. One group added the comment that it 'endorsed the concept of in-service training for seasoned administrative staff at all levels'.

Index